WHO ATE ALL
THE PIES?

WHO ATE ALL THE PIES?

The Life and Times of Mick Quinn

Mick Quinn
with Oliver Harvey

4

This edition published in Great Britain in 2004 by
Virgin Books
Thames Wharf Studios
Rainville Road
London W6 9HA

First published in hardback in 2003 by
Virgin Books

ISBN 978 0 7535 0803 9

Typeset by TW Typesetting, Plymouth, Devon

The Random House Group Limited supports the Forest Stewardship
Council (FSC®), the leading international forest certification organisation.
Our books carrying the FSC label are printed on FSC® certified paper. FSC
is the only forest certification scheme endorsed by the leading environmental
organisations, including Greenpeace. Our paper procurement policy can be
found at www.randomhouse.co.uk/environment

Printed and bound by CPI Group (UK) Ltd, Croydon, CR0 4YY

Dedication
To Mum and Sean – I'll never forget you.
And to Karen, the love of my life.

CONTENTS

1. WHO THE FUCK IS MICK QUINN?

'I am the greatest, I said it even before I knew I was. Don't tell me I can't do something. Don't tell me it's impossible. Don't tell me I am not the greatest. I am the double greatest.'

Muhammad Ali

Walking out through the heavy iron gates of Newcastle's famous St James's Park stadium, I had a smile on my face the size of the Mersey Tunnel. I had just signed a big-money contract to lead the attack for one of Europe's most famous clubs. It meant I would wear the black and white number nine shirt which in Geordieland is revered like a footballing Turin shroud. Newcastle legends Hughie Gallacher, Jackie Milburn and Malcolm Macdonald had all possessed the sacred shirt. Today it is worn by Alan Shearer. If I was a success I would be treated like a god by the Newcastle fans, known as the Toon Army.

It was July 1989, and I was 27 years old. After the formalities of putting pen to paper I decided to have a stroll through the city to get a feel of the place, and to treat Sheila, my girlfriend at the time and the mother of my beautiful twin girls Natasha and Melissa, to a celebratory bevvie. I was wearing my favourite Armani grey-flecked double-breasted designer suit, and handmade Italian loafers. Sheila, her long dark hair bouncing off her shoulders, looked stunning in a cream trouser suit. The sun shone as brightly as it ever does above the Tyne and life felt great. I had finally fulfilled my footballing destiny. The boy from a Liverpool council estate had run to something after all.

I turned to Sheila and said, 'Darling, this is one of the proudest moments of my life. It's what I've been struggling to achieve since I practised kicking a tennis ball against a wall every night when I was a kid.'

She squeezed my hand and said, 'I'm really made up for you, babe. This is a new beginning for both of us. I'm so proud of you.'

I hugged her tightly. We walked hand-in-hand through the gates and on to the street.

Suddenly, we both stopped in our tracks as we heard a rhythmic chanting: 'Sack the board, sack the board, sack the board!' Dozens of folk in black and white shirts were marching towards us. It was a demo by the Toon Army against the men then running the club. As they came closer we could make out the wording on a huge banner carried by two fans in the middle of the throng. In large black letters, it read: WHO THE FUCK IS MICK QUINN?

Welcome to Newcastle.

I had a month to wait before I could answer the question on that banner. My first game was against Leeds, a giant of a football club who, like Newcastle, were languishing in the old Division Two – the equivalent of today's Nationwide Division One. Newcastle had just been relegated from the top flight and the failure had hit the fans hard. Being such a fanatical football city, the supporters wallowed in the good times but suffered terribly in the bad. The city's traditional industries, like shipbuilding, were going through a long, slow death as well, and unemployment was high. Watching their team win on Saturdays helped shine some light into their lives. They hadn't had a real hero with the number nine on his back for years. The leading scorers in the last two seasons had been the Brazilian Mirandinha with eleven goals and John O'Neill with thirteen, and the supporters couldn't see yours truly being a twenty-goals-a-season man, which is the mark of a good striker. I had just scored 54 League goals in 121 appearances for Portsmouth, including 28 in one season, to shoot them into the First Division, but the Toon Army didn't seem very impressed. As I jogged out on to the pitch at a packed St

James's Park, I could feel the atmosphere of discontent on the terraces.

Leeds, as always, had brought down big travelling support, around 3,000 of them, all in full voice. The Yorkshire club had bought seasoned pros Vinnie Jones, Gordon Strachan and Jim Beglin in the close season and they were hoping to get off to a flying start. In contrast, there was a muted atmosphere among the 26,000 Newcastle fans following the previous season's relegation and what they saw as an inadequate rebuilding of the squad. The announcement of my name over the stadium loudspeaker was greeted with a polite ripple of applause. Where was that famous St James's Park atmosphere? I was used to being treated like a hero by the fans at Portsmouth. The Leeds fans were giving me the usual crap, too. Jabbing their fingers at me in unison, they sang: 'Who ate all the pies, who ate all the pies? You fat bastard, you fat bastard, you ate all the pies.' But, with the adrenalin pumping through my veins, it was easy to ignore, and I knew there was at least one friendly face in the crowd: my dad Mick senior had made the trip up from Liverpool to watch my first game. All I kept thinking about was that banner. I wanted to show the Newcastle fans exactly who Mick Quinn was.

When the whistle went, I was like a pitbull terrier straining at the leash. I put myself around for the first few minutes, and when Beglin tripped John Gallacher for a penalty I sprinted over. I grabbed the ball before anyone else could and placed it on the spot. It was a cocky thing to do in my first game, but I was desperate to score a goal – and, fuck it, I had the number nine shirt on my back. I wasn't going to miss this chance of getting off the mark. I had this method of taking pens at the time which I thought was the business. I would turn my back on the keeper, then, when the ref blew his whistle, I would spin round as fast as possible and hit the ball as hard as I could. It certainly flummoxed Leeds keeper Mervyn Day. I clenched my fists in the direction of the Gallowgate. 1–0.

Soon after, the Magpies got a corner. The ball flew in towards the near post and my strike partner Mark McGhee nodded it on for me to head in at the back post. Cue mad celebrations. The Toon Army seemed to be warming to me. Minutes later, a cross came in from the right as I made a darting run into the box. I connected with the ball six yards out and bundled it over the line for my hat-trick. I went nuts and ran towards the Gallowgate, arms outstretched. 'That's who fucking Mick Quinn is!' I screamed, almost tearful. The Newcastle fans went absolutely berserk. A new chant echoed around the famous old stadium: 'He's fat, he's round, a number nine we've found, Micky Quinn, Micky Quinn.' I had won over the Toon Army and would never need to buy another drink in Geordieland again.

In the dying minutes of the game Kevin Dillon, my old mate from my playing days at Portsmouth, delivered a slide-rule pass on the halfway line. I was 30 yards out but I ran between two defenders to the edge of the box and found myself one on one with Mervyn Day. Just like a Western gunslinger, I took my time and let him make the first move. Then I pulled the trigger. I unleashed a right-foot thunderbolt and the ball cannoned into the bottom left-hand corner of the net. I thought the roof was going to explode off the stands. I jogged over to salute the Gallowgate for the fourth time and a bunch of kids in the black and white Magpies strip jumped over the advertising hoardings and mobbed me. Newcastle won the game 5–2 and I had scored my 150th League goal, one of the best of my whole career.

I saluted the Toon Army like a victorious gladiator as I trooped off the pitch with the match ball tucked under my arm. Manager Jim 'Bald Eagle' Smith came charging into the dressing room and screamed, 'You are a fucking bargain, Mr Quinn! Now, go and get us promoted.' Then it was straight to the players' lounge to meet Dad, who had a couple of pints waiting on the table. He'd been there, pushing me, when I was playing schoolboy football or just kicking a ball in the street. I felt so proud that he was there to see one of my greatest days in football.

The beer began to flow and the coaching staff and the other players came over to offer their congratulations. After four or five pints Dad and I headed out for a meal. Our taxi driver turned round and said, 'Do you realise you've made this whole city happy? Until the next game, anyway.'

As we snaked our way through the streets towards the Tyne quayside, folk in the black and white stripes of the Toon Army banged on the windows and yelled their support. Walking into the supposedly sedate restaurant, the diners clocked me, then gave me a huge cheer. Drinks were sent over, menus were autographed. Dad turned to me and said, 'Fuck me, I thought Liverpool was a football-mad city. This is unreal.'

Wine and brandies followed before we made our way back to the city centre hotel that was my temporary home. As we arrived, we saw a billboard in the street for the Pink 'Un evening newspaper with the banner headline QUINN'S STUNNING FOUR-GOAL DEBUT. I pulled it off the wall and strode into the hotel bar. I stuck the billboard on the bar and ordered drinks for everyone. Later, some bird came over and started whispering all sorts of filthy stuff in my ear. She was blonde and wearing a microskirt; she had what you might call a fuller figure. But by this stage I was far too pissed to do anything about it. I wanted to continue drinking but I was desperate for a piss. I was so unsteady on my pins, though, that I could only stagger a couple of feet to a nearby potted palm tree and piss in that. The night porter saw me and I thought, 'Here we go. I'll be thrown out of the hotel where the club's put me up and I'll be in trouble before I start.'

'Sorry, mate,' I slurred. 'I'm absolutely fucking polluted.'

The porter smiled, and replied, 'Mick, after your performance today you can piss on whatever or whoever you like in Newcastle. Just don't try it in Sunderland.'

So I carried on drinking in the bar, every now and then staggering a few paces to the plant pot for a piss, until I could see daylight through the hotel curtains.

That was the start of the most glorious season of my career. I netted 36 goals and became a Geordie hero, writing my name into Newcastle folklore. I will never have to buy a pint in the Bigg Market ever again. No one, not even the era's golden boys Gary Lineker and Ian Rush, scored more that season.

I was born with the gift to score goals. Left foot, right foot, headers. I didn't care if they bounced in off my fucking knob as long as they went in. I had that God-given ability to be in the right place at the right time. Though I wouldn't have beaten too many players over 100 metres, I was faster than Linford Christie over a yard. There is a famous old football cliché that the first yard is in your head. It sounds like bollocks, but some players have quicker reaction times and better special awareness than others. I had that sixth sense. My gaffer at Coventry City, Bobby Gould, once summed up my goalscoring talents like this: 'Quinn is the football equivalent of Polaris when the ball lands in the penalty area. Up comes his periscope and suddenly there is a submarine on the surface of the water and the missile has been fired. Opponents don't realise he's there until it's too late and they're holed below the Plimsoll line. Mick is a silent killer.' Thanks, Bob. I think he meant it as a compliment. Bobby should know I've always tried to make the best possible use of my periscope.

But that wonderful four-goal start didn't only make me a hero in Geordieland, it also set me on a collision course with the man who had inspired me as a boy to play football, the man I'd pretended to be every night as I practised kicking a tennis ball first with one foot and then the other on to the wall on the side of our council house in Liverpool, keeping it below the white line painted there. He's the man Toon fans called the Messiah, but he ended up branding me a Judas.

Kevin Keegan.

2. THE FARM

'All together now, all together now, all together now, in no-man's land . . .'

The Farm, 'All Together Now'

'When they start singing "You'll Never Walk Alone", my eyes start to water. There have been times when I've actually been crying while I've been playing.'

Kevin Keegan

Standing high on the Kop at Liverpool's Anfield stadium is a scruffy lad, only just fourteen. He has a mop of black hair and is wearing a royal blue tracksuit with white stripes down the legs, and white Adidas trainers. With his hands stretched above his head, he sings as loud as he can: 'Walk on, walk on, with hope in your heart, and you'll never walk alone!' Suddenly, Steve Heighway breaks down the right, flights in a beautiful cross and Kevin Keegan, at full stretch, scores with a diving header. The lad goes crazy.

It was the summer of 1976 and, like thousands of other Scouse kids, I was there to worship my hero, the man whose picture was all over my bedroom wall – Kevin Keegan. With me was my little gang from our estate: Kevin McGowan, John Clarke, Mark Laing, Philip Lappin and Mark 'Snowy' Moffat. We were a right bunch of herberts and, as usual, we had all double-clicked – that is, we'd passed two at a time through the turnstiles to save cash. It was 50p to get in and I would always get there early and have a cup of Oxo and a pie. I had started out in the Pen, the kids' area of the stadium, with Dad when I was eight, but I was a big boy now and I wanted to run with the lads.

It was the golden era of Ray Kennedy, John Toshack, Jimmy Case and David Fairclough. Liverpool were the kings of English football and about to dominate Europe in the same way. Football, then as now, was a religion on Merseyside, and the atmosphere with the Kop in full voice was electric. It was still terracing in those days and we were crammed in like sardines. When the crowd swayed you went with it, sometimes with your feet not touching the ground. If you felt a warm sensation down the back of your legs someone had pissed on you. And I couldn't believe the amount of swearing: it was fuck this, fuck that. The whole thing was magic for a teenage kid.

King Kev was my own personal Roy of the Rovers, everything I wanted to be. He always looked cool with that bouncy seventies bubble perm, and he wore the latest trendy gear – monster flares and wing-collared shirts. All he had to do was jog out on to the pitch for the girls in the crowd to go nuts. Lucky bastard. He was also Liverpool's best striker, the man who scored the goals, whose name the crowd chanted and who made the headlines the next day. And gobshite Quinny was telling anyone that would listen that one day he was going to be a goal king just like Kev. 'You fucking wait, lads. I'm going to play for Liverpool and be a big star. Just fucking wait and see.' I was just another cocky Scouse kid looking for a way out of a life of boring dead-end jobs or claiming the dole. Or both at the same time.

As usual, that day I kept up the banter all the way home on the bus. We took the number 12c from outside Anfield and talked football, football, football all the way on the five-mile journey out through the suburbs to a huge, rambling estate of grey tower blocks and row upon row of drab sixties council housing. Welcome to Cantril Farm. That may make it sound like a picturesque smallholding in the country, but in fact it should have been twinned with Beirut. Cantril Farm was built as an overspill estate for families from central Liverpool following the slum clearances after the war. My parents, Mick senior and Patricia, arrived on the estate in 1967, with me, aged five, in tow. They were pleased to move into 16 Round Hey, a terraced, pebble-dashed house with a little wooden porch. Then, most folk were grateful for simple things in life like an inside shitter, a garden, three bedrooms and a cul-de-sac location. It was on the streets of Cantril Farm that I learnt to play football and to look after myself. It was to be home, on and off, for the next twenty years.

We were part of the social experiment, with people moving from the cramped inner cities into purpose-built new towns. The Farm had schools and several little parades of shops with chip shops and a couple of bookmakers. What more could you ask for? The rural theme was kept up by the names of the estate's new pubs: the Barley Mow, the Black Angus, the Ploughman, the Thatcher and the Tithe Barn. Back then, the tower blocks were new and the houses smart, but later it became a haven for crime, drugs and graffiti artists and gained a reputation as one of Britain's roughest council estates. The locals renamed it Cannibal Farm. In 1980 there was even a riot on the estate, as there had been in other inner-city troublespots like Toxteth and Brixton. I don't think the kids on the estate were particularly pissed off about anything, they just thought, 'Well, if them bastards are having a riot, we'd better have one too.' Mum made sure we stayed indoors, out of the way of the burning cars, flying paving stones and riot cops. One of Dad's favourite jokes is: 'Did you hear about the two lions who escaped from Knowsley Safari Park and ended up in Cantril Farm? They were clawed to death outside the Tithe Barn at kicking-out time.' The ice cream van used to come round the streets playing Bob Marley's 'One Love', and the man would sell the punters dope with their choc ices.

There was very high unemployment in the area. We used to get fans from Chelsea and Spurs waving wedges of cash at us at Anfield and singing, to the tune of 'You'll Never Walk Alone', 'Sign on, sign on, with pen in your hand, and you'll never work again.' After Michael Heseltine, then a government minister, toured the estate in the early eighties we were officially declared an impoverished area. It was just home to us, though, and Dad always somehow scraped by and kept the family afloat. Once, when I was about ten years old, I saw someone jump from a window at the top of one of the tower blocks and splat on to the concrete below. There wasn't anyone around, so I walked slowly towards the body, then legged it once I could see it had been turned to a bloody pulp. Very grim. But we didn't feel socially deprived, just the opposite. We loved the friendship and solidarity of the estate and thought that was how everyone lived. We never went hungry, we never wanted for anything.

In the Liverpool tradition, pop music and football were a way out. One lad from the estate called Peter Hooton and his mate Phil Jones started a music and footie fanzine called *The End*. It was sold on matchdays, and it charted the rise of the scally culture of Liverpool. Scallies – short for 'scallywags' – wore trainers 'zapped' from trendy shops whenever Liverpool played in Europe, Slazenger jumpers, straight-legged jeans and cagoules. They were jack-the-lads who had a laugh and didn't give a shit about being on the dole; they were two a penny on the estates. Peter formed a band which, in honour of concrete Cantril, they called The Farm. In the summer of 1990 they had a huge hit with 'Groovy Train', and they followed it up at Christmas with 'All Together Now'. Both top tunes.

There was this kid two years older than me who lived in the house facing our back garden and had the piss ripped out of him terribly. He was very effeminate and used to go to school holding his sister's hand. The lad, called Paul Rutherford, went to St Dominic's Comprehensive with me in Huyton, which was a tough school. He was ribbed mercilessly. Paul took the punishment and didn't let the bullies break him. He later became an international star as Holly Johnson's sidekick with chart-toppers Frankie Goes to Hollywood. It's funny, because all those wankers who gave him a hard time were later proudly walking around Cantril Farm in their FRANKIE SAYS RELAX T-shirts. Paul said later, 'Where you're from does make you what you are. I personally had a very hard time there. I used to get kicked in the face at least twice a night for being a poof and dressing weird, being a punk or whatever. I had a horrible time at school. I don't have particularly fond memories of the place, although it's great when I go back now. You have to move out if you're going to be as successful as you want to be.'

The estate also produced a load of footie players. Liverpool's super sub David Fairclough learnt his trade kicking a ball around on the Farm; other footballers include Manchester City and West Ham's Ian Bishop, Barnsley's Tosh Fielden, Billy Mercer, who was a goalkeeper at Rotherham, and Steven Ward, who was on Liverpool's books. Loads of kids had trials with clubs then ended up playing amateur football.

When us kids weren't playing footie we were out on our bikes. One kid, Joey McLoughlin, brought up on the estate as the youngest of eleven, became a top cyclist and went on to win the national Milk Race in the eighties. We even had a comedian. Craig Charles, who was two years younger than me, also grew up on the Farm. He is best known for starring in the sci-fi comedy show *Red Dwarf* and, now, for presenting *Robot Wars*. He summed up his childhood by saying, 'The working class have to keep laughing. If they don't, they cry.' Cantril Farm was a tough place to grow up, but it seemed to produce a generation that wanted to go out and take on the world.

My dad, Mick senior, was a tough-as-nails docker who was pissing up his hard-earned dosh at the Lorcano dance hall in Liverpool when he saw a beautiful girl with dark features whom he took to be Irish. Dad, though shorter than me, has my brick-shithouse physique; his then strawberry-blond Celtic hair was greased into a teddy-boy quiff like most lads in the days before the Beatles made it big. He went over and asked the glamorous girl to dance. He was blown away by her. Patricia was seventeen, the same age as him, witty, intelligent and exotic; her black hair in fact came from her Mediterranean background. Their courtship was short, and they married at eighteen. A year later, on 2 May 1962, I was born. Surprise, surprise, I was a big baby, weighing in at eight pounds and seven ounces.

They started married life in an old Victorian tenement building in Everton with lots of other families. There was a communal shithouse in the yard. They lived close to mum's parents, Luigi and Elizabeth Silvano. My swarthy good looks actually come from Italian ancestry. It's funny, because Jack Charlton was always saying to me, 'Come and play for Ireland, Mick. You'd be just up our fucking street.' And I think I would have relished their up-and-at-'em physical style, too, and scored a few for them. Problem was, my Irish blood came from my great-grandfather Quinn who hailed from Waterford in the Republic – not enough to make me eligible to pull on the green shirt of Ireland. But with Luigi's blood in my veins I could have played for Italy alongside Roberto Baggio, Paolo Maldini and Gianluca Vialli. Funny, but the Azzurri never asked me.

Luigi was a right character (my family tends to throw them up). He was from Naples, in the mafia country of southern Italy, but with work scarce after the war he swapped the picturesque Bay of Naples for a cramped flat on Merseyside. There weren't many jobs around then, but Luigi was a real hard nut and he turned his fists to professional boxing. Somewhere in a cardboard box we have some faded posters showing the cards for various fight nights in Liverpool. There, in heavy type, is the name Lou Sullivan – Luigi's pro name. As it was only just after the war, it wasn't too clever to use an Italian name, so he opted for an Irish one.

Although I never knew Lou – he died from tuberculosis at the age of just 39 – I like to think I have some of his fighting spirit. I certainly needed to resort to my fists a few times when I was playing. There are some nasty centre-halves out there. Once I even bashed Fash – Wimbledon hardnut John Fashanu. I also love the sport of boxing; Muhammad Ali and Liverpool's own John Conteh are two of my biggest heroes. Ali is not only one of the greatest sportsmen who ever lived but also one of the greatest human beings. John came from Kirkby on Merseyside, which is as tough an area as Cantril Farm. To see a kid from a Liverpool council estate fulfil his dream and become world champion was a real inspiration to me. I got to meet him at a sportsmen's dinner at the height of my career, by which time he'd retired and become a born-again Christian. I went over to him like a star-struck schoolboy looking for an autograph. 'John, mate,' I spluttered, 'watching you go all the way to the top from humble beginnings has been such an inspiration to me. What did it feel like to have the world championship belt in your hands?' I wanted to hear about his years of struggle, sweat and tears, but he said simply, 'I thank God for it.' I felt so disillusioned that I simply shook his hand and went to talk to Barry McGuigan – and that's saying something, because Barry can talk a glass eye to sleep. Meeting your heroes is often a bad move.

Luigi soon hooked up with a beautiful Scouse girl called Elizabeth – my nan, known to everyone as Tiggy. Mum was the eldest of their three children. She was brought up a strict Catholic and had aspirations that she might get an education and a decent job, but girls didn't do that sort of thing in fifties Liverpool. They simply got married and had kids.

The Quinns were a big Liverpool clan with Irish roots, like many Merseyside families. My great granddad, who emigrated across the Irish Sea from Waterford, was said to have worked with horses when still in Ireland. Dad's dad Joseph Quinn had fought bravely with the King's Regiment in France during the Second World War, but he'd been hit by a bullet in the leg, which was left paralysed for the rest of his life. He returned to Liverpool, got a job in the Tizer factory, and met Scouse girl Margaret. They had six kids, the third of whom was my dad, Michael. Joe, who walked with a stick, later worked as a porter in Liverpool fruit market, and he and Margaret lived in cramped lodgings near the Scotty Road in one of the toughest areas in Liverpool. The Quinns didn't have much; Dad married above himself when he met Mum. Money was scarce, and straight from school Dad went to work in the then thriving docks that still handled goods from every corner of the British Empire.

When I was born my parents moved round the corner from the Silvanos into Kerford Street in Everton. Dad still worked in Liverpool docks for £11 1s. 8d. a week. It wasn't a fortune, but we always had a ready supply of stuff from the docks, especially fruit. I ate more bananas as a kid than Guy the Gorilla. Later, Dad was made redundant from the docks and he bought a black hackney cab with the proceeds. Then he settled on life as a pub landlord, which he was born to be good at. He likes a beer and is great at nattering to the punters all day. That was when my parents found that their application for a council house on a plush, brand-new estate called Cantril Farm had been successful. I was five, my brother Mark was three; Sean was to come along in 1970, followed by Tricia in 1974.

3. 16 ROUND HEY

Quinn: From Ceann, the Irish word for 'head'. The name Cuinn means 'intelligent'. In general, Catholics spell the name with two 'n's while Protestants spell it with one. The Quinns are primarily from Antrim, Clare, Longford and Tyrone, where their surname is the most common.

'They hate you if you're clever and they despise a fool, 'til you're too fucking crazy to follow their rules.'

John Lennon, 'Working-Class Hero'

I was kicking a ball as soon as I could walk. If I couldn't find a ball, I used a can. Being a footballer was all I ever wanted to do. From as early as I can remember it was practice, practice, practice.

Dad drew a line on the wall beside our council house, about three feet high. He said, 'Keep the ball below this line using first your right foot, then your left. You'll thank me in the long run.' Using a tennis ball, me, Mark and later Sean did just that for hours on end, day after day, until it became second nature. I used to give that wall some stick. Wallop – that's an FA Cup final winner for Liverpool. Bosh – there's one for England. I kept on banging them in until Dad called us in for tea at 7 p.m. He would then go out for a pint, thinking we were safely inside, but as soon as we'd scoffed down our tea we'd be back out there with the tennis ball. It annoyed the fuck out of the neighbours.

Like many footballers of my generation, I believe playing with a tennis ball from such a young age helped my ball skills no end. When you actually got a proper-sized ball to kick it was easy after playing with a small ball. It's something kids today don't seem to do. In the age of computer games and DVDs, they have so much more to amuse them. Years later I did indeed thank Dad for that line on the wall.

Dad had aspirations for me to become a professional footballer. He was a decent centre-forward himself and had trials for Blackpool, but he ended up playing amateur football on Saturdays for a team called Waterloo Dock. As the name suggests, the players were dockers, or ex-dockers. They were hard players and hard drinkers. My dad could handle himself, and he had to. Two-footed tackles that left stud marks around the throat were the norm, and fights would often break out.

From about the age of five, I went along with Dad. Me and the other kids couldn't wait for half-time so that we could get on to the pitch for a kick-around. I loved getting on to that pitch; it was what I waited for all week. Once, when I was twelve and Waterloo Dock were about to play in a cup semi-final, I jogged on at half-time, as usual, for the kickabout. I went in for a tackle with Joey Harkin, one of the team's star players, and caught him with my studs. I don't like pulling out of tackles. But that day I crocked him for the second half and Dad got loads of shit.

On every away trip we made sure we came back with some goodies. We would empty the kit bag and fill it with veg growing in nearby fields. When we played in Rainford it was carrots and turnips, at Formby there were gorgeous apples. Afterwards, it was back to the pub. Us kids would have to stay outside with crisps and lemonade. We would peer into the bar, and it was like a magical world. All our dads, miserable old bastards normally, were laughing and joking and having the time of their lives. What was it about pubs that made them so happy? They would drink themselves silly. Often we would see them come out to the beer garden and chuck their guts up everywhere. Then they would duck back in and start drinking again. I found the whole thing exciting. So that's how adults have fun. They would just laugh and laugh, and then fall about all over the show. Mum would give Dad a frightful bollocking if he ever brought us back late – which was quite often.

Mum was the boss of the house, and what she said went. She made sure we had everything we needed. When Chopper bikes were all the rage she made sure each of us had one, not the cheaper Chippers. She also drummed into us the need for politeness, good manners and a decent education. I would say to Mum, 'I'm going to be a football star just like Kevin Keegan. I'll be able to buy you anything you want,' and she'd snap back, 'If you really want to earn some money, get an education and a decent bloody job.'

But it never entered into my head that I would be anything other than a top professional footballer. The first step was to get into a team, and the nearest one was the Nevites Close junior team. The Farm had around fifteen teams named after roads on different parts of the estate which formed a little league. Trouble was, you had to be eight to join up and I was just six and a half when I first tried to play. But then, as now, I was on the big side, so I lied and said I was old enough. They were desperate for a goalie so they let me join. I was bollocks in goal, so when they let me go out a few games later I played up front and scored a goal. I can remember the sheer joy as the ball hit the back of the net for the first time. I rushed home to tell Mum and Dad all about it. I met two great mates on that team: John 'Taskforce' Tasker – he was the goalie, a big lad – and Steven Ward, who went on to sign for Liverpool.

Dad really encouraged me with my football and often came to watch. It made me feel so proud to score when he was on the touchline. His advice to me was always, 'When you see the net, let it fly.' Those words stood me in good stead over the years. Mum was at home where she had her hands full looking after Mark, Sean, and then Tricia. It was always Mum we went to if we wanted to talk about puberty or something like that. She was a very moral person with a strong sense of right and wrong. Dad was a man's man, and his stock sentence was 'Stop talking shit.' I'd ask questions like, 'Dad, why is the Earth round, not square?' Without taking his eyes off the telly, he'd grunt, 'Stop talking shit.' He would go out on the piss big style – when he started driving cabs, it was often on a Monday – and come in paralytic with a Chinese takeaway. Sometimes he would go out on two- or three-day benders and not come back. He would go off the fucking radar screen. It left Mum devastated.

Dad was very much the breadwinner, but at home, as I've said, Mum was definitely the boss. He was a bit henpecked, but generally it seemed a loving relationship. Dad would do just enough in his black cab to make ends meet. If he had to make £50 a day to cover himself he would knock off as soon as he had made it. Then it was down the pub or the bookie's. Mum was a good Catholic and a regular at St Albert's Church on the Farm, and as a kid I would go to church every Sunday with her. I was confirmed there. I even went for an audition, or whatever you call it, to be an altar boy, but you had to be a goody two-shoes and a lick-arse so I never made the grade. I stopped going to church when I was fifteen.

If Mum and Dad went out in the evening me, Mark and Sean would have boxing fights and knock ten types of shit out of one another. We had only one set of boxing gloves so we would have one each. I would skip around the front room, trying to shuffle like Ali, and look for decent jabs and little combinations. Mark would come charging at me like a mad water buffalo, trying to knock me out with a haymaker. When we got bored of that we would take two ornamental swords off the wall of the living room and play the Three Musketeers until someone got hurt and started crying. Mark was always more aggressive than me with the sword fights, and I would often stop the game if it looked like getting out of hand.

Mark has fair hair and a stocky build and has always had a rebellious streak. He would roam around the Farm with our lakeland terrier Kai. He absolutely adored that dog and both of them would come back covered in blood after getting into fights. Today he has a nasty-looking bulldog called Kai 2. Mark liked to fight my battles as well, and the kids on the estate didn't fuck with him. I remember one of the teachers at school approaching me and saying, 'Can you ask Mark to calm down a bit? He doesn't take any notice of us.' Basically, they were shit scared of him.

Mark and I shared a room and did everything together. We joined the Scouts together, fought other kids on the estate together and gave Dad lip together. The estate was surrounded by fields and woods, and the pair of us would go ratting and rabbiting with Kai and climb trees looking for birds' nests. But when it came to football, Mark and Sean were Everton while me and Dad were Liverpool. It led to some real screaming matches. We had an uncle Mick and auntie Joan and an uncle Billy on my mother's side who were Everton mad and they brainwashed my brothers to support the blues. On Merseyside there are no set areas that support Liverpool and Everton and families are often divided into blue and red. We would all watch footie on the telly together and argue like fuck the whole way through. Every cup final day we would all get a pozzie on the sofa at 10 a.m. for the build-up. I remember in 1974 me and Dad taunting Mark, singing, 'Keegan two, Heighway one, Liverpool three, Newcastle none.' Mum wasn't fussed about football. She had enough of it just with washing four sets of kit and muddy boots every week.

Sean and baby Tricia looked up to me as the eldest, and I always looked out for them. They used to fetch and carry for me around the house. Sean was very much the golden child of the family. He was a slighter build than me and Mark and had mousey blond hair. He was the apple of mum's eye, especially after he got into De La Salle Grammar, one of the best schools on Merseyside. Everyone knew him as Sinbad because he was always up to something. He was always buzzing about the place with a grin on his face. All three of us boys were sports mad, and because Sean played with me and Mark and tried to match us, he seemed way ahead of all the other kids his age. At school he won everything; his teachers said he was one of the best sportsmen they had ever known. Tricia, also a mousey blonde, had to contend with living in a very masculine household, but she was anything but a tomboy. Mum always looked out for her, and she loved doing girly stuff like playing with her dolls. She used to dress up Kai in a bonnet and baby clothes and push him around the Farm in a pram. The dog loved it and would lie on his back and play along. Old grannies would say, 'Ooh, let's have a look at the baby, love.' They'd pull back the blankets and there would be Kai, ratting scars and all, grinning back at them. It scared them half to death.

I loved TV and would watch any old bollocks, especially sport: football, racing, athletics, rugby, cricket, snooker, darts – anything. But my favourite show was *Star Trek*. Captain James T. Kirk was a big hero of mine, and still is today. I thought it was dead cool that wherever he went in the universe he always found a bird who fancied him, even if she was an alien. I loved the way he always had a little joke with Spock and the rest of them on the bridge at the end of every show. My favourite film, then as now, is *The Wizard of Oz*. I just love the way it takes you to a different world for a couple of hours. I watch it every Christmas. I also loved music from an early age. Dad liked rock 'n' roll, the Beatles and Elvis, and they formed a soundtrack to my early life. Anyone old enough to remember the sixties grew up with the Beatles, but in Liverpool it was something else. They were like the four patron saints of the city, and everywhere you went their music blared out.

I went to St Albert's Roman Catholic Primary School on the estate. I was quick-witted but not really academic. I listened and, with Mum's encouragement, tried to learn, but I was a lad's lad and I was the cock of the school – the best fighter in the place. Despite being the hardest, however, I wasn't a bully. I preferred to have a laugh with the other kids and take the piss. There were fights with rival gangs from nearby Huyton though, and if the old fella found out it was a clip round the ear for me and I would be sent to bed with no tea. My parents were chuffed to bits when I passed my eleven plus, but the nearest grammar school meant me having to take three or four different buses. Dad and Mum were too busy to ferry me around, so it was off to St Dominic's Comprehensive in nearby Huyton. It was a poor area. Lots of families couldn't even afford the uniform, and those kids got teased. Luckily, Mum and Dad managed to kit me out.

School for me meant sport, sport, sport. Mr Mellon and Mr Price encouraged me with my football and athletics. I started playing for Huyton Boys team, for whom England midfielder Peter Reid also starred. We were a great team, but we looked like a bunch of urchins; I don't think Huyton council could afford to buy us a proper kit. We all had different colour strips and odd socks, but when we played the Liverpool lads they all looked like junior Charles Atlases. They were all six foot tall with gleaming new kits that Liverpool had given them. We always gave them a good game though. I also played rugby, cricket, tennis and badminton. A teacher called Mr Duff would organise the tennis and badminton tournaments; I won the tennis and came second in the badminton. My mum's sister, auntie Gina, was keen on tennis and she encouraged me to play. She wrote off to the nearest tennis club, Vagabounds, but of course I didn't have proper whites and looked a bit of a scruff and was turned down. Gina wrote four times but she couldn't get me in. It was a fucking disgrace, really. It's no wonder we're so bollocks at tennis in this country.

I didn't mind lessons, but I used to stare out of the classroom window at the playing fields, longing to get out there and kick a ball around. That was where I really came alive. I knew I had it in me to be a decent footballer, and that was all I wanted to do. One day, when I was fifteen, a job creation counsellor came in and interviewed everyone in the class.

'What do you want to work as, Michael?' he asked me.

'I'm going to be a professional footballer, sir,' I replied. It was the same answer I gave everyone.

He laughed and said, 'Michael, every boy in Liverpool wants to be a professional footballer. Unfortunately, only one among thousands makes it. Now, can you tell me something a little more realistic you'd like to do?'

I told him I was sports crazy and wouldn't mind being a sports journalist.

'Well, you need five O-levels to do that,' he said.

Oh well. I was sharp at school and had spadefulls of common sense, but exams and the academic life weren't really for me.

Soon after that, Dad got me a trial at Tranmere Rovers, Liverpool's third team on the Birkenhead side of the Mersey, who were then in the Third Division. He had played football in the same team as the father of Bobby Tynan, who was now on the staff at the club. Dad said I was a goal machine for my junior team and that Rovers should give me a trial. Bobby came over one Saturday, and that day I scored five in a 7–2 win. Bobby said, 'Mick, your boy doesn't need a trial. Bring him along to training.' So every Tuesday and Thursday Dad drove me to Tranmere and I trained and played for the under-sixteens.

The Wirral-based team had always lived in the shadow of Liverpool and Everton and was a family club with small gates. I wanted the big time and the glamour that went with it, so I also had trials with Liverpool, for whom I'd dreamt of playing since I was a nipper. I went along for training and played in a few games. It was very exciting to be involved with the club I'd idolised for as long as I could remember, but there were so many kids down there that you only got to play for about ten minutes in a game, and after a month the coaches didn't even know my name. I knocked it on the head because I knew I would never get noticed there. I could always go back when I was an established star.

Then, when I was 15, a scout called Jimmy Aspinall heard about the young hotshot from Cantril Farm and came to see me play. Jimmy, now a scout for Liverpool who has discovered a wealth of talent including Robbie Fowler, approached me as I walked off the pitch one day and asked if I fancied a trial for Derby County, then a leading First Division club. I was made up and couldn't wait to show County what I could do. I went down there, scored a shitload of goals, and was offered a £16-a-week apprenticeship with £15 towards lodging costs. I told Tranmere about the offer and they said they wanted me as well. I knew that at Rovers it would be much easier to break into the first team and I could live at home at the same time, but Derby were in the glamorous First Division. It was no contest. I wanted to go straight into the big time.

4. FIFTY PENCE EACH WAY

'A dollar won is twice as sweet as a dollar earned.'
Paul Newman in *The Color of Money*

'Punters are stupid bastards, aren't they?'
Lester Piggott

Dad was sitting on the sofa with the newspaper on his lap, as he did most Saturday afternoons. Earlier, after breakfast, he had marked his racing selections in the paper and had then walked around the corner to Ladbrokes in the little parade of shops on the estate. Now he was waiting for the *World of Sport* ITV 7 to start – the seven televised races of the afternoon.

'Dad, can I have a go?' I pleaded.

Dad showed me how to read a race card. He explained the handicap system, showed me how the weight the horse has to carry was written beside its name, and told me that some horses preferred different sorts of going. I looked through the paper and put my crosses next to the horses I thought would win.

First race, and Dad's horse got a bad start. It was tailed off before pulling up, but mine surged through and finished third. Next race, and coming into the home straight our horses were neck and neck. We were both jumping up and down on the sofa going apeshit. My selection just got up to beat Dad's, and I jumped up and danced around the room. What a buzz! Nearly as good as scoring a goal. I didn't get any more winners that day, but at the tender age of thirteen I was well and truly hooked on the thrill of horse racing. I started picking horses every Saturday and taking on Dad. He got more and more irate as I seemed to do better than him every week. 'You're putting a fucking jinx on me,' he would moan.

It didn't take me long to twig that I could be making a few quid with all the winners I was picking, so I started skipping lunches and using my dinner money for a punt. I also started to skive off school. Me and a mate called Billy Kearns would hang around outside the bookie's until we spotted a friendly bloke who we'd get to put on bets for us. It was usually 50p each way. I made the sort of silly mistakes that beginners make – sentimental bets, silly odds and daft accumulators – but I managed to get a few winners nonetheless. If I lost, I didn't get any dinner, so there was a big incentive to get it right.

Then one day I came home and Mum and Dad were waiting for me in the lounge with faces like thunder.

'You silly bastard,' Dad bellowed. 'You've been having a fucking bet.'

'Michael, how could you?' Mum said, almost in tears. 'I thought we'd brought you up well, but you're gambling at your age. You've brought shame on the family.'

Dad clipped me round the head, stopped my pocket money, and I was grounded for a month.

But it did nothing to put me off. It was too late. Just a few weeks later was the day of the second biggest sporting event on Merseyside after the Liverpool–Everton derby: the Grand National. Me and the rest of the gang – Kevin, Snowy, John, Mark and Philip – took a bus up to Aintree, walked around the course, and on the far side clambered over the fence. We were all dressed up in trackies and trainers and fancied ourselves as right lads. We watched the build-up races, then went and stood by the Canal Turn for the National. I could hear the thunder of the horses' hooves on the turf before I saw the leaders approaching. The hairs on the back of my neck stood on end. As they flew over the huge spruce fence we screamed and danced around. It was my first visit to a racecourse and a magical moment for me.

I started to read the racing cards in the paper every day. My heroes were Lester Piggott and Red Rum. Every punter loved Lester, just like they love National Hunt champion jockey Tony

McCoy today. Winning means everything to them, and both had the ability to be first on horses that shouldn't have won and wouldn't have won under anybody else. Watching Lester on a racehorse was thrilling: stirrups short, reins long, man and horse flowing over the turf in perfect harmony. He had problems with authority and a brilliant win-at-all costs attitude. What a bloke.

Rummy, trained on the sands at Southport by Ginger McCain, was almost as big a Scouse hero as Bill Shankly. I remember watching him win his record-breaking third Grand National in 1977 with tears in my eyes, bouncing up and down on the sofa at 16 Round Hey. Everyone on Merseyside had a few quid on him, including me and the old fella. Rummy was a freak of nature who was bred as a sprinter on the flat. Lester even rode him in a five-furlong seller at Aintree. He ran five times in the National and won it three times, coming second twice, on one of those occasions to dual Gold Cup winner L'Escargot. Just like all my heroes, he had battled his way up from adversity. After failing on the flat he became the most famous British racehorse ever. Years later, when he died, I cried like a baby.

As well as going to racecourses, me and the gang used to cycle for miles to places like Southport and New Brighton. We would hang around the fun fairs and have fights with other lads, then we would piss about on the beach, trying to avoid all the turds. We would nick pens, sweets and wank mags from W.H. Smith's, but we weren't robbing houses or cars or anything like that.

It was at thirteen that I also started getting into birds. I opted to do CSE cooking – or Food and Nutrition as they grandly called it – rather than woodwork because there were fifteen birds and just two lads doing it. I would cycle around the Farm giving it the big one to all the girls. There was a little gang of girls who hung around Round Hey and I went out with all of them at one time or another. It was just kissing and fumbling. I wasn't old enough for shagging.

I also started to get into music big time. I started to learn guitar at school; I thought I was the next John Lennon. If I didn't make it as a footballer I could always be a pop star. I still play the guitar today, and can knock out a mean 'Working-Class Hero'. Me, Kevin and John decided to start a mobile disco as we thought it would be a good way of pulling birds. We called ourselves the Bus Stop Disco and played at local youth clubs and parties. We were three scallies who thought we were cool as fuck. Kev, short and stocky with tight, dark, curly hair, and John, a year older than me and fair with chiselled features, spun the records; yours truly did the banter on the mike between songs. We were well into our soul and dance music and played stuff by Earth, Wind and Fire, James Brown, the Fatback Band and Parliament. Dad could never work out how a kid from Cantril Farm could be so into black American dance music. Kev's older brother got me into it. He put on an Earth, Wind and Fire record for me once and something clicked. A light went on inside my head, and I thought, 'This is the real deal.' They are still my favourite band. Before that I'd been listening to Status Quo, Black Sabbath, Slade and Sweet. Back then it was uncool for lads to dance, but I used to get up and do this thing called The Walk. It was basically walking backwards and forwards with the odd hand jerk and flick of the fingers. I thought I was frigging John Travolta.

I went through a few fashion stages in my teens. At one point we all wore long trench macs and looked like Columbo. I used to wear baggy trousers called Birmingham bags, V-necked jumpers and spoon shoes. Then punk rock took off and we started to wear mohair jumpers and drainpipe trousers. We also introduced a few punk and new wave records into our DJ set from bands like the Sex Pistols, the Jam and Elvis Costello.

At fifteen, I started boozing. First it was cheap cider at discos or hanging around the streets. I used to drink it like lemonade.

Then one day the Bus Stop Disco were asked to play at a couple's 25th wedding anniversary in a local hall. Kevin's uncle Jimmy had a minivan and we drove our kit over in that. The couple really liked our funky records and started to send over complimentary drinks. It wasn't cider but Pernod, whisky, gin and brandy. It was double this and double that. I was really loving it, giving it the big one on the mike and winking at the girls. I was having a ball.

Then the room started spinning and I began to feel very sick. I badly needed to lie down. The last thing I remember that night is collapsing behind one of the speakers in a pool of my own puke. Kevin and Jimmy dragged me to the minivan and put me in the back. I was completely comatose with diced carrot all down my front. On the way home a large wet patch appeared around my crotch. When we pulled up outside 16 Round Hey Mum and Dad heard the commotion and came rushing out.

'You've pissed yourself, you dirty little sod,' Dad bellowed, 'and you've got puke all over your clothes.' I could hear what he was saying but I was too fucked to move. Mum started crying. Dad dragged me into the house and up the stairs, dumped me in the bath and turned the shower on. 'You thought you were the big man who could handle his ale, didn't you? I hope this is a fucking lesson to you.'

'Michael, I can't believe you'd embarrass the family like this,' Mum spluttered through her tears.

I was grounded. I wasn't even allowed to play football, which was the worst punishment they could dish out. I didn't drink Pernod again for a decade.

Just before I left school I joined a local amateur dramatic society. I loved the thrill of performing on stage and got a part as Tony in *West Side Story*. The lads gave me a load of stick, calling me a big poof, but I didn't give a toss, I really enjoyed it. In the play I got stabbed, and I remember acting it up, taking about five minutes to stagger around holding my wound before dropping to the floor. Mum was in the audience and said she was really proud of me. Whether it's on the stage, behind a mobile disco or on the football field, I have always loved playing to a crowd.

When my CSEs approached, Mum begged me to do some revision. I remember her saying, 'Please try, Michael. Suppose this football thing doesn't work out?' But I really couldn't be arsed. In the end I got a grade one CSE in English – the equivalent of an O-level pass – grade four in English Literature, grade two in Food and Nutrition and grade five in Music. I was ungraded in Maths and Geography. But who cares? By the time I got the results I was already an apprentice professional footballer with one of the biggest clubs in the country.

5. APPRENTICESHIP

'There's no place like home.'

Dorothy in *The Wizard of Oz*

'To be someone must be a wonderful thing, a famous footballer, a rock singer, or a big film star – yes, I think I would like that. To be rich and have lots of fans, have lots of girls to prove that I'm a man, and be number one and liked by everyone.'

The Jam, 'To Be Someone (Didn't We Have a Nice Time)'

I had been at Derby four months when seven of us apprentices piled into a Hillman Imp one night to go to a house party. We breezed in and started giving it the big one to all the birds about being footballers with a First Division team. I was knocking back the cider like there was no tomorrow. Well, there's no drinking when you're dead.

It had taken me a few months to come out of my shell at the club and start making friends and having a laugh. All the apprentices would go out on the piss big style on Saturday nights. We often went to the Top Rank nightclub in Derby where I would try to chat up the birds. I was sixteen and oozing testosterone, but I was still a virgin. I was fucking desperate to break my duck as many of the apprentices had already done the business. It was turning into a race between some of the lads, and that night at the house party I was on the hunt for a half-decent bird to help me on my way.

Over the other side of the room I spotted a blonde in tight white miniskirt, white blouse and white stilettos. She was helping herself to a glass of punch from the punch bowl when I made my move. She wasn't exactly Marilyn Monroe, but then I was no Clark Gable – not yet anyway. 'Do you fancy a dance, love?' I asked, clutching my can of Strongbow tightly. She agreed. I was under starter's orders, and after downing a couple more bevvies we started snogging in front of everyone. It wasn't long before I was leading her by the hand outside and into an alley beside the house. A few of the other lads were also out there with girls. I didn't waste much time. With the other apprentices cheering me on, I dropped my trousers and pants and got on with it. It was over in a few quick thrusts but I was off the mark. Weighed in, as we say in racing, although it was more of a five-furlong sprint than a three-mile chase. Soon after that we piled into the Imp and headed for home. On the way back we stopped for a pee, and I noticed that my knob had blood all over it. In the dressing room on Monday my exploits were the big talking point. I loved all the banter and it felt great being Jack the lad.

I really thought I was the big grown-up lad when I left Cantril Farm for Derby County in the summer of 1978. They were a huge First Division club that had won the League title twice in the seventies, the last occasion just three years before I arrived. I already had the moustache that was to be my trademark during my playing days – it was just getting through the bum-fluff stage, but I was desperate to have one as they were trendy at the time, particularly on Merseyside – and with my mop of black hair I looked liked the drummer from Frankie Goes to Hollywood. I didn't go for the perm but had a bushy head of black hair. Looking back at photographs of myself then in the reserve team, it looks like I should be wearing a sombrero in a spaghetti western.

Dad had driven me down the motorway in our battered Ford Granada to the digs the club had arranged in a two up, two down in Cuthbert Street in the suburbs of Derby. Dad was so proud that I was starting out on a footballing career, something that he would have loved to do, and all my friends and family were chuffed that someone from the Farm seemed to be on the path to success. Dad said hello to the old couple who were going to be looking after me, and then I was shown to my room. Wayne Richards, a fellow apprentice, also roomed there. After tea with the couple, I went to bed. As I lay in the darkness my cocksure attitude evaporated. I began to miss my family and all my friends like crazy. I felt lost and lonely. I wasn't as grown up as I had thought.

The next day I joined the fifteen other apprentices for my first day in professional football. We were given a short introductory talk by Ronnie Webster, youth-team boss and ex-Derby player, then we were shown to the shithouses. One of the coaches barked, 'These have got to be fucking spotless every morning or you will get your scrawny arses kicked.' And the old pros made sure there was shit everywhere for us to clean up, just as they'd had to do in their day. We scrubbed the dressing rooms and the baths. Any backchat, or if, God forbid, a spot of dirt was found, and you would be given an almighty bollocking. We also had to put out the players' kit and make sure the four players' boots you were assigned to clean were polished and ready to be put on. I cleaned Gordon Hill's, who later starred for Manchester United. We had to sweep the corridors, too. We didn't seem to be kicking many footballs.

I wasn't used to doing much in the way of tidying up – Mum had always taken care of all that. I hated it, and thought, 'What the fuck has all this got to do with football?' I couldn't see how wiping up the piss and shit of some has-been old player would make you a better footballer. But I tried to knuckle down, keep my gob shut and work hard. After three days I wrote home, saying that the training was hard and that I was bored at night. I wrote, 'The meals are fantastic but not as good as yours, Mum. I'm missing your spaghetti a lot. Although Tricia is a pest, I still miss her, and Sean.' Reading the letter now, I sound like a little boy lost. In truth, I was terribly homesick.

Football was still in the dark ages then. Hooliganism dominated the terraces, crowd numbers had dipped and the only 'foreign' stars in the squad were from Scotland, Ireland or Wales. The advent of Sky TV, which turned football into a multi-million-pound showbusiness world, was still a decade away. Some of the older players at Derby made time for you and treated you kindly; others, mainly those who were in the reserves and hadn't long been professionals themselves, were complete arseholes. Fellow Scouser Roy McFarland, the ex-England centre-back who was a legend at Derby, took me under his wing and looked after me. He used to take me to the dogs and give me a couple of quid for a sarnie and a bet. Gordon Hill, sporting a great Bay City Rollers-style haircut, would take us apprentices into town and buy us chips when we were skint. Bruce Rioch, who went on to manage Arsenal, would give me free records as he knew someone in the business. I was nuts about music, then as now, and couldn't get my hands on enough albums. I liked some chart stuff, but it was still funk and R & B for me. Then Bruce got me a copy of new band the Jam's *All Mod Cons*. Paul Weller was the front man and I loved his snappy mod dress sense with his drainpipe trousers and small-collared shirts. Before that, everyone had been wearing huge flares and wing-collared shirts. Their songs, like 'David Watts', 'A-Bomb in Wardour Street' and 'Down in the Tube Station at Midnight' were great tunes. It was angry music, and being a teenage lad, I thought it was brilliant. Other big stars at Derby at the time were ex-Arsenal striker Charlie George, Colin Todd, Gerry Daly and Don Masson. Tommy Docherty, later to manage Manchester United, was the gaffer. I tried to copy their moves, and if they offered me advice, I listened. Most were happy to help.

But Colin 'Charlie' Chesters, the reserve-team centre-forward, was very much in the arsehole category as far as I was concerned. I saw him walk up to apprentices and head-butt them for no reason. He found it hilariously funny, and I suppose he was dying for you to have a go back. When Chesters first did it to me, I didn't know what to do, so I just took it, stared at him and walked away. He did it to all the apprentices; it was a kind of test. It was just what you needed as a sixteen-year-old lad trying to settle into a new environment miles from home. I wouldn't have minded meeting him a few years down the line, when I had grown a bit bigger, for another game of head-butts.

Head-butting and cleaning up other people's shit were not what I thought football was all about. For me, it took all the enjoyment out of the game when we finally got round to playing it. Perhaps I thought I should have been playing in the first team. But I did learn a lot about the basics of playing the game at Derby. Ronnie Webster gave us a good grounding. He taught us how to get ourselves fit, and showed us basic ball skills like trapping a ball, first touch and second touch. We played five-a-side, games that were full of late tackles and little flare-ups.

Whenever we had the afternoon off, starting a habit that would last for the rest of my career, I would drift off to the bookie's. I couldn't spend much as I was only on £16 a week, so I would often just walk aimlessly around the shops. We'd always have to be back by 4 p.m. for more cleaning before sorting out the kit for the following day. The old couple I lodged with were great cooks, but they also had a curfew, and they reported you to the club if you weren't in by 10 p.m. Not a great prospect for a sixteen-year-old just getting into his boozing and shagging, though we did, of course, manage that night out in the Hillman Imp.

I was beginning to leave my mark on the football field, too. We drew Manchester United in the Youth Cup that season. It was a big game, played at Old Trafford, and the Doc himself got involved. He gave a rousing team talk and finished off by telling us, 'Don't be afraid of them, just go out and play. If you beat United today I will give every one of you a one-hundred-pound bonus.' The Doc was desperate to beat them. I scored, and we won 3–1. It was wonderful to score in such a big game, and great to play at Old Trafford. It made me more determined than ever to become a professional. I also played at Highbury and sent the team sheet to Sean, telling him to keep it for his scrapbook.

I used to go home to Cantril Farm once a month, when I had saved up a bit of dosh, to see the family and go out on the piss with the lads from the estate. I used to bring my record player back in my bag because I was so crazy about music at the time. I couldn't go out unless I put on a bit of funk or R & B. During one of my stays at home I was DJing at the Long Reach in Dovecote between Knotty Ash and Huyton, not far from the Farm, when a girl a cut above the usual caught my eye. She had a cute face, with high cheekbones, beautiful big green eyes and a mane of brown hair combed back and bouncing on her shoulders. She also had a shapely figure and long, long legs. She wore a red mohair jumper, drainpipe jeans and what we called granny shoes with peaked toes and low heels, which I thought at the time was the height of cool.

I said over the mike in my best Smashy and Nicey voice, 'This one's for the girl in the red mohair jumper.' I spun the Jam's 'English Rose', then made my way over to her as casual as you like. Her name was Debbie Williams, and at eighteen she was two years older than me. She worked as a carer in an old people's home. She was a real woman compared to the other birds I'd chatted up and I was absolutely bowled over. We seemed to click straight away. I got her number, and on my next trip home we became an item. Debbie was my first proper girlfriend and it became a big wrench to leave Liverpool and head back to Derby at the end of every visit home. I once gibbed out of a youth-team tour to Switzerland because I wanted to go back to Liverpool. Not only was I homesick, I was desperate to see Debbie, too.

To make my loneliness worse, I had a very frightening experience one night as I slept in my digs. I woke with the hairs on my neck standing on end. There was a chill in the room and my breath was leaving a vapour trail. I craned my neck over my shoulder and let out a shriek. Standing at my shoulder was a ghostly figure in human form. I jumped out of bed and hit the light switch. The apparition disappeared, but I kept the light on all night and hardly slept a wink. It shook me badly. The next morning I told Wayne, the other apprentice lodging there, and he told me that a member of the family had died in my room. I haven't seen a ghost since, but I do believe in the spirit world. It really put the shits up me and made me feel more homesick than ever.

Then, around eight months after joining Derby, the couple I was lodging with grassed to the club that I had been breaking their poxy 10 p.m. curfew. I had been out on the razz with a few of the lads and had banged the door coming in late. The Doc, who would later manage Manchester United, called me into his office for a chat. Despite being only sixteen, I wasn't in awe of him. He would always crack a couple of funnies to put you at ease, but this time there were no gags.

'Michael, we hear you've been taking the piss a bit at your digs and coming in late,' he said. 'It's not the sort of behaviour we expect from an apprentice just starting in the game. You should have more respect for the family who are looking after you.'

'To be honest, Mr Docherty, I've had enough,' I told him. 'I want to quit and go back to Liverpool. I'm missing my family too much. I want to go back and start again. I'm sorry to mess you around.'

He reluctantly agreed, and I was released by mutual consent. Apart from me, only Trevor Morley, who was successful at Aston Villa, and Steve Spooner, who played in the lower leagues, went on to enjoy professional careers from my batch of apprentices at Derby. That shows how difficult it is to make the grade.

Cantril Farm might have been a concrete jungle, but it was still a close-knit community and I missed it so much. I rang home and told Dad what I'd done. He went absolutely nuts.

'What the fuck are you playing at?' he bawled. 'Cantril Farm's full of kids on the dole and you throw away a dream career. You can't get a job around here for love nor money. You must be fucking mad.'

But I had made up my mind, so it was back to my bedroom at Round Hey. I did what a lot of my old school mates were doing and signed on the dole. Roy McFarland sent me a lovely letter: 'Dear Quinny, Sorry to see you finished so quickly. I just thought I'd write to wish you all the best in whatever you plan to do in the future. Don't let your head drop. Good luck. Roy McFarland.' It was wonderful for a player of his stature to think of me, and the letter gave me a real lift. I made sure I treated apprentices with the same respect in the future.

Despite quitting Derby, I was still determined to make it as a pro and I wrote letters to every club in the north-west begging for a trial. I sent one letter to Tranmere manager John King telling him I had made a mistake turning down the club's offer and now would love to take it up. I was shocked when I received his reply: 'You had your chance. Now I don't even want you to come within a mile of the ground.' I couldn't believe he was being so precious. I was a kid who had made the wrong decision at a young age, but he wasn't big enough to give me a second chance.

Debbie and I saw each other the whole time. It was great to be back. Everyone else on the estate seemed to be signing on at the time, too. Unemployment was high across the country but on Merseyside it was especially bad. Away fans, particularly Londoners, would sing at the Kop: 'In your Liverpool slums, you look in the dustbin for something to eat. You find a dead rat and think it's a treat, in your Liverpool slums.'

Despite the knockback from Tranmere, I kept writing to clubs all over the north-west. Eventually, a letter dropped through the door at 16 Round Hey from Wigan Athletic manager Ian McNeill offering me a trial. I went down to Springfield Park and did well in a few practice matches. Ian told me, 'We are the Football League's youngest club but we are very ambitious. You are a very talented young footballer, and if you work hard you will get your chance here.' They offered me a generous apprenticeship at £35 a week with £5 a week travelling expenses. I also received a signing-on fee of £250, but it was hardly big dosh. Dad wasn't earning a king's ransom with his cab and he had three other kids to feed, so as well as taking up the Wigan offer I decided to carry on signing on the dole. I didn't think anyone would notice.

Wigan had only just achieved League status, having been promoted from the Northern Premier League in 1978. They were an ambitious club with a small squad which meant I would taste first-team action sooner rather than later if I was good enough. It was also close to home, and I soon discovered the club was teeming with Scousers. There must have been about eight of us at the club then, and we would share lifts to the Springfield Park ground, reading the racing papers in the car on the way up there and then stopping off for a pint and a game of pool on the way back. Life was looking up again. As Dorothy says in *The Wizard of Oz*, there's no place like home.

6. BABY MICHAEL

'If a player is not interfering with play or seeking to gain an advantage, then he should be.'

Bill Shankly

I was lying on the sofa at home one afternoon drinking a can of lager and eating a butty when there was a knock on the door. I had just come back from training at Wigan, had done me nuts in the bookie's on the estate and was about to have a kip. Mark, Sean and Tricia were at school, Mum was down the shops and Dad was at work, so I was forced to get up and answer the door myself.

'Michael Quinn?' said a stern-voiced man dressed in a smart dark suit.

'Yeah. What's it to you, pal?' I sneered back.

'Mr Quinn, I'm from the DSS,' he said in a deadpan voice, 'and we have reason to believe you have been signing on and claiming unemployment benefit while working full time for Wigan Athletic Football Club.'

Oh shit. My football career looked like going tits up before it had started. I had walked out on Derby and now I looked like being lobbed out of Wigan for signing on. It turned out some nice person in a bookie's in Huyton, next door to Cantril Farm, had heard me talking about playing for Wigan and knew I was claiming dole. Whoever it was had grassed me up to the DSS.

When I told Mum and Dad, they stared at me in disbelief.

'Are you fucking stupid or what?' Dad yelled. 'You've got the talent to go to the top in football but you're going to throw it all away being a dickhead. You got a second chance after Derby and now you've fucked it up again. You don't know how lucky you are. When I was your age I was working down the docks at all hours. I give up, I really do.'

Mum said, 'Michael, if you wanted any extra cash you should have asked. I would have helped you out. How could you be so stupid?'

I felt I had let the family down after they had backed me all the way in my football and been so proud of me getting to a League club. I had a sleepless night, and the next morning I went straight in to see the manager Ian McNeill.

'Mr McNeill, I've made a big mistake,' I mumbled, ashen-faced. 'I've been signing on while playing for Wigan and been found out. I'm so sorry, I've been a complete prick.'

Ian, an easy-going bloke who I always got on well with, stared at the pitiful figure in front of him and burst out laughing.

'Look, Quinny, it ain't the end of the world. Get it sorted and don't do it again. The chairman doesn't need to find out about it. Just go out and score a few goals for me and we'll forget all about it,' he said.

A huge weight had been lifted off my shoulders. The dole office let me pay the cash I had claimed back in instalments and I knuckled down and concentrated on my football.

Wigan, a bustling working-class Lancashire town on the fringes of Greater Manchester, was a great move for me. It was only a short drive away, meaning I could live at home, and it was also a small club, giving me a chance to break into the first team quickly. The town has always been more famous for its all-conquering rugby league team. Springfield Park was a rusty, tumbledown stadium. I always remember a white police horse standing on a grass bank behind the terraces during games. It was hardly the Nou Camp. Now Wigan play in the 25,000-capacity £30 million JJB Stadium, shared with the rugby league club, but back then they were just finding their feet in the old Fourth Division.

I was introduced to a training regime which basically stayed the same throughout my career, whichever club I was at. After each season I would do nothing for three weeks but eat and drink, and my weight would balloon by as much as two stone. As pre-season approached I would cut down a bit on the food and perhaps do a bit of jogging and swimming. Then it was back to the club around 10 July after six weeks off. Training in week one would begin with a fitness test and lots of light exercise and stretching from 10 a.m. to 12.30 p.m. We would return in the afternoon from 2 p.m. to 4.30 p.m. for a three- or four-mile run and more stretching with everyone from apprentices to first-team stars training together. In week two we would concentrate on more stamina work with five-mile runs and other aerobic stuff. I wasn't much of a distance runner because of my large frame, so I would end up jogging along at the back with the goalies and the other big lads. In week three we would work on ball skills and speed work and start playing five a-sides. Then the practice matches started, followed by friendlies and pre-season tours. When the season proper started, the first-team squad would train alone, starting at 10 a.m. and finishing around 12.30 p.m. Often I would stay on and work with the coaches on my heading and shooting skills. At Wigan we were weighed every Monday and Friday, and it was the same at most clubs. Sometimes you could put on as much as six pounds over a weekend if you went massively on the piss and ate a good Sunday roast. If you were over what was considered your ideal weight you were fined, and I was hit with fines a few times, but the cash went into a pot for an end-of-season piss-up so it wasn't much of a loss anyway. If I had put a bit of weight on I would get one of the lads to distract the physio as he weighed me and not stand on the scales properly.

One night after training I went round to see Debbie. She looked pale and drawn.

'Mike, you'd better sit down,' she said tearfully. 'I'm going to have a baby.'

I sat there pole-axed. I was still a kid and was in no way ready for fatherhood. Debbie had come off the pill and I had chanced having sex without a rubber johnny. But I gathered my thoughts, hugged her, and said, 'We'll get through this together, babe. Whatever you want to do I'll support you.' I wanted to do the right thing and had absolutely no thoughts of walking away from my responsibility.

We decided to have the baby, so I went round to break the news to Mum and Dad. Mum broke down in tears. As a strict Catholic, she thought I had brought shame on the family, especially when I admitted that Debbie and I had no plans to marry. Dad said, 'You stupid idiot. You're just starting in life and you do something like this. Why do you always do something fucking stupid just as you start getting a bit of success?' Debbie's family were equally pissed off, but soon they all calmed down and were very supportive. They helped us with baby clothes and to find a council house in Huyton, and contributed a few sticks of furniture. We didn't even have a proper bed, sleeping instead on this sponge thing which was a glorified sofa.

My son Michael was born while I was at training at 11.30 a.m. on 16 January 1980 in Mill Road Hospital, Liverpool, and he weighed in at seven pounds seven ounces. I got a call at the club saying my son had arrived so I dashed back from Wigan and went straight to the hospital. I kissed Debbie and picked up the tiny bundle that was my flesh and blood. I thought, 'Shit, I'm a dad! What am I supposed to do now?' I didn't know whether to laugh or cry. Debbie was nineteen and I was seventeen.

It is something of a tradition in Liverpool, certainly in our family, to call the first-born son after the father, as I was named after my dad. So the baby was known in the family as Little Michael. Likewise, when my brother Mark had his first son he was Little Mark, and our Sean's first kid was named Little Sean. In January 2003, Little Michael had his first son, so now there is a Little Little Michael. It can get a bit confusing.

I didn't tell anyone at Wigan about Michael's arrival in case it was frowned upon. At the time, football clubs held themselves to be moral guardians, and for an apprentice to have an illegitimate child back then was almost taboo.

I started off at Wigan in the reserves. In October 1979 we played Manchester United reserves and I managed to get myself sent off. As our team was packed with Scousers we were bang up for the game. Ref Malcolm Todd had already warned me for clattering someone, and had awarded United a free-kick. I lost my head, and as they prepared to take it I jogged over to the ball, stepped over it, then gave it a hefty back-kick. Out came the red card. I got an almighty bollocking from the coaches and was fined £4 by the club. Despite that, things were going well for me at Wigan. I was training hard and soaking up skills and techniques from the older lads. The coaches told me they thought I had the talent to become a professional footballer, that it would only be a matter of time before I broke into the first team.

But my £35-a-week wage packet didn't go very far. Debbie was signing on and getting child support, but basically we didn't have a pot to piss in. Mum offered to look after Michael so Debbie could go out to work, but we wanted the baby to be with his mother. I would come home from training to dirty nappies without enough cash even to go for my afternoon bet. It was hardly the glamorous footballer's life, but I loved Michael and tried to give him as much as I could. Sometimes Mum and Dad would lend me a few quid to have a punt. Other times I got really desperate. We had one of those TVs where you put 50p pieces in the back to power it. I can remember getting a screwdriver and jemmying the back off to get a few quid for a bet. But I always kept a bit back for the telly – there would be hell to pay if I missed *Star Trek*. Debbie would shout and scream if she knew I'd been down the bookie's, then didn't have enough cash to put a meal on the table. I can't say I blame her.

Gambling seems to be in my blood. People who have a punt don't do it to make money, they do it for the thrill. I would class myself as a risk-taker in life. I love the idea of beating the odds; even if I had a win I would stay on and spunk more money away. It was like a daily fix I needed; the buzz of winning was like a drug rush. I won my fair share of cash, and I don't consider myself a mug punter, but I kept going back.

That April, the gaffer called me to one side after training. 'Oh shit,' I thought. 'Have the DSS got on to the chairman?' But Ian said, 'Mickey, I'm going to give you your debut on Saturday. Go out there, play your normal game and enjoy it.'

Saturday, 12 April 1980 couldn't come quick enough for me. When I jogged out that afternoon for the Lactics against Halifax at Springfield Park in front of 5,076 fans in the old Division Four, it felt like a Wembley final. My family and friends were in the stands, and it was everything I had dreamt of as a kid. I ran around like a man possessed and achieved very little, but in the second half, when we were already 2–1 up, I suddenly sprang the offside trap and was left in a one-on-one with their keeper. I travelled at pace towards him, looking straight into the whites of his eyes. He shit out basically and made the cardinal sin of making the first move. He dived for the ball, I flicked it past him and tapped it into the net from just a few yards out. It was hardly a screamer but I went absolutely apeshit.

I had imagined for years how I would celebrate scoring a League goal. Would I kiss the badge and salute the fans? Whip my shirt off? Run to the corner flag for a John Lennon impersonation? Now that I'd actually scored, all that went out the window. I wheeled away, pushed past my team-mates gathering to congratulate me, and set off screaming and bounding in the air, with arms aloft, towards the halfway line. Anyone who has seen how Ronnie Radford celebrated after scoring his famous FA Cup goal for Hereford against Newcastle will get the idea. Add to that the legendary David-Pleat-in-a-cheap-suit victory pitch invasion when his Luton team stayed up, and you get an idea of my manic celebration that day. My team-mates just stood there, hands on hips, pissing themselves laughing. I didn't give a fuck. I'd scored my first League goal, and it felt like the winner in the World Cup final.

After the game it was back to the Farm for a pub crawl around the estate, starting in the Tithe Barn. It was Dad's local and you were guaranteed a lock-in. Dad was just a punter in there at the time, but he would help organise the stay-behind and he later went on to manage the pub. He is not a man to show his emotions; there were no hugs, no big 'I'm proud of you' speech. He just said, 'Well played, son.' But that was enough for me. I knew he was chuffed to bits. Later I met Debbie and we had drunken sex. It was a great way to end the evening.

Next day my name was all over the local papers. I loved all the attention, it was what I had always craved, and I couldn't wait to get out there and score more goals. I was sub for the remaining games of the 1979/80 season because Ian McNeill wanted to nurse me through slowly, but it was great just to be involved.

That summer the club went on an end-of-season tour to the football-mad Mediterranean island of Malta. Manchester United legend Bobby Charlton, who had become a club director at Wigan, joined the party. Wigan then had a load of Scousers including Frank Corrigan, Peter Houghton, Alex Cribley and Tony Quinn, and roughly the same number of Scotsmen, so the club had a family atmosphere. We got a 6 a.m. flight and the piss-up started on the plane; we were bladdered before we even arrived. We checked into the sumptuous Dragonara Hotel in St Julians, dumped our bags in our rooms and went straight downstairs for cocktails by the pool.

We were all working-class lads and the lavish surroundings went to our heads a bit. Next to us on some sun loungers were Lord and Lady Shit wearing more jewellery than Ron Atkinson at a Ratners sale. Frank Corrigan jumped on a table and shouted at the couple, 'Why don't you pawn them jewels and adopt a kid from Kirkby?' Then, in traditional Scouse fashion for a piss-up, he started a singsong as the rest of the guests tried to sunbathe by the pool. The gaffer rushed over and rounded us up for a team meeting. 'We have been in the resort for under four hours and the hotel manager has already received a string of complaints,' he yelled. 'If you don't start behaving in a manner becoming of professional footballers then the tour will be cancelled and we'll be on the next flight home.' So it was into our rooms to do some serious damage to the minibar.

Next day we were playing a local side and Bobby Charlton had agreed to make a cameo appearance. Malta is Manchester United nuts, and the ground was heaving. In the second half, Bobby made his grand entrance. It wasn't long before the ball came to him nicely 40 yards out and sat up, and with his sweep-over hair trailing in the breeze he hit it like a thunderbolt on to the crossbar. The crowd went mad.

After the game it was back to the Dragonara for drinks. We hit the casino, which has a glass floor so you can see the ocean below, and settled down to watch the show. Hollywood star Robin Williams, who was in Malta filming *Popeye* and staying at the Dragonara, had agreed to do a stand-up routine. We heckled him but he gave it all back and was absolutely hilarious. Afterwards, Robin and his wife joined us for drinks.

She said, 'Robin has worked so hard filming *Popeye*. Every morning he sits for seven hours while his make-up is applied before he even begins on set.'

I could see tough Scotsman Colin Methven, a miner before he joined Wigan, looking at her with a look of utter disgust on his face. 'Hard work?' yelled the hard-as-nails centre-back in the broadest of Scots accents. 'If he thinks fannying around having make-up put on is hard work, he should try shovelling coal down the pit for eight hours.'

'Yeah,' I joined in. 'Or be in a family of four in Liverpool living on sixty pounds a week.'

Robin, to be fair, laughed along with us. He even agreed to sign a Maltese one-pound note for me. We then decided to move on and find another bar, where I offered to get the beers in. They came to £11. I handed over a tenner, and the only cash I had left after that was the note Robin had signed. I looked at it, thought 'Fuck it', and handed it over. Easy come, easy go.

Despite being just a teenager I managed to keep up with all those heavy-drinking pros, but the next day I got in a spot of bother. We went for a lunchtime bevvy, then I went back to my room for a wash. I got my kit off, lay in the bath, set both taps running on full, then passed out. Luckily, Alex Cribley came back to look for me and found me slumped in the bath with the water up to my mouth. It was straight out for a stiff drink after that one. Thanks, mate, for saving my life. Alex, a lovely bloke who like me sported the Scouse tache, is now the physiotherapist at Wigan.

The next season, still only eighteen, I became a first-team regular and signed a new contract. I promised to 'play in an efficient manner to the best of my ability' for three years. I was to be paid £140 a week in the first year, rising to £160 in the second and £180 in the third. I also received £10 travelling expenses a week. Bonuses stood at £10 for a draw, £20 for a win, and £25 for a first-round victory in the FA Cup rising to £2,500 a man if we won the final. The chairman must have had a sense of humour. I again started off in the reserves where the bonuses were £1 for a draw and £2 for a win.

I had at that stage of my career what I would describe as a Wayne Rooney-type physique. Just like the Everton wonderkid I was a man trapped in a boy's body. I was twelve and a half stone and bigger than many of the old pros I was up against. I also had Rooney's aggression, and it gave my career a flying start. I scored my first League hat-trick in October 1980 against

Doncaster Rovers, and at last my life seemed to be running smoothly. There were big changes afoot at Wigan, too. Freddie Pye, one-time chairman of Manchester City, took over the club and brought in Ken Bates, now Chelsea's outspoken chairman. They wanted to inject the cash that would take us out of the Fourth Division.

On 8 December, I was lying in bed when I heard Mum shouting 'Oh my God!' downstairs in the front room. I ran down the stairs into the lounge, terrified that she'd hurt herself. 'John Lennon's dead,' she wailed. I was knocked for six. I sat there and listened to the news reports in stunned silence. Lennon was like Liverpool's very own Shakespeare. People were crying in the streets and the whole city was in mourning. I had been brought up with the Beatles. Paul McCartney could certainly knock out a decent tune, but John was a natural born rebel, a visionary and a creative genius. One of my biggest heroes was gone and I was devastated. I went up to my room, picked up my guitar and began playing 'Working-Class Hero', then 'Jealous Guy'. The tears welled up in my eyes.

Lennon's death coincided with things taking a turn for the worse at Wigan. After a string of bad results Ian McNeill was given the boot in February 1981 and he was replaced by ex-Nottingham Forest and Liverpool star Larry Lloyd as player–manager. In a sport full of bullies and lunatics, the six-foot-three-inch Larry, who had won just the one cap for England, was as far as I was concerned King Rat. On his arrival at the club the squad was directed to the players' lounge to be introduced to him. We expected him to give us the usual managerial spiel about having his own ideas, everyone having a clean slate and how the club was going places. Instead, Larry slammed the door open, nearly taking it off its hinges, strode in and bellowed, 'Hello, I'm Larry Lloyd. If you don't like what I'm going to say then I'm going to head-butt you.' Everyone looked at one another in amazement. Nobody knew whether he was being serious or whether he was joking, but judging by his bulging eyes and wild, jerky hand movements, he certainly looked as if he meant it.

We soon found out that Larry was every bit as formidable as he'd first appeared. On one occasion we came in at half-time after what was admittedly a poor performance to Larry going bananas. He smashed all the tea cups against the wall above our heads as we sat on the benches, and ranted, 'You were a fucking disgusting shower of shit out there!' He pointed to my fellow Scouser Tony Quinn and screamed, 'You fucking stank out there, get in the fucking shower!' Tony, who was sitting next to me, got up and left. I was frowning at the weird sight of Larry having virtual convulsions, so he turned to me.

'What's the fucking matter with you, Quinn?'

'Well,' I replied, 'if you got off our backs, we might be able to play.'

'Get in that fucking shower! You're off!' he screamed.

So I joined Tony in the baths. There was just one problem, though. Those were the days of just one substitute, so with two of us off Larry was sending his team out for the second half with just ten men. One of the coaches noticed, and as the ref waited to restart the game he dashed in to tell me I was back on. Eventually I emerged, nice and clean, to play the second half.

On another occasion Big Larry had a pop at Graham Barrow, a six-foot-three-inch bluff northerner who had worked his way up through the tough world of seventies non-League football. Larry was niggling at Graham in training, saying this was wrong and that was wrong, when suddenly Graham snapped and squared up to Larry in front of all the lads. Pointing to the other side of a ridge at the training ground, Graham screamed, 'OK, big man, you and me over there now. No one has to watch, just you and me. Come on.' A terrified-looking Larry turned down the kind offer.

I found my form in the Fourth Division towards the end of that 1980/81 season, and the goals were flying in. I was still eighteen, but I could handle myself. You have to be fairly tough to battle your way through the lower divisions. I had already learnt some tough lessons. If somebody went down the back of my leg with their studs, I'd turn around and give them a mouthful. If they did it again I'd clatter them in the next tackle. If they wanted to get up and make something of it, fine, I'll stand toe to toe.

My contract was up for renegotiation that summer, and after the fourteen goals I'd scored in my second season in League football I felt I was in a strong position. I stuck to my guns and held out for more cash. Assistant manager Fred Eyre said I was the 'oldest teenager he had ever met'. As a result my wages went up from £140 to £200 a week with £50 expenses. That was a lot of lolly for an eighteen-year-old, and it came just when I needed it most to support Debbie and Michael.

I was playing for a professional club, but football in those days was anything but professional. One time we were playing Doncaster and ex-Liverpool player Brian Kettle got his leg broken in an horrific tackle. All the lads were standing around dead concerned when suddenly these two St John Ambulance men pushed through with a stretcher. One was the spit of Benny Hill – the little specs, the flat cap all skew-whiff. Brian was writhing in agony so Benny and his mate stuck him on the stretcher and set off in wobbly fashion towards the touchline. They hadn't gone a couple of yards before they tipped the stretcher over, sending Brian screaming to the hard turf. Despite Benny's best efforts, Brian refused to get back on. Instead he hopped off the pitch, clutching his broken leg and effing and blinding at the medic. I could hardly carry on playing I was laughing so much.

There were some real characters at Wigan. Goalie John Brown would come into the dressing room at half-time, take his teeth out and light up a fag. The physio, a lovely guy called Duncan Colquhoun, was a former player whose only piece of kit looked about 50 years old. He would attach sensors with some gel to whichever part of your body you said you had injured, then light up a fag and read the *Sporting Life*. Kitman Kenny Banks was another great bloke who thought he was guarding the crown jewels. To get a new pair of socks or, God forbid, a pair of boots out of him took hours of begging. He protected the stuff with his life. His behaviour, I later found, was typical of kitmen at all clubs.

I used to invite loads of family and mates from Cantril Farm to the games at Wigan as it was just up the road, but we were allowed only two tickets per player for guests to get into the players' lounge. I liked to treat everyone to a beer after the game, so I got a mate at Liverpool University to print up 50 tickets from the original for each home match and handed them out to all my pals. My lot all liked a drink and there would be queues at the bar three deep, all of them boozers from Cantril. I can remember one of the Wigan stewards saying, 'Since you joined the club, Mickey, this place has been full of fucking Scousers.'

'Yeah,' I replied. 'Weird, innit? I must be pulling in the fans.'

Dad would come up with my old mate from our kids' football team John 'Taskforce' Tasker. A big lad, John would always make sure we stopped for pie and chips on the way back from the game. So it's John I have to blame for eating all the pies.

The following season, 1981/82, in which the club was eventually promoted to the Third Division, I was played out of position. It was either wide on the right or behind the front two, and I managed just six goals. Then, in the summer, Larry brought in ex-Everton man Eamonn O'Keefe, Notts County's Les Bradd and the experienced Peter Houghton. They were all vying for the striker's job; I'd only just turned twenty, and as a kid I was expendable. Just before we were about to start our Third Division campaign I was told I was being offloaded to Stockport County. I was absolutely gutted. I loved the club, I was really settled there; with all the Scousers there, it felt like a home from home. Some of my happiest memories in football are from my Wigan days. I thought I was about to move up a division, but no, it was back to the Fourth with County. Wigan chairman Freddie Pye was a former chairman of Stockport, and he'd apparently let me go to them as a favour because they were so skint. It was hardly my dream move, but they offered me a grand in my hand to go, and at least I got away from Big Larry, who went on to be a great managerial success. I last heard he was managing a pub in Nottingham.

7. THE CLASS OF '84

*'If you're in the penalty area and don't know what to do with the
ball, put it in the net and we'll discuss the options later.'*

Bob Paisley

Footballers like to think they are boss drinkers, boss gamblers
and boss shaggers. By this stage in my career I was getting a
reputation for all three. My move to Stockport County in 1982
didn't curtail my social life. The Greater Manchester club was
close enough for me to carry on living on the Farm and to see
all my old mates. I now had a well-established routine for my
afternoons, which was basically the bookie's, then a bar for a
pint or a game of snooker. Then more ale in the evening.

I was now the proud owner of a £700 electric-blue Ford
Capri, the ultimate eighties shagging wagon, bought with the
grand I got for the transfer. It was my dream car, but I kept
crashing the fucking thing. One time I spun it 360 degrees on
the M62 coming back to Liverpool after a night game and
smashed the front in on a bank. I was messing around sliding
it on a frosty road – showing off, really. There were no other
cars around and I hadn't been drinking. I had to limp back to
Cantril Farm on one headlight.

My ale partner at the time was fellow Scouser Alex Cribley,
who had been at Liverpool University before joining Wigan, and
his brother Peter, a talented singer and guitarist who was a
teacher at my old school. We would go on monumental
piss-ups, often in the lively pubs in the Dock Road in Liverpool.
In those days a good all-day session meant as many as fifteen or
twenty pints. Then I would start on the vodka. For a late drink
we went to a club called The Cabin where all the nurses,
firemen and cops drank. The booze was cheap and I've always
had a thing about women in uniforms. Stockport is only a small

town, so if we went out on the piss there people would recognise us. It was my first taste of stardom, albeit on a small scale. The first time a bird comes up to you and gives you the eye and a bit of chat just because you hoof a ball about on a field is a real eye-opener. I had my 21st at The Cabin – just me and Alex. After a heavy night, I always made sure I was the first into training the next day to sweat all the booze out.

Stockport manager Eric Webster had sold the Fourth Division club to me by saying it was a great springboard for a young player's career. Because County were on the doorstep of Manchester United and City they played their home games on a Friday night so they didn't clash, which meant the matches attracted lots of scouts from other clubs. I took a pay cut to play at Stockport as they really didn't have two pennies to rub together.

Eric, who as well as being manager also seemed to be kitman, groundsman and tea lady, was a real character. Even if we lost he would come into the dressing room cracking funnies. After one game in which we had been demolished 4–0, Eric came in whistling and joking.

I said, 'Gaffer, we've just been tanked. Why are you still cracking jokes?'

'Mick,' he replied with a smile, 'I've fourteen full-time professionals. I can't drop anyone, we've got no money to buy anyone, so I might as well keep laughing. If I don't I'll cry.'

My target was always twenty goals a season, as it is for most strikers, but I had a slow start to 1982/83 and spent the first few games on the bench. Five or six games into the season we played local rivals Bury; I came on as sub and scored in a 2–1 victory. From then on I was in the team and scoring goals.

At the same time I was moonlighting for another side – the History Department of Liverpool University. I had a mate at the college who ran the faculty's football team but they were only in the inter-department second division. The first division teams got transport to the pitches and warm showers, the second division didn't, so my mate asked me to help his side get promoted. I registered for the team as Kevin Dalglish – one name from each of my footballing heroes Kevin Keegan and Kenny Dalglish – and turned out for them every Wednesday night. Amateur football on Merseyside is of a very high standard, but this lot were a bunch of Nigels and Jeremies just having a kickabout in their spare time. I was a League footballer playing in front of thousands every week. It was a joke. I would waltz through the opposition, beating every man, then bang the goal home. In the first game I scored fifteen times. As the weeks went by a few eyebrows were raised about this star goalscorer Kevin Dalglish. People were asking why they had never seen me at lectures, but I just shrugged and said I liked to study in my room. I got the team promoted, then called it a day. Fuck knows what would have happened had I been injured playing for them, or had someone recognised me.

It was about this time that my relationship with Debbie began to disintegrate. Debbie was my first love, someone I shared many highs and lows with, and of course we shared the joy of having baby Michael. We had met when we were kids ourselves, when we barely knew what life was all about. The love had gone, though; it was sad, but it was time to move on. We obviously kept in touch for Michael's sake, and Debbie is still a friend today. I went back to my old bedroom at 16 Round Hey. It was like being a kid again. Mum loved having me back and fussed over me the whole time, cooking and doing my washing. I gave Debbie a few quid for Michael and spent the rest on gambling and ale.

I was shagging around, but I was getting bored of one-night stands. Despite never having married, I have always enjoyed being in a steady relationship. One night I went to the Coconut Grove bar in the Tuebrook area of Liverpool with a gang of lads. It was a real eighties bar, with plastic palm trees, dry ice and

Wham!'s 'Club Tropicana' being played on rotation. I was going through my Del Boy phase – cigars, cocktails and a string of naff chat-up lines. On the other side of a palm tree, a stunning girl with a curvy figure, lovely legs and dark Celtic looks caught my eye. I thought she looked like a better-looking version of Irene Cara from the hit movie *Fame*. I strolled over through the dry ice, puffing on my cigar, and asked her to dance.

'What do you do, then?' she asked in a lilting Scouse accent.

'I'm a professional footballer actually,' I replied, as cool as you like.

She laughed, and yelled to her mate, 'Hey, Mary, have you heard this one? We've got a right one here. He reckons he's a professional footballer.' Then she turned to me and said, 'Yeah, love, and I'm Joan Collins.'

Sheila Hutchinson, nineteen, was a nursery nurse who lived close to Anfield. Her sharp, typically Scouse humour and beautiful looks blew me away. I got her number and soon my Capri was a common sight outside the Hutchinson family home. The only problem was that the alternator in the car was on the blink, so our nights out began and finished with us bump-starting the motor, which didn't go down that well with Sheila, tottering on her high heels.

By the end of that first season at County's Edgeley Park I'd scored 23 goals and the scouts from bigger clubs were beginning to take note. Eric told me Blackpool were interested in signing me and briefed me on what County chairman Alan Kirk would say about the proposed move. Eric said the club was desperate for cash and that Alan would tell me that Blackpool, then playing alongside County in the Fourth Division, were a sleeping giant with an FA Cup pedigree. Alan, a loveable bloke desperate to balance County's books, repeated the spiel word for word.

So it was off to Blackpool to meet manager Sam Ellis. I went round to his house and his missus cooked up spaghetti

Bolognese while we talked football. He offered me a pay rise and said I would be first choice up front, but I was desperate to play at a higher level and get out of Division Four so I turned the offer down. Blackpool weren't so much a sleeping giant as completely catatonic. 'Was it anything to do with the missus's spaghetti Bolognese?' Sam said afterwards, sounding put out. Whenever I bumped into him down the years he would always say, 'If it wasn't for my wife's spaghetti Bolognese you'd still be at Blackpool.'

Back at Stockport, the goals kept coming. Against Crewe Alexandra away at Gresty Road, a big local derby for County, I fired in a hat-trick. When the third went in I sprinted over to our supporters and leapt on the rusty old fence that in those days hemmed in the crowd. As 200 ecstatic County fans surged forward to mob me, there was a huge screech of twisting metal. The supporters turned tail and ran back up the terraces as the fence threatened to crush them. I leapt off just in time to prevent taking out all of our away support. My most embarrassing game at Stockport was getting knocked out of the FA Cup 3–0 at non-League Telford. With ten minutes to go, when it was obvious we were beaten, I stopped playing and concentrated on kicking lumps out of their players, but they were playing so well I couldn't get anywhere near them. I'd rattled in seventeen goals for County in that 1983/84 season when Oldham Athletic made an approach for me.

I didn't take much persuading. Oldham were in the old Second Division alongside clubs the size of Leeds, Manchester City, Wolves and Middlesbrough. Their manager Joe Royle, a Scouser and ex-England and Everton star and now manager of Ipswich Town, had done everything in the game and was someone I admired. He was a typical old-school manager, a man's man, who I immediately warmed to. He achieved wonders with Oldham, with successful cup runs and, eventually, promotion to the First Division. Joe paid £52,000 for me –

a good bit of business for Stockport – and told me, 'Mick, I think you are a raw centre-forward with bundles of potential. You need to work hard, listen to what the coaches say, and I believe you will soon be in the First Division. I know you're aggressive, Quinny, but what I need from you is controlled aggression.'

I arrived at the club in January 1984, at the same time as goalie Andy Goram, who went on to play for Scotland. Andy, who had a broad Lancashire accent and was known as the Bury Werewolf, also played cricket for Scotland. Later he joined Glasgow Rangers and was diagnosed with mild schizophrenia; away fans used to sing, 'Two Andy Gorams, there's only two Andy Gorams.' Oldham also signed ex-Luton and Newcastle star Darren McDonough and fellow Scouser and ex-West Ham and Everton midfielder Mark Ward. All three of us liked a pint and a punt, and we became known as the Class of '84. Joe Royle used to call me and Mark Wham! because we had all the trendy gear and were continually poncing about with our hair.

My wages went up to £300 a week, so I treated myself to a new motor. I bought a big fuck-off white Ford Granada for £2,000 – a lot in those days. The rest of the lads called it The Ambulance. I always loved big cars, perhaps because Dad drove a huge Zephyr Zodiac. In the early eighties, as now, footballers compete with cars, birds and clothes. The dressing room was all about banter related to these three things; it was all 'I shagged this or that bird' or 'I won this or that bet'. Image is all important, and back then the sophisticated urban soul boy look was what all the lads strived for. In my case that meant a mullet hairstyle: short at the sides and on top but long at the back. Still, compared to others at the time like Chris Waddle, Barry Venison and Mark Hateley, mine was very much a baby mullet. It was also the beginning of my shellsuit days. I liked white or cream trackies with a nice Lacoste T-shirt and some big flash white trainers. On my car stereo I played Luther Vandross,

Alexander O'Neal and Stevie Wonder. I thought I was dead cool.

Soon after arriving at Oldham the Class of '84 decided to have a day out at nearby Haydock races. For days we planned the trip, and it was the talk of the dressing room. On the morning of the meeting we were in the changing rooms early, gathered around the *Sporting Life* trying to decide on our wagers for the day. Joe had sussed out what was going on and, for a laugh, extended training. When he finally let us go we made a mad dash for the changing rooms to get suited and booted. We had a horse in the first that we fancied and it was going to be a close call to make it in time. We dashed out to The Ambulance in the car park, still doing up our kecks and putting on our ties. I leapt into the driver's seat and, as the other lads piled in, stuck it into reverse and with a screech of rubber spun her round. Unfortunately, Andy, who had clambered in the back, hadn't closed his door. As I did my best Starsky and Hutch spin, the door caught a concrete bollard and was ripped clean off its hinges. 'Andy, you prick!' I screamed. 'You'll have to hold the fucking thing shut now. We haven't got time to piss about, we've got to make the first.' I sped off towards the motorway with Goram holding the back door of The Ambulance nice and tight. We made it for the first, but wished we hadn't. The horse was well beaten.

I used to share a lift from Liverpool to Oldham with Mark Ward and Joe McBride. One afternoon we were driving down the motorway in Joe's white convertible Golf GTI when this saucy-looking blonde overtook us in the fast lane. 'Fucking hell, Joe, she looks a bit of a sort,' I said. 'Let's catch her up.' Joe put his foot down and we pulled up alongside her. We were giving it all the tongues and hand gestures and she was responding, so I grabbed a piece of paper, wrote 'Do you fuck?' on it in big letters and held it up against the window for her to see. We could see her scribbling on a piece of paper as she sped down the motorway, then she held it up: 'Yes, and oral.' Laughing hysterically, we motioned to her to come off at the next exit where Wardy and I had left our motors. When she pulled up in the car park, we got a better look at her. She was blonde, in her mid-thirties and wearing a short skirt. Wardy and I decided she was a bit on the old side for us and called it a day, but as I pulled out of the car park and headed for home I saw the blonde easing herself on to the back seat of Joe's GTI. Away win for McBridey.

I was still living with Mum and Dad on the Farm, meaning I was close to Little Michael and seeing Sheila whenever I could. At that time my brother Mark, who now had a family of his own, won a trial with Stockport. He was a great midfielder, a tough tackler with a left foot that was so sweet he could open a can of beans with it. During one game Mark scored a cracking goal, but in the second half the bench signalled that he was being brought off. A larger than usual crowd starting going absolutely nuts and Mark started clapping and showing his appreciation. In fact, the reason for the applause was that his replacement was club skipper Tommy Sword, who was returning after a lengthy absence caused by a broken leg. Mark had trained every Tuesday and Thursday at his own expense, and as he was earning good money as a joiner, he eventually hung up his boots. He had the ability to make it as a pro footballer, he was more skilful than me, but he had a very short fuse with both coaches and other players.

My little brother Sean looked like being the most talented of us all. He broke through the ranks at Liverpool and won himself an apprenticeship when Kenny Dalglish was boss. Like me, he played up front. He had my touch and eye for goal, but he was slighter than me and had more pace, not to mention a real zest for life and the cocksure nature that every goalscorer needs. Sean was so well thought of he had the honour of cleaning Ian Rush's boots. Rush was then at the height of his goalscoring powers and was hero-worshipped by the red contingent on

Merseyside. Then one day Mum got a letter from Dalglish's office: Sean had only gone and nicked a pair of Rushy's boots. Dad confronted him.

'Sean, Liverpool have written to us to say a pair of Rushy's boots have disappeared. Tell me you haven't been a prick and lifted them.'

'Sorry, Dad,' he said. 'I gave 'em to my mate Billy. He loves Rushy so much, he was made up.'

'What? You didn't even flog them?' Dad shrieked.

Dad was in a rage and said he was going to march Sean straight down to Anfield to apologise to Kenny. Our Mark could see that Dad was at boiling point so he insisted he went with him and Sean to the club. All three of them were shouting and screaming at one another in the car all the way to Anfield.

When they got there, they knocked on Kenny's door and went in.

'Mr Dalglish,' Dad said, 'Sean nicked Rushy's boots and we're here to apologise. Don't worry, we'll make sure he gets punished big style for this.'

Before Kenny could say anything, Mark turned to Dad and said, 'Why don't you calm down and keep your mouth shut? You're just making it worse.'

Dad swung round to Mark and said, 'You shut up and let me handle this.'

'Look, Dad,' Mark continued. 'Just leave, will you?'

Kenny, his mouth agape, looked on as Mark and Dad bickered with each other, each insisting the other calm down. It was like a scene from Harry Enfield's Scousers sketch.

That evening Sean scored four goals as the youth team beat Manchester United reserves 5–1, but he was always a bit of a tearaway, his career stalled and he didn't last much longer at Liverpool.

Most players need a bit of luck to reach the top. I had always had a real hunger to succeed. Yes, I was out on the piss a lot, but I made sure I was in early for training and working harder than everyone else. When I was playing at shitty little grounds in the Fourth Division in front of one man and a dog, I always ran my bollocks off in every game and never pulled out of a tackle. I knew how skint many of the fans were – I had been there myself – and the least us players could do was try our hardest.

I established myself as a first-team regular at Oldham in my first season with them. Willie Donachie, who was the coach and played as full-back, was someone I respected a lot, and when he took me to one side and told me I had the ability to play in the First Division I was very flattered. I remember him saying, 'Quinny, you have an instinct for scoring goals that is born and not made. Very few players have that, and if you work hard, you can go all the way to the top in the game.'

I always worked better for people who believed in me, and I arrived a week early for pre-season in the summer of 1984. Willie said I trained 'like a beaver' that season. I had set my sights on playing in the top flight alongside the country's best players. I must have been going places because I was made poster boy in the old *Match* football magazine. Only problem was my picture was labelled Jimmy rather than Micky Quinn.

Reaching the Second Division was a real milestone for me. Playing at Maine Road, Molineux and Elland Road really whetted my appetite for success. And, despite rising two divisions, the goals kept coming. The Class of '84 was also hitting top form in the partying stakes. A professional footballer's best night of the year without a shadow of a doubt is the players' Christmas party. It is planned in meticulous detail weeks in advance. The back room of a pub is hired and strippers are booked. It is kept to players only, and bar staff are told in no uncertain terms that if anything ends up in the papers they're for it. The married lads dread it and some make crappy excuses to get out of it. The party always begins with a few bevvies and the girls do their stuff. Then the birds send the pint pots round and everyone puts in a few quid for 'extras'. This usually involves them shagging a couple of apprentices on stage with the rest of us gathered around and cheering them on. In those days lads would often be virgins. But you try getting a hard-on in front of 30 baying footballers. It ain't easy, but it all adds to the fun of the party.

My most memorable Christmas party was while at Oldham in 1985. We started in the afternoon, as usual, in the back room of some dodgy boozer – the owners wouldn't thank me for reminding them which – and then a couple of real sorts did their thing on stage. One of the strippers gave an apprentice a blowjob while the other shagged another lad. Then the real drinking began and it was off for an extended pub crawl around Oldham. We were young, we had cash in our pockets and we were cocky bastards who were treated like celebs in the close-knit northern town.

By pub number six I had downed ten pints already. I stuck Thin Lizzy's 'The Boys Are Back in Town' on the jukebox and began strutting my stuff – with eleven-stone Mark Ward on my shoulders. Andy Goram joined us on another player's shoulders. As we danced around we were sloshing beer all over the place. Then, as I attempted a Michael Jackson-style spin – not easy with Marky Ward on your shoulders – I slipped on some ale and did the splits, landing arse over tit on the floor. I immediately felt a sharp stabbing pain in the back of my thigh that even the booze couldn't dull. I had only pulled a fucking hamstring. It was a disaster. I was Oldham's top striker and the busy Christmas fixture schedule, which often decides a club's fate for the season, was about to start. I looked up from the floor and said, 'Andy, me leg's fucked. What am I going to do?' In his broadest Lancashire accent, he growled, 'Shut up you soft shite and have another beer.' The lads propped me on a bar stool and did their best in the way of medical treatment – they stuffed ice cubes down my boxers on to my thigh.

The night was still young so the pub crawl carried on, with the lads chair-lifting me from boozer to boozer because I couldn't walk. We ended up in a Manchester nightclub. When the word went round that a gang of footballers had arrived, the birds were immediately swarming all over us. I got talking to a half-decent sort. She wasn't exactly Claudia Schiffer, but at least she was blonde. Well, sort of blonde. She had one of those wet-look perms with highlights. She had a stunning figure and was wearing a black skimpy dress that I couldn't wait to see her out of. I bought her a couple of bevvies and I was under starter's orders. I'd only gone and scored with an injury. The lads shouldered me to a cab waiting outside the club, and it felt like I had scored the winner at Wembley. Back at her gaff we didn't waste any time and went straight to the bedroom, but I was in such pain with my leg that I couldn't give her one in the missionary position. She had to get on top and ride me – and very nice it was too.

When I opened my eyes in a strange bed the next morning I was hoping it had all been some alcohol-fuelled dream. But no, my leg was still absolutely killing me. I would have to go to the club and face the music. I took a cab straight to the ground where the physio confirmed my worst fears: I had done a hamstring and would be out for seven weeks. Joe Royle had done everything in football and knew immediately what the score was. He knew it was a drinking injury, not a training-ground knock, but he very kindly put out a press release saying I had injured myself falling down the stairs at home and sadly would miss several games. As I said, the Christmas party is always a great night out.

Towards the end of that 1984/85 season it was time again to upgrade the motor, and this time I got a second-hand 320 metallic blue Beamer on the drip – higher purchase, that is – for £5,000. In the close season I drove the BMW into Liverpool for a night out with 'Snowy' Moffat, one of my childhood friends from Cantril Farm. We had been for a bevvy and were heading into Liverpool on the East Lancashire Road when I ignored a couple of red lights. Then I noticed a cop car in my rear-view mirror. We came to another red light so I jumped it to see if he would follow. He did. Surprise, surprise, I saw flashing blue lights in my mirror. I was breathalysed and I failed. Later, at the Liverpool Magistrates Court, I pleaded guilty to drink driving and was fined £100 and given a one-year driving ban. Back then drink driving wasn't the social no-no it is today, but no excuses, it was a bloody stupid thing to do. It was an error that would return to haunt me.

My playing days at Oldham came to an end one day near the transfer deadline date in March 1986. Joe Royle called me into his office.

'Mick, Portsmouth have come in for you,' he said straight away, 'and we need the money. The long and short of it is we have to sell you to balance the books. I don't want you to leave because I think you're a great goalscorer, but Portsmouth are a bigger club with great support who have been on the verge of the First Division for a few years. I think it's a great move for you.' He later told the *Daily Telegraph*, 'Quinn doesn't feel that you necessarily have to play in the game all the time to be effective. Sometimes he can't head a ball unless there's a chance of a goal, and then he heads the ball rather well. Sometimes he can look slow, but when there's a chance of a goal he's lightning quick. He reminds me of a player at Hull City called Ken Wagstaff. They used to say about him that he doesn't do this and he doesn't do that, but you regularly saw his name on the scoresheet.'

So after scoring 34 goals in 80 appearances for Oldham I was off down south. I was nearly 24, and it was time, at last, to leave the comforts of Cantril Farm.

8. THE DIRTY DOZEN

'What about that Alex Higgins? . . . He's off his tits. All that money and fame and shit and he's blown the lot. What a way to go. I hope that happens to me. One big fucking blow-out. Top.'

Oasis singer Liam Gallagher

'After a time, you may find that "having" is not so pleasing a thing, after all, as "wanting". It is not logical, but it is often true.'

Dr Spock in *Star Trek*

The Portsmouth team I joined were the footballing equivalent of the Dirty Dozen, a bunch of reprobates who, because of their attitude or unruly behaviour, didn't fit in at other clubs. It was a rogues gallery; most of the lads liked a drink and a few also fancied themselves as ladies' men. Going to an away fixture with Pompey, as both the team and the city are known, was like going on tour with seventies rock band Led Zeppelin: on the coach there would be tins of lager, barley wine, bottles of scotch – the works. There would be card schools, too, and when we overnighted the shaggers among the lads would be sniffing after everything in a skirt. Manager Alan Ball once screamed at us after one particularly drunken away trip, 'I've created a Frankenstein's monster of a team!' He then added, 'But I can destroy you as well.' The ethic at Fratton Park was work hard and play harder, and it was one of the most successful teams in the club's recent history.

It seemed like most people on the playing staff at Pompey had been in some sort of trouble, and there was a real assortment of hard nuts and tough tacklers. Many of the lads hailed from the north – I don't know whether that was by accident or design. Pompey striker Mick Channon told *Shoot!* magazine later: 'The club's disciplinary record had brought them a lot of bad publicity. It is true that they'll gladly fight the world on the football pitch but basically they are a good bunch of lads who deserve a crack at the First Division.' Among those lads was Birkenhead's Kenny Swain, who was part of Aston Villa's European Cup-winning side; midfielder Kevin Dillon, who was a real character; skilful forward Vince Hilaire; midfield hardman Mick Tait; England star Paul Mariner; and Jamaica-born six-foot-two-inch defender Noel Blake. Howard Wilkinson once said, 'Blake's even got muscles in his spit.' Once, Blakey – whose middle name, incidentally, was Lloyd-George – said he was going home to Birmingham. Two days later some of the lads went out for a Sunday lunchtime pint. We were sitting in the beer garden when someone shouted, 'Look, it's Blakey's motor!' We all turned round and there was Blakey's smashed-up black Toyota Supra going up the motorway on the back of a breakdown lorry. He eventually turned up in one piece.

I decided not to tell Portsmouth that I had been banned for drink driving while living up north. I signed in March 1986 and my court date was set for May, but why blot my copybook before I'd even started? So they'd given me a Toyota Corolla club car.

Mick Channon, already into his racehorses and an assistant to trainer Ken Cunningham-Brown, would come into the changing rooms with his wellies on covered in horse shit and the *Sporting Life* under his arm. He would walk past the reserve team's dressing room every morning on his way to the first team's dressing room, pop his head in and say in his best bumpkin tones, 'Mornin' reeserrrves!' The lads who were out of favour with the first team and forced to change with the reserves would grimace with anger. Mick would laugh and shout, 'Quinny, they hate it when we call them reserves.' It was an in joke between me, Alan Ball and Mick. Later, Bally bought a racehorse and put it into training with Mick. He called it Mornin' Reserves.

If Bally ever had a pop at Mick or a moan that he wasn't working hard enough, he would shoot back, 'Football is my hobby, racing is my career.' And so it proved. Mick and I hit it off immediately both on and off the field. He has a sharp humour, but behind it is a man who is incredibly driven and talented. Mick said of me in an interview at the time, 'I could see straight away that Quinny was a natural goalscorer. He's not the prettiest player you will ever see, but once he's inside that penalty box he's deadly, especially with his back to goal because he can turn past defenders so well.' That was a wonderful compliment coming from someone of Mick's standing in the game. He added, 'Mick is a Scouser and has the sort of humour one associates with a Liverpudlian.' Which can be translated thus: I had an unofficial role as first officer of dressing-room banter.

We had a saying about Kevin Dillon that he wasn't happy unless he was sad. We were playing Blackburn once and Dills was back in the side after being left out by Bally. He hit a volley from 35 yards, a real Exocet which almost burst the net. Instead of celebrating like mad like most other players, he calmly turned and walked slowly back to the halfway line, shrugging off the congratulations of his team-mates. At half-time Bally went over to Dills and said, 'Well done, mate, that was a super goal.' Dills turned to him with a scowl on his face and replied, 'I saw your face on the ball and hit it as hard as I could.'

We had a little drinking and gambling clique at Pompey known as the Gremlins. After training we would go to the bookie's together before retiring to either a snooker hall, the Cowplain social club or a boozer, then on to someone's gaff to watch the racing. Portsmouth fans' favourite chant is the Pompey Chimes, but we were known as the Pompey Crimes. The *Sun* ran a piece under the headline POMPEY CRIMES: SHAME OF TOP SOCCER CLUB. It detailed our abysmal disciplinary record. In the 1986/87 season when we were promoted, we had 64 players booked and six sent off; the following season 51 were booked and five sent off; and during 1988/89 there were over 60 bookings and four dismissals. The FA had to keep summoning the club to explain its disciplinary record. The paper said: 'Portsmouth are today revealed as the club who make Wimbledon look like a bunch of choirboys.'

We certainly weren't the sort of team you'd like to meet in a dark alley. We idolised the stars of the day who lived life on the edge, as we liked to think we did. Our heroes were Alex 'Hurricane' Higgins, film star Ollie Reed and snooker pisspot extraordinaire Bill Werbeniuk. Canadian Bill often sank 40 pints a day, which earned him the nickname the Hoover from Vancouver. He famously won a mammoth drinking competition with darts ace Big Cliff Lazarenko. Once, the Gremlins showed up at the Fosters snooker tournament in Portsmouth to cheer on Bill. Afterwards we went for a drink with him, and a protracted booze session ensued. Bill told me that he needed the booze to steady his queue hand because he suffered from a condition that gave him the shakes. While other snooker stars were in demand to play exhibition matches up and down the country, Big Bill was once hired for £500 by some blokes in Middlesbrough simply to go on the piss with them. We made Bill honorary president of the Gremlins for the evening. The drinks were flowing and we were buying all sorts of cocktails and liqueurs and mixing them together. We were just getting warmed up when Bill stood up and said in his Canadian drawl, 'Wow, man. I've met some drinkers in my time but you guys are fucking unreal. I'm going to bed.' The Gremlins gave him a bit of ribbing and clapped him out of the room. We had seen off Bill Werbeniuk, and we laughed about it for months afterwards. If there was ever a social function or charity do in the evening, I would always offer my services. I would do anything for a piss-up.

Alan Ball was a manager I immediately respected and admired. He is a man's man with a quick wit, not afraid to speak his mind. He was also nuts about horse racing, so we had a few things in common. As a player he had, of course, won the World Cup and gone on to win 72 England caps, so he gained instant respect from the players. Bally, like many redheads, could be very emotional, and he hated losing. He once banged his head on the dressing-room wall after we lost a game.

Bally made an effort to help me on the training field, especially with my positional sense and judgement of crosses. He knocked a few of the rough edges off my game and helped me make the step up to Division Two football. One of the first things he said to me on the pitch at the Moneyfields training ground was, 'Did that Joe Royle teach you the far-post run?' I told him Joe had, so Bally taught me the darting near-post run. It helped improve my goalscoring, as did Bally's tough training programmes, which helped to burn the pints off. Bally was quick to sing my praises. 'A goalkeeper has to be on his guard at all times with Quinn around,' he told the *Sun*. 'I've never seen anyone get as many shots and headers on target so consistently. I tried to make him more aware of his responsibilities outside the box, but it was like telling a ten-year-old he's got to like cricket when he loves football.'

There were only eleven games to go of the 1985/86 season when I arrived, and the club was battling for promotion. It had missed out on goal difference the previous season, so expectations were high. I made my Pompey debut away at Charlton Athletic on 15 March, playing up front alongside Mick Channon. Mick scored that day, but I failed to hit the net. Ten days later I was given a rousing reception by Pompey's lively supporters for my first home game, against Millwall. For some reason there has always been a lot of rivalry between the two clubs. It was a niggly game, with John Fashanu – also known as Fash the Bash – going in especially hard for them. He went up for one challenge with Kevin Dillon and caught him in the face with his elbow. We all raced in and there was a lot of pushing and shoving and threats – what's known as 'handbags' in football speak. By chance, Fash then signed for Wimbledon who we were due to face just four days later, so all the Pompey lads were chalking their elbows, ready for another bruising encounter. Sure enough, early on in the game our south London-born defender Billy Gilbert went into a fifty-fifty tackle with Fash and hit him like an express train somewhere around the waist. The game ended 1–1, and Billy and Fash were still glaring at each other as we walked down the tunnel.

They were in front of me as they trooped towards the dressing room, and then I saw Billy fall to the ground. The spirit of my granddad Luigi Silvano, the pro boxer from Naples, flashed through me. I shoved past a couple of other players and caught Fash square on the jaw with a decent right hook. He, too, fell to the ground, and then all hell broke loose as 22 players piled in for a mass brawl. The police and stewards eventually broke up the huge ruck and we filed into the dressing room. Bally went apeshit. 'That was fucking disgraceful!' he screamed. 'You've behaved like animals and let the club down. I want to know exactly who started it.'

Everyone looked at the floor, but I thought, 'Fuck it, I was sticking up for Billy,' so I stood up and said, 'It was me, boss. I chinned Fash because he dropped Billy in the tunnel.' I could see Billy frowning on the other side of the dressing room.

Bally yelled, 'Is that right, Billy?'

'Well, I did go down in the tunnel,' Billy replied, 'but Fash didn't hit me. I tripped and fell down the stairs.'

Oh shit. The manager was apoplectic.

I scored six goals that season but we narrowly missed out on promotion again, finishing the season in fourth place just three points adrift of Wimbledon in the days before the play-offs. Everyone at the club was shattered. The lads thought they had let Bally down big style. A crestfallen Bally told us, 'What the club has achieved over the last two years simply has not been good enough. The hard fact is we are still in the Second Division. Everyone knows we have to work harder.'

In my few short weeks at Pompey I had already fallen in love with the city and the club. Just like Liverpool, Portsmouth is a proud working-class city and a big sea port where people are passionate about their football. In the summer, Sheila and I moved into a lovely red-bricked four-bedroomed detached house with a huge garden in Waterlooville, an upmarket town just outside Portsmouth. As usual, I was living above my means. Although my pay had gone up to £950 a week, I was spending it as fast as I was earning it. I was going on monster punting sessions every day – it almost seemed compulsory. I could do £400 a day if I didn't get a winner. I loved the thrill of trying to beat the odds. With beer money on top of that, I struggled to pay the mortgage every month. Sheila was quite rightly pissed off. I was out on the razz most afternoons and travelling to away games every other weekend. She had been forced to move down south with me where she had no friends. It was tough for her – it's not easy being a footballer's partner.

It's especially difficult when the footballer in question is out shagging all the time. Portsmouth is a fairly small place, and if you're starring for the football team you are treated like a rock star. Women would throw themselves at me. If I was in a club, gorgeous women would come straight up to me and whisper in my ear, 'I want to fuck you.' Others would slip me pieces of paper with their phone numbers on them. I felt like Rod Stewart. It's not something I'm proud of, but despite still living with Sheila I did succumb.

There was a Bernie Inn-type pub in Waterlooville where I would go for a beer with some of the lads. Serving behind the bar was a shapely brunette called Cindy. She was nineteen, a real laugh, and after closing one night I went back to her flat and we had wild, drunken sex. Later I would pop into the pub for a pint and then cop off with her when she knocked off in the afternoon and evening. She used to come round to the house in Waterlooville when Sheila was out and cut my hair. I was at home one evening with Sheila when Cindy rang up out of the blue. I hadn't seen her for a while and thought the whole thing had fizzled out. Sheila was upstairs when I answered the phone.

'Mick, I'm really missing you,' Cindy whispered. 'When am I going to see you again?'

'Look, love, it's over,' I said firmly. 'I'm trying to make a go of it with Sheila. I love her.'

Cindy started weeping, gently at first, but then really wailing. I heard a click on the line.

'But I really love you, Micky. I'll do anything if you take me back. I beg you.'

Then I heard another click on the line. To my horror, I realised someone had picked up the extension upstairs, heard our snippet of conversation, then put the receiver down again. Sheila. Fuck. Beam me up, Scotty. A shiver went down my spine as I heard the sound of Sheila bounding down the stairs.

'Cindy, I've got to go, love. Bye.'

I slammed down the receiver, then all hell broke loose.

'You dirty, double-crossing bastard!' Sheila screamed, her face contorted in rage and tears streaming down her face.

'Sheila, I can explain. You know what fans are like. She's deranged, she's been stalking me,' I pleaded. 'You know I love you.'

After a couple of hours of bare-faced lies, I thought I had talked her round and we went to bed. But Sheila wasn't stupid.

The next day I was at morning training as usual, and afterwards I decided to have a booze-and-horses afternoon with a few of the lads. Micky Tait, Micky Kennedy, Kevin O'Callaghan and I first went to the bookie's, then I invited them round to my house to watch the racing on the telly. As I strode through the front door with the lads behind me, my jaw hit the carpet. The house had been stripped bare. All the furniture had gone, every last stick of it. It turned out that Sheila had got her brother to come down from Liverpool with a removal van and gut the place. But we didn't let it stop us. She had left the fridge, and that was still stocked with cans of beer. I found a radio and we all sat on the carpet supping beer and listening to the racing results.

I actually had four birds on the go at the time. They were all barmaids, which says a lot about the life I was leading at the time. In truth, I was leading a celebrity lifestyle. I was a working-class kid from a Liverpool council estate who'd suddenly been given wodges of cash and was a hero to thousands of people. I was in my mid-twenties and had lived in the cosseted world of football since the age of sixteen. Your bum is wiped for you, and you don't need to grow up. Women threw themselves at me and I simply couldn't resist. Instead of banking the cash and concentrating on training, I went out and lived the high life. God knows what it's like for today's footballers, who earn far more and have much higher public profiles than we had. I eventually managed to entice Sheila back with lots of solemn promises to improve my behaviour. Despite all the aggro, we were in love.

As one of the club's most high-profile stars, I received a lot of letters from fans asking me to meet them, or to attend this or that function. Despite my wild lifestyle I tried to make time for the fans; after all, it was their hard-earned cash that paid my wages. I loved working with young kids and meeting disabled or disadvantaged youngsters. Just by turning up and signing a few autographs you really made them happy. I met up with some kids with Down's syndrome two or three times and had a kickabout with them. It was wonderful to see the joy on their faces when I juggled a football around and then passed it to them. I tried to clear a few afternoons a month to do this sort of stuff. It was nothing to do with the club – in fact, they didn't even know I was doing it. I think if you do stuff like that you should do it because you want to help others, not so that you can boast in the papers about your 'charity work'. In 2001 I was at a Pompey game commentating for The Quay, a local radio station, when I was approached by a couple of guys with Down's syndrome. It was the kids I had visited all those years ago. They said how much they had enjoyed my visits and what a great player they thought I was. I was choked up. It shows just how much good footballers can do. They are heroes to people, and the smallest gestures can mean so much to the fans.

It was during my first year at Pompey that I became a racehorse owner for the first time. Mick Channon had offered me the chance of owning a 'leg', or quarter share, in a horse. It was the logical progression to spending hours in the bookie's. Getting more closely involved in racing was a dream come true. I loved going to Mick's yard and watching the horses work on the gallops, and then getting close to them in the stables afterwards. I admire the power and athleticism of a thorough-bred and enjoy the thrill of watching it pit its strength and speed against another – especially if the one that crosses the line first has got a trouserful of my money on it.

Land Sun, a two-year-old colt, was my first horse. He was a quirky little thing who ran 23 times as a two-year-old and won four times. He was a real moody git and would pull himself up sometimes. The first time he won he trotted up at 33–1 at Wolverhampton. It was a glorious day. I had a few quid on him and was made up when he romped home. My party adjourned to the owners' and trainers' bar for some victory bubbly. With me were Micky Channon, keen gambler and ex-Bolton star Frank Worthington sporting his Mexican bandit-style beard and mullet hairstyle, and ex-Manchester City star and one-time racehorse trainer Francis Lee. With me looking great in a leather jacket and a thick moustache, we looked like extras from *The Magnificent Seven*. We must have cut quite a dash in the parade ring, though Wolverhampton on a winter's afternoon is hardly Ladies' Day at Royal Ascot. At the bar, some of the tweed-and-corduroy brigade looked down their noses at us. I heard one well-known trainer sniff, 'It appears you have to be a footballer to train a racehorse these days.' I thought, 'Fuck 'im. We've got as much right to be here as he has. His shit stinks just like mine.' In my loudest and broadest Scouse, I shouted at the barman, 'Another bottle of champers, please, dear boy, and one for yourself.'

Paul Mariner didn't know what had hit him when he joined Portsmouth in the summer of 1986. Marrers was one of the biggest names in English football. He had won 35 England caps and FA and UEFA Cup-winning medals at Ipswich before joining Arsenal. He linked up with us on a pre-season tour to the Isle of Man and Blackpool. When he joined us on the ferry, The Gremlins' party was in full swing and we were already bevvied up. Bally always wore a flat cap, so every member of the first-team squad had gone out and bought one in his honour. We stayed in a bed and breakfast in Blackpool and went on the piss from 10 a.m. By the time we got on the ferry to the Isle of Man we were fucked. Mariner was introduced to the squad and offered a beer. Then the lads broke into a chant of 'Billy Big Time, Billy Big Time, whoa!' Blackburn, playing in the same tournament, were also on the ferry. Mick Kennedy, who was a real hard nut, had a fight with one of their players. They had a bit of history. The look on Paul's face was one of horror. You could see he was thinking, 'What the fuck have I joined here?', but he eventually became a key member of the Pompey Dirty Dozen.

That August one of my aunties had been visiting from Liverpool. She needed to get back to the station quick as one of her kids had been taken sick. The club Toyota was still parked invitingly outside the house, so I decided to drive her there myself. I sped into town, but as I flashed past a lay-by a cop car pulled out behind me and the blue light started to flash. The two policemen warned me I had been speeding and gave me a ticket to produce my documents. The only problem was that my driving licence was still suspended by order of the Liverpool Magistrates, and I wasn't insured. The police charged me and I was bailed to appear in court in six months' time. I felt sickened by my own stupidity. I could afford a taxi, so why hadn't I fucking taken one? I had finally settled at a decent-sized club, was banging in the goals and now was going to bugger it all up. I decided not to tell the club because I was terrified of being booted out. I wasn't ready to go back to Cantril Farm, so I kept quiet, hoping I could get through the court case without the press or the club finding out. The Toyota stayed parked outside the house, and I threw myself into training and the pre-season friendlies.

Despite narrowly missing out on promotion in the last two seasons, the bookies had local rivals Brighton ahead of us in the betting to go up in the 1986/87 season. Bally used this for a bit of kidology. 'The Lord said to me a couple of years ago, "Come forth",' he said. 'Well, we have done, twice. I'm delighted they're tipping someone else for promotion apart from us. I'll tip them as well if you want. I seem to be able to put a block on us any way. So let's hope I can put a jinx on Brighton. Yeah, I fancy them. This team will be as consistent as it has been for the last couple of years. I don't think Liverpool have bettered our consistency over the last two seasons. We haven't been out of the top six, or indeed the top two, for long periods of time.'

Inspired by this, early wins against Blackburn, Huddersfield and Birmingham took us to the top of the league. After twelve matches I had scored nine goals and was playing some of the best football of my career. I just pushed being stopped by the police to the back of my mind and pretended it hadn't happened. I was bagging two goals in so many games that the lads gave me another new nickname: Noah, because the goals were coming two by two. But our defence was also superb. We let in just three goals in the same period, and goalie Alan Knight had kept an amazing nine clean sheets. Knightie, a legend in Portsmouth, was still keen to improve, and after training he often spent an extra half an hour with workaholic Bally, practising his keeping.

Things went a bit awry when we got stuffed 3–1 at Leeds, but we bounced back with a 3–1 win over Derby at Fratton Park on Trafalgar night in October with all three goals coming from yours truly. That was when the fans borrowed a song from sixties stars Manfred Mann for me: 'Come on without, come on within, you ain't seen nothing like the Mighty Quinn.' It was my first hat-trick for Pompey and my sixth as a pro. It was a special night for me. It was good to get one over on my first club Derby where I had been so homesick as a kid. Also, the game was on my sister Trisha's birthday and the day before my mum's. I'd spoken to Mum before the game and she'd said the only thing she and Trish wanted as a present was for me to score a hat-trick. It was a great feeling to make my family proud of me.

Despite living down south, I was still a regular visitor to Liverpool. Michael was growing up fast and I saw him as often as I could. He was a good-looking kid, like his dad, and he had a lovely nature. I liked to bring him back some of the Pompey shirts I had worn for keepsakes, and for his school to auction off. Although I was only up in Liverpool on the odd weekend, Dad, Mum and Mark made sure they kept an eye on Michael. Our family always look out for one another.

Then we faced West Bromwich Albion at Fratton Park. The linesman made a couple of iffy offside decisions in the second half, and young striker Paul Wood and I told him so. I screamed, 'Open your fucking eyes, lino, you useless fucking c***!' Not very pleasant, but I didn't think he was doing his job properly. Woody gave him a similar broadside. We beat Albion 2–1 and took the applause of the crowd before heading for the showers. Waiting at the dressing-room door, however, were two burly policemen. We were told by them that our language was unacceptable. Our names and addresses were taken and we were given a warning. Then, to our utter surprise, Woody and I were frogmarched from the ground. That day, eleven people were ejected from the ground – nine rowdy fans and two foul-mouthed football players. It was commonplace in the eighties for fans to be ejected from grounds, but players? That was a new one. I said at the time, 'To be honest, this is farcical. I thought it was a joke when I was showering and the lads said this policeman wanted to see me. They let me dry and change, then led me away. I agree we have to clean up the game, but I didn't do anything drastic like drop my shorts or abuse the crowd.'

The incident got me a lot of negative headlines. The *Sun*'s read SOCCER PAIR KICKED OUT BY COPS – POMPEY DRESSING ROOM DRAMA. Later, a Hampshire Police spokesman revealed that had Woody and I shouted the abuse during the first half we would have been sent packing in the interval. This was in the days of teams being allowed just one substitute, so if Woody and I had been lobbed out of the stadium at half-time Pompey would have had to continue the game with just ten men. This was also the age of rampant hooliganism. Can you imagine the effect on the hardcore Pompey element if we'd jogged out with ten men for the second half? 'What ho, we're down to ten men. What a wonderful piece of community policing. That'll teach those scallywags Quinn and Wood.' I don't think so. Chief Constable John Duke was unrepentant. 'The action was part of the general policy and strategy of trying to make this a family game.' Bally saw it differently, saying, 'If we had run out with only ten men it could have caused a riot. We would have had to make an announcement on the intercom to tell the crowd what had happened. The police can now virtually run a football match. I love football desperately, but I think it has probably got as low as it can ever go if this continues.' The Portsmouth Constabulary sent one of their officers down to the club a month later for clear-the-air talks with all the players. They would see much more of me over the next few months.

A few weeks later we played Grimsby, and after twelve games with the club my strike partner Paul Mariner finally got off the mark. A classic it wasn't. It took a couple of bobbles before Marrers knocked it in off a defender. We were racing towards the big time and the First Division, and I was the club's leading scorer. Then an almighty spanner hit the works.

One December evening, Sheila came down with a really nasty dose of flu. We didn't have any painkillers or medicine in the house, so at about 7 p.m. I got behind the wheel of the Toyota and headed for the chemist in Waterlooville. I was driving over the 30mph limit, and soon a white car came up close on my tail. Then the blue lights started to flash. Oh shit. The local police knew all the Portsmouth players drove Toyotas. I was given a ticket to produce my documents at the local police station, but they knew full well I didn't have two vital documents: a driving licence and a certificate of insurance. I hadn't yet appeared in court after being stopped without a licence in August. I was well and truly in Shit Street.

9. PORRIDGE

'A gambler never makes the same mistake twice. It's usually three or more times.'

US gambler V.P. Pappy

'I decided to keep my head down, keep my nose clean.'

Lester Piggott, on being imprisoned for tax evasion

I was mobbed by photographers when I arrived at Portsmouth Magistrates Court on 19 January 1987. It was a frosty morning, but as I smiled nervously for the cameras my hands were clammy and I could feel sweat running down the small of my back. I made sure I looked smart in a dark Ralph Lauren suit, white shirt and red striped tie. Sheila, who was being wonderfully supportive, looked stunning with a sheepskin jacket over her figure-hugging brown jumper and trousers. It was a big story. I was the Second Division's top scorer with 21 goals already that season and Portsmouth were looking good for promotion.

Inside, I waited uneasily on the bench for my case to be called. The place was full of reporters, fans who were worried about the fate of their top striker and supportive friends and family. I was absolutely crapping myself. Manager Alan Ball was with me; he had kindly agreed to speak in court on my behalf.

I was eventually called to the dock and I confirmed my name and address. I pleaded guilty to driving while disqualified, driving without insurance and speeding the previous August. Three weeks earlier I had admitted a similar charge before another court. I picked out Sheila's face in the public gallery and smiled nervously in her direction. I was in deep shit and had been forced to shell out £2,500 on a top brief called Michael Kent. He stood calmly before the court and outlined the mitigating circumstances. 'Mr Quinn realises he has jeopardised a brilliant career,' he added. Bally then went into the witness box. He told the magistrates, 'There's no limit to where Mick can go and what he can achieve, even to the point of international class.' I thought, 'Bloody hell, Bally. Did you really swear on the Bible and just say that?' Bally went on, 'If Mick lost his liberty it would set him back an awful lot. This has affected his work, but hopefully everything will be all right and he can keep scoring goals and that will help us get into the First Division. If he lost his liberty it would be a tragic blow to him and the club.'

The court adjourned for sentencing. I would find out if Bally's plea had been successful the next day. I had been warned by my legal people that the least I was facing was a big, big fine. At worst, I would be jailed. A restless night followed.

Next morning I was asked by the security guards to stand in the dock as magistrate Mary Yoward prepared to pass sentence. I had been an idiot. I had twice driven while banned and as a famous footballer I'd inevitably been spotted and caught. It was time to hold my hands up and take the punishment on the chin. Mrs Yoward, middle-aged and middle class, looked down her nose at me from the bench. I imagined that her worst nightmare was a Scouse footballer with more money than sense. She cleared her plummy voice, fixed her glare on me and said, 'Michael Quinn, you have flagrantly breached the order of this court on no fewer than two occasions.' She paused for effect, then added, 'We find we have no alternative but to send you to prison. I am sentencing you to 21 days. Take him down.'

The blood drained from my face and my throat was instantly bone dry. Everything seemed to slow down; I felt like I was in a dream. In the background I could hear Sheila sobbing loudly. The security guards led me from the dock towards a door that led to the cells. As I moved past the public gallery, Bally caught my eye and gave me a wink. That little gesture meant so much to me in the hours that followed. He was saying, 'Get on with it, son. Do your bird, come out, and we'll take it from there.' It was a wonderful boost to see a friendly face at a time like that.

The guards led me to a holding cell beneath the court. Gradually, the realisation of what had happened began to flood in. Quinny had fucked up again. Though I didn't know it at the time, there was mayhem outside the court. Sheila, wearing a dark suit and white blouse, was mobbed by the press as she tried to leave the building. Tears streamed down her face as she fled to a waiting car. She didn't deserve to be put through that.

I was one of the first top footballers of the modern age to be jailed, and the press were eagerly hoovering up quotes. My solicitor, Brian Statham, told the throng of reporters, 'This is a sentence for who Mick is rather than what he has done. Mick will take this sentence on the chin and will not appeal.' Bally also faced the press afterwards, and again stood by me. 'People associate jail with a person who is not very nice,' he said, 'yet Mick is the warmest man you could wish to meet. He is devastated, and my thoughts are only for him at this time. We are obviously disappointed for the boy, but these things happen.' Vince Hilaire said later, 'He is greatly missed as a bloke as well as a player. I'll visit him and take him the match reports and magazines.' Another Pompey player who didn't have the balls to give his name told *Shoot!* magazine, 'It was Quinn's own fault. He was banned for drink-driving when he played for Oldham, but didn't tell our chairman John Deacon about it when joining the club last year. He thought that what had happened a couple of hundred miles away wouldn't matter.'

Down in the bowels of the court a wave of dark depression was beginning to engulf me. I had let the club down, but more importantly I had brought shame on my family and Sheila. There was a rap on the cell door. It was a security guard saying there was a phone call for me. It was my old childhood mate John Clarke from Cantril Farm. He'd lived only a few doors away from us in Round Hey and I had known him since he was five. John had gone on to be a prison warden and, hearing the news, had managed to get a call through to me. He explained to me the prison process and what was about to happen to me. He said he'd try to have a word with the screws at whichever nick I was taken to and make sure I was looked after. It was great to hear a friendly voice at this time, and it's something I will never forget.

After a couple of hours I was told I would be taken to Winchester Prison. It was the beginning of the most harrowing few weeks of my life. The flashbulbs from a dozen press cameras lit up the night sky as the black maria pulled through the gates outside the court. I was slumped in a corner of the van staring straight ahead. I shared the van with several other prisoners, but I wasn't in the mood for polite chit-chat.

After arriving at Winchester nick I was taken to a holding cell where I was to go through the degrading experience of being processed. My designer Ralph Lauren suit, trendy red-striped tie and Italian handmade shoes where taken from me and replaced with huge bell-bottom trousers, striped regulation shirt and spoon-shaped shoes. I was no longer Mick Quinn the pampered pro footballer and terrace darling, I was prisoner 78459.

I was led to my cell by a screw who warned me that the prisoners had heard they were being joined by a celebrity con. I was carrying my pillow cases, sheets and blankets and passed a group of prisoners playing cards and reading papers. They looked at me like I was dog shit. In my cell, sitting on the top of a bunk bed, was my cell mate, a rough-looking geezer, hollow-cheeked and unshaven. As I took in my new surroundings the door behind me clanked shut and the keys rattled as the lock turned. I was doing bird.

Built in 1846, Winchester Prison was hardly a modern correctional facility. The Category B jail was like something out of a Charles Dickens novel. The grey/white walls of my cell, which was roughly ten feet by eight feet, were peeling and etched with graffiti. It stank of piss. The prison didn't even have a football team.

I chatted to my cell mate for a bit. He was on remand for beating up his wife but she had dropped the charges. Then an envelope was shoved under the door with QUINN written on it in red biro. Expecting a welcome from a Pompey fan on the wing, I opened it quickly. On a church pamphlet was the message: 'There's a lot of loving that goes on in prison. We are not all bad. If you fancy some loving tonight see me in the chapel behind the big organ after tonight's service.' I nearly shat myself. I was missing Sheila but not that much, so I stayed in my cell. As the night wore on, other lags made sure I knew they were there. They would bang on the cell door and scream 'Millwall!' or 'Saints!' or whatever team they supported. Others just yelled, 'Do your fucking bird!'

After lights out, I put my head under the itchy, smelly blankets and thoughts began to rush through my mind. I was ashamed that I had let down all the people who loved me. My family in Liverpool, Sheila and Little Michael. There was also Alan Ball, who had gone out on a limb to speak up for me in court; my team-mates fighting for promotion; and Portsmouth's fans, who hero-worshipped me. I had put my wonderful lifestyle on the line. The flash clothes, the top-of-the-range cars, the beautiful house – they had all been taken away from me. All the hard work and years of training I had sweated through to take me from Cantril Farm to the top of my sport could have been for nothing, and for what? For being a prat and driving when I was banned. As I tossed and turned a wave of deep depression engulfed me. I promised myself I would never end up behind bars again. Despite the stench and the noise, I eventually drifted off to sleep.

A loud banging on our cell door at 6.30 a.m. shook me awake. My cell mate warned me it was slop-out time – that is, time to empty the buckets you had used as a toilet overnight. I kept my head down and joined the Indian-file queue for the latrine. As I readied to empty my bucket one of the lags behind me clipped my heels, jabbed an elbow in my back and sent me sprawling. My chamberpot spattered piss all over me. Behind me I heard the sarcastic cry, 'Penalty, ref!' Another voice growled that familiar refrain, 'Do your fucking bird, Quinn.' Other lags joined in the laughter. I might have been the big tough guy on the football field, but in the nick I am not ashamed to say I was scared shitless.

The next ordeal was breakfast. As I queued up for my powdered scrambled egg I noticed a lifesize cardboard cut-out of a PG Tips monkey with a football under its arm. Some nice fellow had scrawled on its chest in marker pen DO YOUR BIRD, QUINN. As I sat down to eat, a huge, shaven-headed, tattooed monster dropped a beetle in my food. 'You're a Scouser,' he hissed. 'You must like beetles. We love you, yeah, yeah, yeah.'

I was shown the newspapers and saw my mug grinning out from them. It was big news; I was one of the first well-known footballers of the era to be jailed. The *Sun* even devoted a piece to my sentence in its editorial column. Under the headline OWN GOAL, it said: 'Portsmouth soccer player Mick Quinn was twice caught driving despite a drink offence ban. He richly deserves his 21-day jail punishment. Instead of supporting the sentence, Portsmouth's manager Alan Ball bleats that it is a "tragic blow" for the club. If Mighty Mick had killed someone, that would have been pretty tragic too!' I was feeling bad enough as it was, but I felt too sick to eat after reading that. I was a national talking point and it really hit home to me how serious my situation was. I could only imagine the sort of grief it was causing my family and friends.

I went back to my cell and descended again into a deep, dark depression. I tossed it over and over in my mind, and the more I thought about how I had put the career I had worked for on the line, the worse I felt. I decided to work out in my cell, both to keep in trim and to keep my mind occupied. I did press-ups and sit-ups until I was exhausted. We were banged up for 23 hours with just three twenty-minute stints outside for exercise, so my punishing work-outs in the cell became a twice- or even three-times-a-day routine.

Later, a friendly lag came into my cell and offered me some advice. He told me I needed to get a supply of Mars Bars and fags which, when used as bribes, would help keep the nutters at bay. The betting currency inside was also Mars Bars. For once I managed to curb my impulse to have a gamble. With my recent form with the horses, it was a good move. One day I saw the punishment meted out to a bloke who owed a huge Nigerian guy two and a half Mars bars for a gambling debt. The Nigerian dragged him into a cell and cut him up with some sort of sharp object. Blood was literally dripping off the walls. It scared the crap out of me. The friendly lag also warned me to go on a vegetarian diet as things like pies were cooked overnight and often had mice droppings on them in the morning.

I kept myself to myself. I had 21 days to get through and I didn't want any trouble that might put my release date back. I palled up with a few Pompey supporters who helped protect me from the bullies, and I listened to the sob stories of other lags. There were violent burglars, drug dealers and wife beaters. One thing they nearly all had in common was that they believed they were innocent. My spirits were continually lifted by a stream of letters from Pompey fans ranging from kids to grannies, and all were positive.

A couple of days after I arrived I was told I had a visitor. It was Pompey chairman John Deacon, no less. As I walked to the visiting area I felt chuffed that the chairman himself was backing me. I sat down and thanked him for coming, but instead of a cosy keep-your-chin-up chat, he said gruffly, 'I don't want you saying anything that might embarrass the prison or Portsmouth

Football Club.' I could see he was disgusted that I had shamed the club by ending up behind bars, but I wasn't looking for sympathy. I had done wrong and now I was paying for my crime. But at that moment I really needed to hear a friendly voice from the outside world. Little did I know that Deacon was trying to offload me to Aston Villa.

Sheila, accompanied by my strike partner Paul Mariner, also visited me. As I sat down in my prison clothes Sheila broke down and wept, and I could feel myself welling up too. Then Paul took a close look at me – and I must have looked a right sight in my bell bottoms, striped shirt and spoon-shaped shoes, all too big for me – and started laughing. He began with a giggle, but he was soon howling hysterically. It was infectious, and gradually Sheila and I joined in. It was the one warm moment during my time inside.

My first Saturday soon came, and Pompey were playing Brighton in the League. I listened on a borrowed radio to the scores. Although we won 1–0 I felt bad that I had let the rest of the lads down. I later learnt that the last thing Bally had said to the lads as they left the dressing room was, 'Go and win it for Quinny.' He told the press afterwards, 'The whole of the team was devastated when Quinn was sent to prison. They think the world of him, and it's made them extra keen to beat Brighton to give him something to cheer him up. Quinn's a smashing lad without an ounce of nastiness in his body, so there's no better way to give him a lift.' A week later the lads faced Wimbledon in the FA Cup fourth round at Plough Lane. Again I listened on the radio as Portsmouth were stuffed 4–0 in what Alan Ball called the worst performance he had ever been involved with in football. Again I felt ashamed and frustrated that we were tamely knocked out of the cup while I, the club's leading goalscorer, was banged up.

During my second week inside I was told that I would have to serve just fourteen days of my sentence as a result of good behaviour. I was overjoyed. As I walked back to my cell, a huge musclebound freak accosted me in the prison shop. He was that rough he had HATE tattooed on *both* knuckles – but you couldn't see them because they were dragging along the ground. He stared at me and demanded, 'Are you Mick Quinn?'

I mumbled, 'Yeah.'

'Do you play for Portsmouth?' he growled.

I thought, 'I don't need this. I've got two days of my sentence to serve and I'm going to end up in a scrap with some maniac Saints fan,' but the bruiser simply lurched forward, grabbed my hand and said, 'Right on, bruv. Get out there and score the goals to take us into Division One.'

Two days later I exchanged my prison gear for my designer suit. I walked out of the prison gates blinking in the sunlight and ran straight into Sheila's arms. We hugged for what seemed like an age. I asked her to take me to Southsea on Portsmouth's seafront. We stopped off at our house in Waterlooville to get my training gear. There was a huge WELCOME HOME banner draped across the garage. Down on the beach I put my shorts and trainers on and started to run, slowly at first, then faster and faster until I was sprinting. I whooped with joy and took down the cold sea air in gulps as I ran along the beach for five miles. I was free, and it felt good to be alive again.

10. HE'S FAT, HE'S ROUND, HE'S WORTH A MILLION POUND

'You meet a better class of person in pubs.'

Oliver Reed

Just four days after my release in early February I was back in the first team for a visit to our promotion rivals Ipswich. It says a lot for Alan Ball's integrity that he stuck by me. I got a great cheer from Pompey's travelling faithful, but the home fans gave me a bit of stick. Every time I touched the ball they made mock police siren chants, and there were a few choruses of 'Mick Quinn is a jailbird'. I thought it was quite amusing, and I had expected a few taunts. It just spurred me on to play better, and we beat them 1–0.

Afterwards I had to face a press conference about my mid-season 'holiday'. Mindful of chairman John Deacon's warning when I was behind bars, I was careful about what I said. 'I'm just relieved that it's all over,' I told the reporters. 'I'm just relieved to be out in the fresh air again. It's changed me. I think I've matured as a man. It was silly what happened and I wouldn't advise anyone in a similar situation to do that. I can assure the fans it won't happen again. I let myself, the fans and the club down. When I was in jail I had over eighty letters from all over the country, from youngsters to old-age pensioners. There wasn't a bad one among them. Kiddies were sending in pictures of me in the Pompey strip. It was brilliant, and it kept me going. I would like to thank everyone who sent letters. I couldn't reply to all of them because I was only allowed one letter a week.'

Days later, Mick Channon told *Shoot!*, 'In a perverse way Quinn's spell in jail might be a turning point for Portsmouth.

The millstone has been lifted from his neck and you can be sure he'll be raring to go.' A week after that we faced Hull City at Fratton Park. I felt determined to pay back everyone who had stood by me: Sheila and my family, Bally, my team-mates and, not least, the fans. I was given a hero's welcome by the crowd and I repaid it with my 22nd goal of the season. The whole ground echoed to the chant of 'The Mighty Quinn'.

In March my youngest brother Sean arrived at Portsmouth for an apprenticeship after I had a word with Bally. Like me, Sean played up front. He had my instinct for scoring goals, and unlike me he had pace, too. Typically for Sean, he scored in his first game then got sent off in the second. He had done enough to impress, though, and he was taken on. But, perhaps because his big brother was the star striker at Pompey, he started to act the big-time Charlie before he had barely settled in. He was out on the piss the whole time and coming in late for training; he was moaning about having to clean the bogs and the senior pros' boots. It was typical Sean. He had the talent to go right to the top but he didn't have the patience to wait for it to happen. Sean lived life in the fast lane, and soon the club let him go and he was back off to Liverpool. But it had been great to have a laugh with Sean for a few weeks and spend some time with him – something I hadn't had much of a chance to do since moving south.

In April we stuffed Millwall 2–0 and needed just one more point to make it mathematically impossible for third-placed Oldham to catch us. On Bank Holiday Monday we could tie up promotion with a point against play-off-chasing Crystal Palace at Selhurst Park. Over 10,000 Pompey fans made the trip to south London hoping for a promotion party. With three minutes to go substitute John Salako raced down the wing and knocked in a cross to Ian Wright, who scuffed it into the net. The nerves were jangling again, but 24 hours later Oldham lost to Shrewsbury, which meant we were home and dry and back in the top flight for the first time in 28 years. At the time Portsmouth were the only League champions – they'd won the title in 1949 and again in 1950 – to have sunk to the Fourth Division and climbed back up again. That night the players went to Kenny Swain's house for a champagne piss-up and got absolutely mullered. We were surprised to be told that we were expected in for training early the next morning.

There were a few grumbles from some of the lads when we arrived in the changing rooms the next day. Most of us were hung over, and with one game of the 1986/87 season left we were expecting Bally to keep up his workaholic approach with a hard slog on the training pitch. The gaffer called a meeting. 'Training today,' he told us, 'will take the form of a piss-up in the Pompey pub. Well done, lads.'

It was 10 a.m., and we wandered over to Fratton Park's own pub, which is handily attached to the ground, and began the mother of all benders. Soon the players were linking arms and singing the Portsmouth terrace anthem: 'Play up Pompey, Pompey play up'. Fans and the media soon heard that Britain's newest Division One outfit were on the razz. When they arrived they couldn't believe their eyes. We were absolutely smashed. Kenny told Radio Solent, 'Yes, this is a different form of training and we have to remember we have a big game on Saturday. And I wish you'd take that bloody microphone out of my pint of beer.' We didn't need to buy a drink for the rest of the day. Paul Mariner had been in a local snooker club that Tuesday night when he heard we'd been promoted. A tired and emotional Paul admitted, 'It's all been a blank since then. I came over in a purple mist.'

That Saturday a huge crowd crammed into Fratton Park hoping to watch us seal the Division Two championship against Sheffield United. The official gate was 28,001, but it looked more like 35,000. The atmosphere was electric, and it was wonderful to see the old stadium heaving, great for a traditional footballing city like Portsmouth to be back in the top flight after so long. Many of the lads saw the game as an interruption to our promotion party. I had been on the piss solidly since Tuesday; it was the closest I've been to actually playing while pissed, but I still bagged my 28th goal of the season. The fans rewarded me with a rousing chorus of 'He's fat, he's round, he's worth a million pound, Micky Quinn, Micky Quinn!' The million-pound bit I agreed with, but the rest wasn't quite so flattering. Still, to have 28,000 people singing my name left a lump in my throat. The game finished twenty minutes late after a premature pitch invasion had to be cleared by cops and snarling Alsatians. We eventually lost 2–1 and Derby were champions after beating Plymouth.

After the game the party started once again with a vengeance. The champagne began to flow in the dressing room and everyone was on a huge high. Bally was choked up. He said, 'The reception we received out there today was rivalled in my life only by the reception England had when we won the World Cup. It was unbelievable.' I had a quiet moment to myself as I took my boots off. I had finally made it to the big time after years of sweating my nuts off in the lower divisions. My dream of playing at Anfield, Goodison and Old Trafford would now come true. After my stretch inside, I hoped my family and friends would now have something to be proud of again. My goals had helped secure a place for Portsmouth, a club I loved, among football's elite. Things were looking up.

I was jolted out of my thoughts by Vince Hilaire spraying champers all over me. The dressing room was bonkers. Soon I was sipping bubbly in the communal baths with the rest of the lads. Paul Mariner was just as happy that his hometown club Burnley had missed being relegated from the Fourth Division. We grabbed Bally and dunked him in the baths fully clothed, still wearing his trademark flat cap. It was then drinks in the players' lounge followed by a round of pubs and clubs into the early hours.

The next day we assembled at the ground for an open-top bus ride to an official reception at the Guildhall Square. Over 7,000 fans had packed the square with thousands of others unable to get in. We were greeted by the Lord Mayor of Portsmouth and other local dignitaries. I felt terrible. My mouth was as dry as the Sahara and my head was pounding. Wandering into the Guildhall I spotted the refreshments and cracked open a bottle of lager. The lads followed suit. Soon we were pissed again.

Bally was the first man to address the heaving crowd. His voice brimming with emotion, he shouted, 'On behalf of everyone at the club, we do indeed love you. The way you've backed us and stood with us, the least we could do is get you into the First Division.' Then he added, ominously, 'And we are going to stay there, don't worry about that.' The gaffer then introduced the team and let us address the fans one at a time. It was a big mistake. By now we had got well stuck into the complimentary booze and some of the lads were struggling to string a coherent sentence together. When asked to sum up the season, Vince Hilaire told the crowd, 'I've got a little appeal. If anyone sees a pair of sunglasses lying around, they're mine. I came into the Guildhall with them but they're gone. Whoever's got them I want them back, please.' Then he screamed, 'Give us a P, give us an O, give us an M, give us a P, give us an E, give us an S! That got you, didn't it?' When it came to his turn, Mick Kennedy slurred his way through an Irish rebel song, to the amazement of the fans. Paul Mariner said, 'Thank you very much for coming here today, you little beauties! Next year we will win the championship, the FA Cup, the European Cup. Whatever you want to give us, we will win it.' Stepping up to the mike, I yelled, 'I love you all. I love all the people that supported me when I went on holiday for two weeks. All those goals are for you.'

Chairman John Deacon then took the microphone. 'I want you to know that every one of the players here today will be here playing at Portsmouth next season,' he pledged to the thousands of loyal Pompey fans, but Mick Tait, a big mate who would have given his right arm to play in the big league, even for just one game, went in the close season. Even after banging in 28 goals my own future at Pompey was in doubt.

I won a Player's Football Association Award for being the Division Two striker of the year. It was voted for by other players, so it was a great honour. The whole Pompey team was invited, but Mick Kennedy refused to go. He was hated by other pros because of his behaviour on the field. He would pull shirts, tell other players he had shagged their wives and had been accused of spitting. It was all gamesmanship, though. Mick was the nicest guy off the pitch, but it was probably a wise move not to attend. I donned the old penguin suit for the do at the swish Grosvenor House Hotel in London's Park Lane. I got absolutely bladdered on lager and champagne and could hardly stand when it was my turn to collect the award from PFA chairman Gordon Taylor. Other winners that night were Glenn Hoddle, Ian Rush, Tony Adams, Alan Hansen and Kenny Sansom. I was rubbing shoulders with the superstars of the game and I felt I was finally where I belonged. Roll on Division One.

11. THE GREMLINS ARE COMING

'I hate people saying I'm a shit. I'm not. I'm a c***. There's a great difference. A shit is a rotter, intentionally nasty, and I've never been that. I've never deliberately caused a lot of misery. I'm not cruel. A c*** is a c*** by mistake – it's accidental.'

Journalist Jeffrey Bernard

Sweden was a dream come true for the Gremlins – blondes everywhere. Pompey went off to Scandinavia in the summer of 1987 for a pre-season tour and we made the average Viking raiding party look like a Sunday school outing. We arrived at Heathrow early and got stuck into some serious duty-free shopping. The lads had heard about the high price of booze in Scandinavia, so we all stocked up on wine and spirits. We made our way to the plane and waited for take-off. I was sitting up at the back quietly reading a newspaper when Bally came rushing down the aisle.

'Where the fuck's Noel Blake, Vince Hilaire and Terry Connor?' he shrieked. 'The plane's about to take off!'

'Boss,' I replied, 'the last time I saw them they were queuing up to get booze in duty free.'

The captain put out a last call for them but we started taxiing on the runway and then took off without three of our star players. Bally was going spare. They eventually turned up in Stockholm – with their booze stash in tow.

We trained hard, and hit the ale in the evenings. I managed to score on the tour in every sense of the word. I banged in a hat-trick against Swedish Fourth Division side Leksand and I also pulled one of the gorgeous locals. She was a sexy redhead who cleaned the rooms in our hotel. I started having a laugh with her during the first few days of our stay and eventually she agreed to meet me for lunch on our day off. All the lads were sitting on the hotel veranda facing the street when she pulled up in a massive white Cadillac and whisked me off. The looks on their faces were a treat. She had a toddler and took me to meet her family. They got the photo albums out to show me pictures of her when she was pregnant. I was surprised when her dad handed me the pictures and she was bollock naked in them, but that's Scandinavians for you.

On my last night she took me for a romantic drive to a beautiful, clear lake surrounded by thick pine forests. She suggested going swimming, peeled her clothes off, and walked slowly into the cold water, causing hardly a ripple as she immersed her lithe body. I followed her gingerly to the water's edge with my boxers on. I dipped my foot in and squealed, 'Fuck me, it's freezing!' My voice echoed over the still water. My Swedish beauty laughed seductively and called me to join her in the water. Clasping my bollocks against the cold, I made the plunge. I swam out to her gasping with the cold and we began kissing and petting. After a few minutes she led me by the hand out of the water and up into the pine forest. She laid me down on a blanket of moss and performed mind-blowing oral sex on me. Weighed in, weighed in. She later cooed, 'If you come back to visit me in Sweden you can have everything else.' She wrote to me a few times when I got back to England, but I never returned to Scandinavia for the full works.

I phoned Sheila later that evening.

'I suppose you've been letching over all them blondes over there?' she asked.

'Why do you always assume I've been shagging, Sheila? Actually I had a quiet meal with a couple of the lads,' I lied. 'I didn't even have a drink. We are over here on a serious training camp.'

I was a good liar, but I did feel guilty about how I was treating Sheila. She deserved better than that. But I was living this crazy rock-star lifestyle and I couldn't seem to stop being unfaithful. In truth, I was immature and still living for myself. It is difficult to grow up in the cosseted world of football.

Back at the hotel the lads were downing the duty-free scotch they had bought at Heathrow, so I soon forgot about doing the dirty on Sheila again. Vince Hilaire had an extra bottle so he traded it for a hardcore Scandinavian porn movie. The only video player in the hotel was in one of the conference rooms, so Vinnie stuck it in that and got an eyeful. Unfortunately, so did every other guest: the video piped the blue movie into every TV in every room in the hotel.

I should have been looking forward to my dream of playing Division One football, but another almighty spanner had hit the works. After a decade-long slog around the football grounds of England I thought I had finally made it into the game's elite and would be playing at Anfield, Goodison, Highbury and Old Trafford, but that summer Pompey signed not one but two new centre-forwards. It was a massive kick in the teeth. Bally splashed out £285,000 for striker Ian Baird. The Yorkshireman had been the top scorer with Leeds the previous season and Bally believed he had the experience to lead the line in Division One. He also brought in another striker, Terry Connor, an England under-21 star and Brighton's top scorer in three of the past four seasons, for £200,000. Good players, but hardly Keegan and Dalglish.

More insulting was the news that they were trying to offload me to Millwall for £300,000. It was obvious that Pompey didn't think I had the ability to succeed in the top flight despite my 28 goals getting them promoted the season before. I felt sickened, they had knifed me in the back, and I demanded to be put on the transfer list. The papers said Coventry and Celtic were interested in signing me for £500,000, but nothing firm came in. Then Millwall agreed a £320,000 deal with Pompey for me, but I turned it down because I didn't want to go back to playing in the Second Division again. Bally managed to talk me round with promises that I was still very much in his plans, but I started the 1987/88 season as a substitute. One of our first matches was against Tottenham. As the game started I saw Spurs' prolific striker Clive Allen on the bench. During the game I did a few stretches next to him on the touchline.

'How many goals did you score last season, Clive?' I asked.

'Forty-nine,' he replied. 'How about you?'

'I got 28 of the fuckers despite my two-week holiday in Winchester nick. It's a funny old game, isn't it? Both leading goalscorers on the bench.'

To put it bluntly, I was fucked right off. I agreed with the principle of strengthening the team, but I had spearheaded our promotion success. I thought after all my goals it was up to other players to come in and win the shirt from me. I should have started the first few matches, but I think Bally felt obliged to play the new boys after shelling out all that cash on them.

Bally and I had it out in the pages of the local paper, the *Portsmouth News*. Twiddling my thumbs on the bench or playing with the stiffs, as the reserves are known, was not for me. I needed to be centre stage, scoring goals and making headlines. It was so frustrating to have made the top flight and then not to get in the team. I wanted the fans who had idolised me to know that I was desperate to play. I told the *News*, 'I believe in my ability to play at this level and score goals – all I want is the chance. The last thing I want to do is leave Pompey because I love it here. But I also want first-team football.' Bally countered, 'It's up to Mick. If he does enough to make me pick him and then does enough when he plays, then he has got a future here. We need all the good players we can get – it's as simple as that.'

The public appeal worked, and I was back against Charlton Athletic on 14 September. Ian Baird was sent off, and I came off the bench to score the equaliser in a 1–1 draw. I told the now defunct *Today* newspaper, 'The boss told me to wait for my

Above Me and our Mark, aged seven and nine respectively. (Private collection)

Left Quinn Family Robinson. Sean, Mark and me holding baby Tricia. (Private collection)

Right Mum Patricia outside 16 Round Hey on The Farm. I miss her so much. (Private collection)

Left Me and Mark look right pair of cherubs. (Private collection)

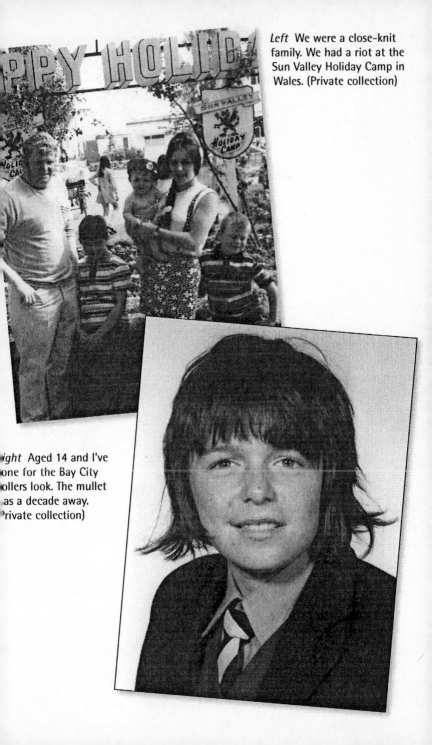

Left We were a close-knit family. We had a riot at the Sun Valley Holiday Camp in Wales. (Private collection)

Right Aged 14 and I've gone for the Bay City Rollers look. The mullet was a decade away. (Private collection)

Left I soon became a terrace darling at Pompey. The fans would serenade me with: 'He's fat, he's round, he's worth a million pounds, Micky Quinn, Micky Quinn.'

Right Pompey v Saints in 1988. The game is the South Coast's version of Barcelona v Real Madrid. (© *Popperfoto*)

Below Alan Hansen was the best centre back I ever played against. Note the different physiques. (© *Popperfoto*)

Left 1990, with Newcastle's famous number nine on my back I'm being tracked by Oxford's Steve Foster wearing his trademark silly headband.
(© *Popperfoto*)

Below I was known as 'The Mighty Quinn' in Geordie Land. They were my happiest days in football. (© *Popperfoto*)

bove A shellsuit is a
must-have outfit for
very true Scouser. I
till bash out a few
ennon tracks on the
uitar. (Private
ollection)

right The 'tache
wouldn't have shamed
 Mexican bandit. Here
m doing a spot of
nodelling for a gents
utfitters. (Private
ollection)

Left My fiancée and soul-mate Karen Davies. (Private collection)

Right Every stable needs a really good horse and Dragon Flyer is mine. I'm hoping she'll take me to the big time. (© George Anderegg)

chance and take it when it comes. I've done what he asked and now I hope he gives me a run in the side.' But when Sheffield Wednesday visited Fratton Park I was out of the team again. It was always easy to spot when I was being dropped: Bally wouldn't ask me for racing tips. I went nuts and told reporters after the game, 'I've got back in the side and proved I can play and score goals, and now I've been dropped again. I'd like to play for a team who wants me to play for them. I'd leave, but reluctantly, because I've settled down south.' I wasn't the sort of player who could just draw his wages, go on the piss and play in the reserves. I needed to be in the limelight, scoring goals.

There were reports that Leeds were interested in signing me, but, again, I forced my way back into the side. Results were going against us. After one desperate performance chairman John Deacon came bursting into the dressing room and screamed, 'Considering how much I paid for you, Connor and Baird, I think you are a total waste of money.' After he had gone, a flabbergasted Bally said, 'I can't believe that has just happened at a professional football club.'

After one match Mick Kennedy and I were picked at random to undergo a drugs test. The procedure was farcical. No one supervised us properly and Mick couldn't fill his test tube with piss because he was so dehydrated after the game. He could only produce a dribble, so he topped it up from a can of lager; he knew he was clean and he didn't want to bugger about all night. Of course, the test came back negative. Sport needs to get its house in order as far as drugs are concerned, and the best way to do that is with regular and thorough tests. I was surprised my urine sample didn't have a cocktail cherry and an umbrella in it – I was drinking a fair bit at the time.

One cold November morning defender Clive Whitehead came to pick me up for training. Since my ban the other lads had mucked in and given me a lift to and from the training ground. Clive, who had joined Pompey in the close season from West Brom, had dark bushy eyebrows and the eighties footballer's identikit tache and mullet. In fact, from a distance he resembled yours truly. We got to Moneyfields and I jogged out in my shorts and began warming up. I was stretching the hamstrings when I felt a tap on my shoulder. 'Michael Quinn, I am arresting you on suspicion of driving while disqualified.' I turned, and two uniformed police officers were standing there. I thought it was a kissagram or a wind-up from one of the lads, but then they flashed their warrant cards. 'Not guilty!' I screamed. 'I have not been behind the wheel of a motor since you had me up in court. I think you've got the wrong moustache. You've fucked up, and I want an apology.' Clive backed me up. 'It was me that was driving,' he said. 'For my sins, I do look a bit like Mick – and Bob Carolgees from *Tiswas*.' There's only two Micky Quinns. In the end, the cops admitted their mistake and I got an apology in the local paper, even though it was only a paragraph long. I should have followed it up with a claim for harassment, but it wasn't worth the hassle. When we had to assemble for the team photograph for the club Christmas card, all the lads played a trick by turning up with Mick Quinn masks on. If I ever got in trouble with the police again it would be like the end scene of *Spartacus*.

Cop: 'Which one of you is Mick Quinn?'

First player: 'I'm Mick Quinn.'

Second player: 'No, I'm Mick Quinn.'

Third player: 'Listen, I'm Mick Quinn.'

The shots were actually taken, but in the end the club thought it might be taking the piss out of the Old Bill a little too much. But the picture was leaked to the newspapers and everyone got to see it anyway.

By now my gambling had become obsessive. I was betting every day, doing as much as £500 an afternoon. I would read the *Sporting Life* in the changing rooms after training and then head for the bookie's. I never like to place huge bets, but I'd have, say, £50 on every race while I was in the bookie's. I'd bet mostly on horses, plus football and the odd dog race. The buzz I got from winning was amazing; it was like the feeling people must have when they take drugs. I needed a fix every day, and one race wasn't enough. I had to go through the whole card.

Saturday was always difficult for me – so many great race meetings, but I had to play in a football match, too. I found the solution when I bought a tiny handheld portable telly. I would put my bets on early doors then head for the ground and get changed; when Bally gave his team talk I would duck into the shitter and watch the races on my little telly with the sound down. I remember Bally saying, 'It's weird. My team talks seem to give Quinny the shits.' At half-time I would be back in the bog to catch up on the results.

Pompey were languishing at the foot of the table, so Bally decided to take us on a break to Jersey to try to turn the season around. When we arrived on the island Alan gathered us together and said, 'We're over here to relax, to forget about the pressures of the First Division and bond as a team. I don't want any poor behaviour or drunkenness.' That night Bally sat down to dinner in one of the best restaurants on the island. The first course arrived, and he had just raised a fork to his mouth for the first bite of his meal when he felt a tap on his shoulder. A six-foot-five-inch policeman was standing behind him. 'Are you Alan Ball from Portsmouth Football Club?' the officer asked. 'We've just detained one of your players.' Noel Blake had apparently gone berserk in a bar and got into a fight with some locals. Police had arrived and dragged them apart.

Bally was furious. The next day he took it out on us by organising a knackering training session on the beach. He had us doing doggies. He walked along the beach dropping a traffic cone every 40 yards until he had dropped five, then he made us sprint 40 yards to the first traffic cone, back to the start, then

80 yards to the second cone, back again, and so on. Bally was strutting up and down the sand, flat cap on his head, stopwatch in hand, screaming his head off at us. He didn't notice the tide was coming in, he was so furious. The training session ended with the water lapping around the cones.

That night we all got completely shit-faced in the hotel bar. Bally joined us and was drinking as hard as the next man. Bally was a great character to go for a beer with because he had an endless supply of funny anecdotes. It got to 3.30 a.m. and the night porter, a Scouser, announced that he'd finally had enough of serving 25 bevvied-up, lairy footballers, and that the bar was closing. 'You've got to be joking,' I screamed at him. 'Come on, pal, don't be a fucking party pooper. We'll get you one in as well. Come on, mate, how about a bit of Scouse solidarity?' The other lads started to give him some stick too, but he wouldn't budge. So me, my room-mate Mike Fillery, Eamonn Collins and Vince Hilaire continued the piss-up with a bottle of scotch in Vince's room. By 5.30 a.m. we were well and truly bladdered and headed for bed.

Two hours later there was a banging on our door. My head was pounding and my mouth was as dry as Gandhi's sandals, but I got out of bed to answer the door. It was Gordy the kitman.

'Bally wants to see you both immediately,' he said.

Mike and I put on our trackies and staggered into the meeting room where Bally stood motionless, staring at the floor and not saying a word. Barry Horne barged through the door moments later, went to sit down, missed and slipped to the floor in a drunken heap. Bally, his face expressionless, kept staring at the carpet. Then he began to speak.

'After the performance in the bar last night we are no longer welcome in the hotel,' he barked, stern-faced. 'Not only that, but apparently the local bigwigs are so pissed off with our behaviour since arriving that they want us thrown off the island for causing havoc. Gentlemen, if this gets out it will be a big story in the national newspapers. Can you imagine it? "Pompey Pisspots Wreck Holiday Haven". The chairman will have my bollocks.' He paused, then added, 'But the good news is I've had a chat with the hotel boss and sent his wife the biggest bouquet of flowers I could find on Jersey. The even better news is that I've cancelled training for the day. I want everyone down in the bar in five minutes for a hair of the dog and a bonding session.' You have to hand it to Bally, he had class.

When I got home, Sheila said she wanted to talk to me about something serious. 'Mick, darling, I'm pregnant,' she said. Days later she went for a scan, and afterwards I got a call on my mobile. 'Darling, it's only twins!' she said excitedly. The pregnancy wasn't planned, but it was a pleasant surprise, and a sobering thought. After putting Sheila through so much, I realised it was time to knuckle down and make a better job of fatherhood than I had with Michael. With two more mouths to feed I would have to make an effort to cut back on the boozing and betting. I also wanted to be there as much as I could for the twins.

I hugged Sheila tight and said, 'I'm really made up, darling. We're going to have a little family now. I can't wait.' Marriage, however, wasn't on the cards. We no longer lived in an era where you were booted up the aisle if your girl fell pregnant. Sheila and I were married in all but name. I wasn't big on the sanctity of marriage anyway, and I didn't need a piece of paper to confirm my love for Sheila.

Also, around this time I got a bombshell piece of news that didn't exactly endear the idea of marriage to me: Mum and Dad had split up. I had been too busy down south with my career to notice the signs, and I was really knocked back when I heard. After 25 years together Mum had finally had enough. The old fella had gone on one too many three-day benders and she had kicked him out. Dad moved into some flats on the Farm and Mum stayed at 16 Round Hey. After years of playing the dutiful housewife she was looking to break free. She was a very intelligent woman and regretted not going to college, so now she applied to do a course in Sociology at Liverpool University. It was real *Educating Rita* stuff. I missed most of the fall-out from the split, being down in Pompey, but it was very difficult for Sean and Tricia.

I had always been closer to Mum when I was living at home. It was she who had taken the most interest in my schooling, she who I went to if I needed to talk about things. As the eldest, I had a special bond with her. But with Dad now living apart, I was forced into a closer relationship with him. If I rang him we had to talk together rather than the phone being handed to Mum, so at least something positive came out of it.

In February 1988 table-toppers Liverpool had visited Fratton for what proved an emotional afternoon for me. Kenny Dalglish, one of my heroes, was the Reds' manager. I was in awe of him. I had three early chances to put us ahead but I fluffed them all, and Liverpool took charge of the game. John Barnes, then at the height of his powers, scored both goals in a 2–0 win that was their 27th game unbeaten on the trot. It was a dream just to play on the same field as the team I had worshipped as a boy. But it was only a small glimmer of light in a dark season which drifted towards the inevitable relegation. By the time Newcastle visited in May the fans had had enough. Supporters blamed chairman John Deacon for not funding Bally's rebuilding plans, and 'Deacon out! Deacon out!' echoed around the ground as we lost 2–1. I did, however, play at Old Trafford on the last day of the season and scored a penalty as we were thrashed 4–1. Their scorers were Bryan Robson, Peter Davenport and Brian McClair with a double. I ended the season with a modest tally of fourteen League and cup goals – not bad when you consider I was in and out of the team for much of the year, but it had been a frustrating and disappointing season. The club had not invested in new players, and they hadn't played me enough.

12. ANOTHER QUINN DOUBLE

'You will find peace of mind if you look way down in your heart and soul. Don't hesitate cause the world seems cold. Stay young at heart cause you're never, never, never old at heart.'

Earth, Wind and Fire, 'That's the Way of the World'

Standing by Sheila's hospital bed, my stomach was in knots. I had played a friendly match and made a dash to Liverpool's Oxford Street Hospital in time to see my twin babies enter the world. Sheila had gone north for the birth to be near her family – plus we wanted our kids to be born Scousers. Sheila was only small, so she had an epidural to ease the pain. I looked away during the gory bits, but I could still see what was happening as it was reflected in the doctor's glasses. A wave of love engulfed me as I held my beautiful twin girls Melissa and Natasha in my arms. The ninth of August 1988 was a magical day: another Quinn double.

I was 26 and a dad of three, and the twins' birth brought about a period of calm and responsibility in my life. I couldn't stand in a bookie's every afternoon any more. We had two new mouths to feed and I could no longer blow so much of my wages on booze and horses. Sheila needed all the help she could get, so I made the effort to come home earlier and give her a hand. I knew what to expect, having been through it with Little Michael. My partying slowed down and I changed nappies, the lot. We would make eight bottles of milk to last them through the night, but they never woke at the same time so it ended up like a relay. We didn't have any family down south so it was down to us to take care of them. Football and racing took a back seat as I spent time with my young family.

Pompey had a great start to the 1988/89 season, beating promotion favourites Leeds and Leicester, but again, I was in and out of the side. I came off the bench to score against Bournemouth, then scored the winner away at Ipswich, but with my contract up at the end of the season I wanted to move. Being on the bench wasn't putting me in the shop window for a new club.

That season, England's youth team were due to face Czechoslovakia at Fratton Park, but when the Danish referee measured the goalposts he found we'd been playing all season with the crossbar six inches too low. 'No wonder I kept hitting the fucking woodwork,' I said. God knows who was behind that little scam.

The results soon began to fall away, and with the fans blaming the board, chairman John Deacon was replaced by Jim Gregory. Jim had a car sales business but he still refused to give me a club car. I think that was probably wise with my driving record. Jim was a real character. He would come into the players' lounge, have a drink with a huge Havana cigar, then bet any player £500 that he could beat him over twenty yards having given him a ten-yard start. So me, Jim and striker Warren Aspinall lined up in the street outside Fratton Park. It was a dead heat, so we agreed to disagree. Fuck knows what the fans thought as they walked past.

Jim appointed John Gregory (no relation) as manager. John, who had played for Derby and QPR, was a disciplinarian who also had some new ideas about training. He was always immaculately turned out and always looked quite pleased with himself. He brought in ex-Chelsea player Steve Wicks as his number two. Steve, to put it bluntly, was a poseur and loved himself. If John and Steve had been made of chocolate they would have eaten themselves.

I was very upset to see Alan Ball go. No manager would have achieved what Bally did with the team of misfits he had. He liked to say we could charm the birds out of the trees with our football, but it was his man-management and tactical nous that held it all together. We weren't so much rebels without a cause as rebels without a clue. He produced a spirit and camaraderie that made us one of the most consistent teams in the country, and but for a lack of cash, I think Pompey could have established themselves as a First Division team. They certainly had the fan base to do it.

Still, John made me skipper, which was a very proud moment for me, and he wanted me to sign a new contract, but the old camaraderie of the Alan Ball days was over and John was building his own team. I didn't think the team was good enough at the time to get out of the Second Division, so I turned down a new contract. I decided it was time for a new challenge and hoped a top-flight club would come in for me. Portsmouth had put a £1.5 million price tag on my head which, though flattering, I thought was a bit over the top. Gregory certainly didn't think I was overpriced. 'Spurs paid £1.7 million for Paul Stewart, and Dean Saunders cost Derby a million, so why not?' he told the papers. Everton, West Ham, Manchester City and Watford were said to be interested. City made three attempts to sign me but they wouldn't meet Pompey's asking price. There were also overtures from clubs in Turkey and Belgium, but with two young daughters it wasn't the right time to move abroad.

In the pre-season in 1989, I was out of contract. I spoke to Watford, but then I got a call from Kevin Dillon who had moved from Pompey to Newcastle United. He said the club had sounded him out about me and that they were very keen on signing me. I was on my way to Geordieland.

13. NEWCASTLE

'You don't understand Newcastle United unless you realise the hero wears the number nine shirt.'

Cardinal Basil Hume

St James's Park towers above Newcastle like the Coliseum in Rome. As you drive over the Tyne Bridge into the football-mad city the arena dominates the skyline to the extent that the whole of Newcastle seems to live in its shadow.

Geordies love their football. And with just one team to support, it gives the city a sense of togetherness. There is no divided loyalty such as there is in Manchester with City and United, on Merseyside with Liverpool and Everton, and in Glasgow with Rangers and Celtic. When Newcastle win the whole city is happy, and when the Geordie fans love you, they love you to death. When they don't there is nowhere to hide; it's like living in a goldfish bowl. Just like my home town Liverpool, Newcastle is a tough, working-class city that is coming to terms with the loss of its industrial past. Despite the WHO THE FUCK IS MICK QUINN? welcome I got from the fans, I was confident that it would soon feel like home to me.

I arrived in Newcastle in July 1989. The club was then languishing in the old Division Two – today's Nationwide Division One – a shameful place for a club of Newcastle's stature. The era of Kevin Keegan, Paul Gascoigne and Chris Waddle had passed, and manager Jim Smith had brought me in as part of his plans to re-establish the Magpies back in the top division after their relegation the previous season. I had scored 54 League goals in 121 games for Pompey and now felt ready to play in England's top division again, and this time I wanted to make a bit more of a splash.

Jim, known in football as the Bald Eagle, had a proven track record in management. He had taken Colchester, Birmingham and Oxford to promotion and QPR to the Milk Cup final – now the Worthington Cup. He was also my sort of manager. A blunt northerner from football's old school, to describe him as dour makes him sound too cheerful. When I arrived I was ushered into Jim's office at St James's Park. The Bald Eagle was watching racing on the telly. 'Hang on a mo, Quinny,' he said, 'I'm just going to ring a bet through.' I thought, 'Me and Jim are going to hit it off just fine.'

When he'd finished, he said to me, 'This is a massive club that is desperate for success. Last year Brazilian Mirandinha was leading the line, but we had to keep subbing him and he didn't score enough goals. I need someone to come in and score twenty goals a season.'

'No problem, Jim. I've done it before in this division and I'll do it for you this season,' I replied in a cocksure manner.

Jim, now Harry Redknapp's assistant at Portsmouth, looked taken aback by my supreme confidence. No one had scored twenty goals in a season for the Magpies since the days of baggy shorts and rattles.

Because I was out of contract, my transfer fee was decided by an FA tribunal. Pompey wanted £1.5 million for me, but Newcastle were offering £250,000, so the tribunal decided something roughly in the middle, £680,000, was a fair price. Coming out of that tribunal, the Bald Eagle yelled, 'Fuck me, the chairman is going to go nuts. I was only allowed £350,000.' Pompey chairman Jim Gregory thought he had been ripped off. 'We'll buy him back off you now for a profit,' he said. That seemed to shut Jim up. As part of the deal my agent Mel Stein had got me what I considered decent dosh for the time, £1,000 a week, and I also trousered a nice £85,000 signing-on fee – good money for Division Two but a bit dangerous for someone whose first impulse after training every day was to go straight to the bookie's.

I was given the hallowed number nine shirt, and when I did an interview with one of the local Newcastle papers the reporter made it clear to me just how important the number nine shirt was. In the article he quoted famous Newcastle fan Cardinal Basil Hume, who was once head of the Catholic Church in England. I had never heard of him, but to be fair to the cardinal he seemed to understand his Geordie football. Apparently he had once said, 'You don't understand Newcastle United unless you realise the hero wears the number nine shirt.'

Geordieland is like a nation within a nation, and it needs its own idols. If you wear the black and white shirt for Newcastle then you are a treated like a movie star in the city. Every kid wants your autograph, punters in every pub want to buy you a drink and women throw themselves at you. If you wear the sacred number nine shirt you can times that by three. Quite naturally I absolutely adored my time in the north-east, which began in a hotel in the city centre while I looked for a house for Sheila and the kids and got myself acquainted with the bars and clubs of Newcastle. It was a big wrench for the family to uproot from Portsmouth on the south coast, but football can be a nomadic existence.

The lads at Newcastle weren't such a close-knit bunch as they'd been at Pompey and there weren't quite so many pisspots, but they were nice lads and I soon made good friends. My strike partner was Scotsman Mark McGhee who had also arrived in the summer for £200,000. At 32, Mark was in his second spell at Newcastle having been lured to the all-conquering Aberdeen side put together by Alex Ferguson before starring at Celtic. Mark, now manager of Millwall, was my perfect foil. A big, gruff British centre-forward from the old school, he was strong, held the ball up well and also scored his share of goals. I was the fox in the box, mopping up the stuff he created. Mark was married with kids and lived near me when I moved to Hexham in Northumberland. We would travel to training together and have a pint in the local pub, the Golden Hart. Another vital cog in the team was ex-Oxford midfielder

Kevin Brock. He was a busy player who was a great crosser of the ball, and he gave me much of the ammunition for my shots. Kevin said at the time, 'I just put the ball into the box and Mick goes for it. People think I'm aiming for his head, but I know he will get on the end of it – even if it's only a half-decent cross.'

Scotland skipper Roy Aitken joined later. His first training session was a real scream. Back then, Newcastle trained at Benwell, which seemed to be the highest as well as coldest and windiest place in the city. That day a freezing high wind that came straight from the Arctic circle was blowing across the park. Jim organised a game with the first team playing the reserves. The stiffs always like getting one over on the stars of the squad, and that day, with conditions Captain Scott would have balked at, they were playing like eleven Peles. Early on, the ball came to Roy; he went to control it, but it bobbled and he sliced it into touch. The Bald Eagle screamed, 'Fucking Scotland World Cup star, you're having a laugh, aren't you?' Great way to greet your new signing. It was typical of Jim's sense of humour.

Goalie John Burridge – Budgie to his friends – was a real character. He was advancing in years, but he was one of the fittest guys playing football. Budgie loved working out and even used to eat baby food because he said it was high in protein and helped him bulk up. On the way to games he would listen to motivational tapes he had made: 'You are a great goalkeeper. You will tip any shots from long range over the bar. You will catch all corners.' And, to be honest, he was a good keeper.

Before the first game of the 1989/90 season against Leeds I was in a city-centre pub where I picked up a copy of the fanzine written by Newcastle United Independent Supporters, called *The Mag*. I decided to have a read and see what they thought of their new signing from Portsmouth. Were the fans who held up the WHO THE FUCK IS MICK QUINN? banner at the demonstration just a couple of jokers who didn't represent what the rest of the supporters felt? Reading *The Mag* over a pint, it certainly didn't seem so. Among other things, they described me as a 'fat failure' and 'the Bob Carolgees of English football'. Cheers, lads. I obviously wasn't the fans' first-choice signing to become the next Wor Jackie or Supermac. It made me realise I was going to have to do something special to turn the fans around. The 'fat failure' jibes didn't affect my confidence at all, as they never did throughout my career. I believed in my ability to score goals and I couldn't wait for the season to start, for a chance to prove the doubters wrong.

Then came that glorious first game of the season against Leeds. I was so pumped up I believe I would have scored on any ground against any opposition. I had something to prove and no one was going to stop me. To score four goals at any time is special, but to do it in your first game when everyone believes you will fall flat on your face is such a buzz. Nothing is better than proving people who doubted you wrong, whether it is teachers who laughed in my face when I said I wanted to be a footballer, coaches who sneered at me or people in racing who laughed when I said I wanted to be a trainer. My four goals in my debut game for Newcastle sent the fans on the terraces nuts and I became an instant Geordie superstar.

After that game, the goals continued to fly in. Away at Oxford I scored with a looping header. With this, my ninth goal of the season, I became the first player in Newcastle's history to score in the first five matches of a season. On 21 October I scored my second hat-trick of the season away at Brighton. I was on the sort of run strikers dream of. Everything I touched seemed to hit the net. By the time of that Brighton game I had already scored fourteen goals that season. Afterwards, Jim Smith finally admitted to reporters that he had got me on the cheap. 'When I first spoke to Alan Ball about him, he said Quinn was the best finisher he had ever seen,' he confessed. 'We thought we were overturned to some degree by the tribunal over the £650,000 fee, but he may be cheap.' Jim liked to term me 'an ugly duckling type of footballer'. I think by that he meant I was the sort of player who didn't look much but blossomed into something decent in the end. Either that or he thought I was an ugly bastard. Later, Jim was very complimentary about me, saying, 'Quinn does his best work in the box. He is the best finisher I have ever worked with, and that includes the likes of Trevor Francis, John Aldridge and Frank Worthington.' Even Newcastle fanzine *The Mag* was apologetic after branding me a 'fat failure'. It was a measure of the dire times at the club when they joked, 'Scoring four goals in the same season, let alone the same match, is the stuff legends are made of.' The club was in financial turmoil at the time, and commenting on the resignation of two directors *The Mag* added, 'The vice-chairman's job would be a fitting reward for Quinn's achievements, and his legal experience would also be beneficial.'

By September, *The Times*, no less, was reporting that Jack Charlton, the Ireland manager, was trying to recruit me. Big Jack had been to see me play and hoped I would be eligible because of my great grandparents having come from Waterford, but FIFA ruled that I would need at least one Irish-born parent to qualify. I was very flattered to have been considered for Ireland and I believe I could have done a great job for Jack in his up-and-at-'em side. It later emerged that Tony Cascarino managed to play for Ireland for years despite not having an Irish grandparent.

As well as praise, success also breeds jealousy. It was Malcolm Macdonald, who was also a Geordie hero in the black and white number nine shirt and who later had a well-publicised battle with the bottle, who decided to have a pop at me. Malcolm told a newspaper that I simply leant against a goalpost and let the other players do all the hard work before popping up on the goal line for another tap-in. I had never denied that all my best work is done in the box, but Malcolm's attack seemed bitter and small-minded. His motivation was either sour grapes or money.

Either way, it was a shitty thing to say. But it just made me want to go out and score more goals and make him look like a fool.

My success didn't turn me into a big-time Charlie, thank God. If I did get too big for my boots, my family and friends from Cantril Farm, where I was still a regular visitor, would rip the piss out of me. Plus, I had spent long enough dragging myself up through the divisions to know that you had to keep working hard if you want success, and I was soon joined on Tyneside by Sheila and the twins and I moved out of the hotel to a house on the Whitebridge Park Estate in Gosforth. We decided we were too close to the city centre there, that we would have young fans knocking on the door at all hours, which isn't ideal when you've got two young children, so we bought a lovely four-bedroomed cottage in Hexham in the rolling Northumberland countryside. As well as being handy for Hexham racecourse, it was also home for many of the players, including my strike partner Mark McGhee, Roy Aitken, Kevin Brock and Darren McDonagh. It had been a stressful move for Sheila, who as well as looking after the twins had also masterminded packing the furniture and bringing it up north. A mate from Pompey, Big Dave who now works for Capital Radio, found a lorry and drove all our stuff up. It was a huge operation. Hexham was quite out of the way and Sheila didn't know anyone in the area; on the other hand, I had a squad of 30 blokes to go out on the piss with.

There is no such thing as a quiet beer in Newcastle, and if we went on to a club it was often the wonderfully named Tuxedo Royale. The Royale, on a ship moored on the Tyne, was Newcastle's premier nightspot. One night I pitched up there with a few of the lads and that year's Miss World, Miss Argentina, was hosting a gala evening. I had heard all about George Best's exploits with beauty queens and, fortified with alcohol, I fancied my chances. She was taller than me in her stiletto heels, and her diamante ball gown hugged the perfect hourglass figure. She had dark hair and beautiful Latin features, and she looked absolutely gorgeous; as she was wearing a sash with MISS WORLD on it, I knew it wasn't just the beer goggles working.

'Watch this, lads,' I yelled above the disco beats. I composed myself and strode over to her purposefully. 'Hi, babe, my name's Mick Quinn,' I slurred into her ear as the music blared in the background. 'You look wonderful, a million dollars. I was just wondering whether you fancied a shag?' She turned, looked into my eyes and smiled. 'Here we fucking go,' I thought, but in a heavy accent she replied, 'How you say? I don't speak English.' I laughed, thanked her and returned to the lads giggling at the other side of the dance floor. 'She's thinking about it,' I bragged. At least I'd had a pop. It was the talk of the dressing room for days.

As the goals flew in my social life in Newcastle also gathered pace. I didn't offer Sheila as much support at home as I should have done, and the strain began to mount. Being with a new team, I felt I had to socialise with the lads to get to know them better, so whenever anyone suggested a beer, a game of snooker or a round of golf, I didn't turn them down. I had always been a lad's lad and the team took precedence over my relationship. As a result Sheila was often left at home twiddling her thumbs.

I made a couple of good mates in Newcastle who are still friends today. World Cup Willy, named after the football mascot, was a racecourse tic tac man – that is, the bloke who signals the odds to the bookies with bizarre hand movements. He was my partner in crime on all my betting missions. Big Deggsy looked after me when I went out in Newcastle. He is a man mountain, and he stopped any would-be Charles Bronsons having a pop at me when I was out on the piss. I was also enjoying going racing and had palled up with National Hunt jockey Neale Doughty, who won the 1984 Grand National on Hallo Dandy. He loved his football and I loved my racing. Neale and I toured the local tracks at Hexham, Sedgefield, Carlisle and Newcastle, and he would give me the benefit of his knowledge on race riding, going and how to spot when a horse looks well. In return, I would invite Neale to stay with me when Newcastle were playing at home. He would watch the game, then we would go for a curry and on the piss big time into the early hours. He then used to get up at 5 a.m. to go riding out. I don't know how he did it.

I was also back in the betting shop every day, after a respite when the twins were born. I liked to have £40 or £50 on every horse, dog race or football game I had a punt on, but I literally spent the whole afternoon in the bookie's so if I went on a big losing run I could do as much as £2,000 in the afternoon. For some big-shot gamblers that would be peanuts, they do much more than that on just one race, but it was enough on my wages. Sheila would say, 'We need a new washing machine and the kids need new shoes but you decide to spend your wages in the betting shop. Your career is not going to go on for ever and you should be putting cash away for the future,' but it went in one ear and out the other. My philosophy has always been 'live now, pay later'. I always believe something will turn up whichever way life turns. It may be irresponsible, but that's the way I have always been. As a result, my relationship with Sheila was a ticking bomb waiting to explode.

When I had a big win I always treated Sheila and made sure she got a big bundle of cash, and I also liked to treat the family back in Liverpool. Still, despite earning a grand a week, we sometimes struggled. We had two big mortgages to pay, one on the Hexham house and the other on the flat in Southsea, plus I was pissing a large chunk of my wages up against the wall every week. The country was in the trough of the property slump and the Portsmouth flat had slipped into negative equity. In another great piece of Mick Quinn economics, I handed the keys of the flat back to the building society, losing £25,000 on the spot. At the time, I came from the Nick Leeson school of financial management. Today, the seafront apartment would be worth a small fortune.

Thankfully, the goals kept hitting the net. To commemorate my scoring feats a pub in Newcastle called the Dog and Parrot began to serve a special brew named after me. Surprise, surprise, it was strong and full-bodied. The *Sun* also did a lifestyle piece on me. Here is my Fav File:

TV programme: *Channel 4 Racing*
Pop group: Living Colour
Food: Pasta
Drink: Lots
Film: *Gremlins*
Film stars: Jack Nicholson and Raquel Welch (and not for her acting)
Comedian: Racing tipster John McCririck
What would you do if you won a million pounds? Buy a Derby winner.

That season we travelled away to Leeds, and on the way to the dressing room we saw Vinnie Jones, who was then playing at Elland Road, in the club gym doing weights. It was a silly way to prepare for a game, and Budgie, Newcastle's own muscleman, couldn't resist having a laugh with him. He charged into the gym and said to Vinnie, 'Get out the way and let me show you how it's done.' Budgie, in his club suit, added ten kilos to what Vinnie was lifting and then started pumping iron with his arms going like a hummingbird's wings. Then Budgie jumped off and told Vinnie, 'OK, big guy. Your turn.' Vinnie couldn't lift it at all and he ran off into the dressing room. We all pissed ourselves laughing and went to get changed. Later, Vinnie went to warm up to the strains of the *Rocky* theme tune. He was trying way too hard with his tough-guy image.

During the game there was a poor tackle, and players from both sides started to push and shove one another – real handbags stuff. Vinnie came sprinting over from the other side of the pitch, but as he approached I stuck my arm out, stopping him in his tracks, and yelled, 'This has got fuck-all to do with you, so piss off.' The sheepish self-styled hardman replied, 'I was just trying to break it up.' He then walked off with his tail between his legs.

We had an amazing end to the season winning seven in a nine-match unbeaten run, but we failed to win automatic promotion after losing on the last day at Middlesbrough. Leeds and Sheffield United went up, while we had to slug it out in the play-offs with our deadliest rivals Sunderland. The Tyne & Wear derby is one of football's fiercest confrontations, but this match was about more than local pride: a Wembley appearance and the possibility of a First Division place awaited the winners. This game meant so much to the people of the north-east that you could feel the tension when you were out and about in Newcastle.

It had been a long, hard season, and going into the game I wasn't a hundred per cent fit. I was nursing a hamstring strain, but as England's leading goalscorer in all divisions that season I wasn't about to watch our biggest game of the year from the stands. The first leg was at Roker Park, and, understandably with what was at stake, it wasn't a classic. Actually there was no footballing skill whatsoever on display; the contest boiled down to 22 blokes kicking the crap out of one another. We went back into the dressing room feeling we were home and hosed. We would now take them back to St James's Park for the second leg in front of our fanatical supporters. Again, for the return leg I wasn't firing on all cylinders because my hamstring was giving me gyp. In the first ten minutes Mark McGhee hit the Sunderland post; the ball rolled across the goal line and came out. Not long afterwards they broke away and scored, and that was it. We couldn't get back into it, and late on they made sure with a second. There was a pitch invasion; some Newcastle fans burnt their shirts while others left the old stadium in tears. A black cloud descended over the city.

I was floored, emotionally and physically. Sitting in the dressing room you could hear a pin drop. Everyone just sat there looking at the floor. There was little Jim could do to lift us, and we got changed quickly and went home as soon as we could. It was one of the lowest points of my career. McGhee and I had netted 61 goals between us, but it was still not enough to win promotion. I had scored 36 goals; only Hughie Gallacher in the twenties and Chilean George Robledo, one of the first foreigners to play in English football, in the fifties had ever beaten that tally in one season for the club, but the gloss had been taken off because we were still in the Second Division. We had won nothing and achieved nothing.

It took me all summer to get over the crushing blow of missing out on promotion. I took Sheila and the kids to Barbados. It was some much-needed quality time with the family, and I spent it chilling out, lying on the beach, stuffing my face and getting pissed. I must have put on about two stone in a fortnight. Three weeks before we were due back for pre-season training I started to work on my fitness again. I cut down on the boozing and jogged and stretched every morning. I was burning to play in the First Division again after my taste of it with Portsmouth. I loved Newcastle, and I dreamt of wearing that number nine shirt against Liverpool and Manchester United.

That summer Jim Smith had said he would let me go for 'a ridiculous amount of money', but when Wimbledon offered £1 million it was turned down. They later upped the offer to £1.2 million, but Jim wouldn't budge. I was more than happy to stay and fight to win promotion with Newcastle in 1990/91, and I was straight back in the groove, opening my account against

Plymouth. Afterwards I bragged to the *Sun*, 'I'll be disappointed if I don't score 30 goals this season.' I've never really had a problem with confidence.

I invited Dad and my brother Mark, who brought along a couple of his dodgy mates, to one home match. Afterwards we bumped into Paul Gascoigne in the players' bar. Gazza was then at Tottenham, but as they didn't have a game that day he had come home to watch his team. We had a beer with him and he was a real laugh. After a couple of drinks he said his farewells, and as he walked away from the table one of Mark's mates shouted, 'Hey, Gazza, don't you want this?' For a laugh he had dipped Gazza's wallet without him noticing. Gazza was dead impressed.

I played against Gazza once when he was a kid at Newcastle and I was at Portsmouth. He got the ball in Newcastle's eighteen-yard box, laid it off, got it back, beat a couple of men, then sprayed it wide to a black and white shirt on the right. He then made a fantastic run into the box and smashed the cross into the back of the net. He followed the ball in, stuffed it up his shirt, then ran back to the centre spot, put the ball down and sat on it. We stood with our hands on our hips with looks of utter amazement on our faces. He not only had supreme talent but the impudence of genius. Gazza was something special.

As Gazza knows, north-east derbies are some of the best games in British football, but they had never been kind to me. I had yet to find the net in nine matches against Sunderland and Middlesbrough. I'd had some real tussles with big Gary Pallister, who later played centre-back for Manchester United, and we'd usually ended up kicking ten types of shit out of each other. So when we faced Boro in the Rumbelows Cup in October 1990 I was more revved up than usual. I went into one challenge with their goalie Stephen Pears and gave him what I consider to be a good old-fashioned shoulder barge, but the Middlesbrough players surrounded me and there was lots of pushing and verbals. World Cup referee George Courtney reached into his pocket and pulled out the red card. Afterwards, the Bald Eagle said, 'Quinn had a little go at Pears and my players say the keeper did the same, but it was handbag stuff,' but two days later he'd changed his mind. Now I was 'totally unprofessional', and he clobbered me with a £1,000 fine.

A few weeks later and it was becoming obvious that the season had already gone tits up. We had won just one League game in the last ten and had slumped to sixteenth in the division. We'd also suffered a catalogue of injuries, and the fans were starting to turn on Jim. I spoke up for him in the press, saying, 'If we don't pull our weight for Jim, he's got no chance. The table doesn't look that pretty, but we're still only five points off a play-off position. It's not the end of the world.' But Jim's days as the manager of Newcastle United were numbered.

14. A DEAD CERT

'You gotta ask yourself one question: "Do I feel lucky?" Well, do ya, punk?'

Clint Eastwood as Harry Callaghan in *Dirty Harry*

Sheila was steadily getting more frustrated with the amount of time I was spending either at the races, in the bookie's or on the piss. I was getting paid handsomely, but much of it was ending up in the bookie's satchel. If that was not enough, I had started the Mighty Quinn Racing Club. For a few quid a month ordinary working people could own a share in a racehorse and could watch it run and visit the stables. I knew how much cash you needed to own a thoroughbred and I wanted to make it easier for people to get involved cheaply. The club had a hundred members, lots of runners and quite a bit of success, but I found it difficult to balance the books and the cash from members didn't even pay for the horses' training fees. Muggins here picked up the shortfall.

One morning in March 1991 the almost constant arguing exploded into a bloody fight in the kitchen of the Hexham house.

'You're a fucking waste of space!' Sheila shrieked at me. 'You're earning good money but instead of spending it on the kids or the house you give it all to the bookmakers.'

'At least I go out to work,' I snapped back.

'You think you're the big man,' she bawled, 'but you're a loser. What are you going to do when you retire? Spend your life in a bookie's?'

She paused for breath, then launched into me again.

'You say you love me but you're not even man enough to make a decent woman of me and marry me. You think you're the big man but you're really a pathetic coward.'

By now I knew exactly how to wind Sheila up. Instead of calming the situation, I once again poured petrol on the flames.

'Why would I want to marry you anyway?' I goaded her. 'It's just moan, moan, moan.'

An enraged Sheila then grabbed one of the carving knives from its plastic holder on the work surface. Instead of taking the opportunity to apologise, I wound her up again.

'If you're going to cut me, then fucking cut me!' I screamed as I placed my hand on the work surface, palm down. 'Or haven't you got the fucking bottle?'

She lurched forward, eyes aflame, and I felt the cold steel blade slice against the bone on the back of my hand. Blood started pissing everywhere. Sheila quickly came to her senses and wrapped my hand in tea towels, but soon they turned crimson. There was blood all over the work surface and the floor. My hand began to throb with pain and I realised I was in real trouble – and I was supposed to be jogging out to face Brighton at St James's Park in seven hours' time.

I needed treatment, so I decided to go and see the Newcastle physio. Sheila couldn't drive so I drove myself with my hand wrapped in a towel. The physio took one look at the congealed bloody mess and took me straight to the Nuffield Hospital in Jesmond near the stadium. The doctor said the blade had been millimetres away from severing the tendons in my hand. I was injected four times with a local anaesthetic, once between each finger, and given nine stitches. It was horrific. The surgeon told me I was in no state to play in a football match, but I didn't want to let the rest of the lads down or the fans so I asked the doctor to gave me some painkillers.

I set off for the game as white as a ghost. I told Jim and the press that I'd cut my own hand in a kitchen accident at home while chopping bacon ribs. 'I missed the bacon ribs and slashed my hand,' I lied. 'There was blood everywhere and I was in a lot of pain.' I got a few curious looks but they let it pass. The hand hurt a lot, and to be honest I didn't have a great game. I got a few painful knocks on the wound and failed to score. I shouldn't really have played but I thought a domestic argument, albeit one as violent as that, shouldn't prevent a player from turning out for a team that pays him a huge salary. Sheila had lost it for a moment, but I was just as much to blame for winding her up. Amazingly, Sheila and I patched things up once again, for the sake of the girls, but it didn't take a social worker to know that the relationship was in deep trouble.

It wasn't just me who had a rough time that day. The game itself was a miserable affair watched by Newcastle's lowest crowd for a League game in nine years – just 12,682. Difficult to believe this was just over a decade ago.

Days later I was in the headlines again after going out on the piss with Gazza. Paul was staying in the north-east because Tottenham wanted him to rest his injured groin. We were facing Wolves at home on the Saturday, and the day before I met Gazza for a game of snooker with a lad called Paul Moran who had joined Newcastle on loan from Spurs. I had a couple of beers, nothing silly, and got an early night, but after the Wolves game we all went out on the piss big style and ended up in the Boat bar. Later, someone grassed on Moran saying they had seen him drinking with Gazza at the England star's working men's club the Dunstan Excelsior on the Thursday. This broke the club's rule about not consuming alcohol 48 hours before a game and Moran was sent packing back to London after only sixteen days on loan. I, being the model pro, was not affected.

In the FA Cup that year I scored what I regard as my greatest ever goal. We'd already beaten Middlesbrough 2–0 and had been drawn against my first club, Derby County, at home. England goalkeeping legend Peter Shilton was between the sticks for them. The ball came to me 30 yards out, I looked up, spotted Shilts off his line, and without pausing hoofed it with my right foot. The ball soared high over Shilts' head and then, as he desperately scrambled back towards his goal line, it began dipping viciously before hitting the net, followed by a flailing Shilton. I stood triumphantly with my arms aloft, fists clenched, and screamed at the heavens, then I turned and saluted the fans going berserk on the Gallowgate. It was better than an orgasm. Mick Quinn only scores tap-ins, my arse. Unfortunately we came unstuck in the next round in a replay against a very strong Nottingham Forest team under Brian Clough.

In the League the team was not winning enough matches either, and the gates were down to as little as 12,000. When the punters start voting with their feet the game is up. In March 1991 Jim Smith fell on his sword saying the club was 'unmanageable'. He was replaced by my second manager to have won a World Cup, Argentina and Spurs legend Ossie Ardiles. I was gutted for Jim as he was a manager and a man I respected. He was hampered by boardroom squabbles and a lack of cash with which to rebuild the side. Still, Jim later said that his time at Newcastle was one of the most enjoyable of his management career and that my 36 goals had been one of the high points. 'Mick Quinn was a great fellow, a great character. He was a tremendous finisher, and when he was fit he was a fabulous player who played attacking football, and that is the only way to play up there. The fans have been brought up on it with all their heroes – Macdonald, Milburn, Keegan – and that is what they love to see. I'm not sure Mick was always as fit as his racehorses but he was a great lad to have around, especially as he scored 36 goals in one season.' The 1990/91 season predictably petered out and we finished eleventh, but I was still the club's leading scorer with a respectable tally of twenty.

After football, there was always the horses. At this time, one day at the races in particular had to go like clockwork for me. My horse Mighty Lady, a two-year-old filly, was running at Sandown and I couldn't see her being beat. The more I looked at the form of the other horses in the race, the going and how she had been flying at home, the more I knew I had to stick my bollocks on her to win it. And if I was going to have a big punt I naturally wanted to be at the Surrey course to see her run, plus in those days you had to pay tax on bets placed in betting shops while racecourses were tax free. The only problem with my monster gamble was that I lived in Hexham, Northumberland, a 600-mile round trip from Sandown, and I had to train with the team in the morning and make it back for training at 9 a.m. the next morning. No problems, I'll jump on a plane.

The morning of the big race and I had everything planned. Mark McGhee gave me a lift from home to the training ground. I had a bit of banter with the lads and told them I wasn't sure Mighty Lady would win; I didn't want everybody and his mate plunging on and bringing the price down. Straight after training I showered and changed into a double-breasted grey-checked Armani suit and took a taxi to the airport. On the way I stopped at the bank and took out £5,000 in crisp new notes. I thought it best not to tell Sheila how much I was going to put on, she'd only moan and panic. I'd tell her after I had won, when I could give her a huge wodge of dosh for a luxury holiday and buy her and the kids new outfits. Suited and booted, and with cash in hand, I arrived at Newcastle airport. I settled on the plane with a couple of miniatures and the *Sporting Life*. Poring over the form confirmed what I already knew: Micky was on a winner. Today, old son, you're going to hit the fucking jackpot.

I got a cab from nearby Heathrow round the M25 to Sandown and met up with the horse's trainer, my old mate from Pompey Mick Channon.

'Mick, I'm going to have a little bit on her today,' I said. 'Has she travelled well?'

'She's in great form, Micky,' he replied. 'The horse has done everything we've asked of her at home and will run a big race.'

It was all I wanted to hear.

Standing in the parade ring at one of the country's premier racetracks was, and still is, a great buzz for a boy from Cantril Farm. Rubbing shoulders with aristos, captains of industry and oil-rich Arabs felt great. My horse looked in great health: her coat shone, her eyes sparkled and she seemed to skip over the ground. The other fancied runner was Lucid, owned by Lord Caernarfon and trained by Lord Huntingdon. Mighty Lady was owned and trained by footballers from more humble backgrounds, but that would make victory all the more sweet.

As Mighty Lady cantered down to the start under jockey Mouse Roberts, I made my way to the rails bookmakers – the guys who literally have their pitch on the rails and take all the big bets. I got the £5,000 on at 11–2. It was the biggest bet I had ever laid by a long chalk, or would ever lay again.

I made my way quickly to the stands. The race was a five-furlong sprint so they wouldn't be hanging around. As I did so, the PA system crackled into life: 'They're under starter's orders – and they're off!' My heart was thumping like it was coming out through my chest. Mick had his binoculars focused on Mighty Lady but I was too twitchy to watch properly.

'What's happening, Mick?' I screamed.

'She's got a great position on the rails and is just behind the leaders. She's going well.'

The commentary boomed out: 'And turning into the home straight Mighty Lady has gone a neck clear, but Lucid under Mouse Roberts is fighting back. Mighty Lady is running on and looking like she's going to get up.'

I felt physically sick with excitement. 'Come on, Lady!' I screamed until I was hoarse.

The Tannoy continued to blare: 'And as they flash past the line Lucid has just got up to beat Mighty Lady by the shortest of short heads.'

Oh fuck. Oh shit.

I walked to the parade ring in a daze and watched the horse walk into the spot reserved for second. Why didn't I have a bit of each way? Soon afterwards Mick took me to the bar and bought me a stiff drink. I think he could see that all the colour had drained from my face. It was lucky Mick put his hand in his pocket because I was totally skint. I thanked Mick and said I had to dash. I was too proud to ask him if I could borrow some money for the cab fare to Heathrow. He shouted after me, 'You should back mine in the next, I think it will win,' but I couldn't even draw any money out at a cashpoint because the bet had taken me over the limit.

As I wandered through the crowd towards the exit, a hand tapped me on the back and a Geordie voice said, 'Mick, mate, you're my hero. I watch you every week from the Gallowgate. It is an honour to meet you.'

'Cheers, mate,' I replied. 'I don't suppose you could lend me a score?'

I'd like to thank that fan, whoever you are, because he helped me get back to Newcastle. I later sent him back the dosh – with two tickets for the next home game. Mick's horse in the next race obviously romped home. All I got was an almighty roasting from Sheila; I was in the dog house for days. But soon I was back in the betting shop.

Ossie wanted to build a new young side over that summer of 1991, and by August he'd made a number of changes to the squad. He offloaded McGhee and Aitkin and brought in young guns like Lee Clark, Steve Watson and Steve Howey. Talks on a new contract for me began, and Ossie called me into his office for negotiations. I had made it known that I was anxious to play in the top division.

"Ello, Mick. Tell me waddaya want,' Ossie said in his thick Latin tones as soon as I walked in the door.

'Well, a pay rise and a top-of-the-range BMW would be nice,' I said with a smile.

'OK, Micky, you got it,' he replied, to my complete surprise. It was the easiest contract negotiations I had ever had.

Good as gold, he bumped my wages up to £1,200 a week and gave me a bright-red 528 injection 20K BMW. We shook hands on the deal with the motor and I didn't think to get anything in writing. I was chuffed, as the rest of the lads were driving shitty little Mondeos and Peugeots. I suppose I was acting like Billy Big Bollocks, but if you're doing the business on the park, as I had done for Newcastle in the past two seasons, then you deserve to be rewarded. The club knew my worth and wanted me to stay, so why not take what was on offer? Ossie also recognised my popularity with the fans and asked me to act as a spokesman at some press conferences and on other public occasions because his English wasn't great.

His footballing philosophy was attack, attack, attack, and fuck the defence. We played Tranmere in one of the cups and it was a draw – 6–6. I got a hat-trick and so did John Aldridge for Tranmere. Sometimes there would be nine of us going forward with just one defender and the goalie staying back. Success couldn't last on that basis, and as our form began to dip so the fans began to stay away.

In October we faced my old club Portsmouth at Fratton Park, now managed by Bald Eagle Jim Smith. I always liked to do well against my old clubs, and though I had nothing to prove to the fans, I wanted to make sure they knew I was still the man. But Pompey took an impressive 3–0 lead and we weren't really at the races. The game was drifting towards the final whistle when we broke down the left and a furious cross came in which bounced on the wet turf and spun past goalie Alan Knight. I was racing in at the far post and realised that if I slid in at full stretch I might score, but I would also collide with the upright. Either that or I could just let the ball run past; the result of the game was not in doubt anyway. I made the split-second decision, slid in and scored, but as I did so my knee smashed into the post. There was a sickening thud and I could feel the throbbing pain of ligaments tearing. I was carried behind the goal for treatment and after a few minutes was able to walk back on to the pitch again, but moments later the knee locked completely and I dropped to the turf in agony. I had torn my cruciate ligament and was rushed to Newcastle's Nuffield Hospital for an operation the next day. I was gutted because I had started the season so well. I hated being injured, too.

When I speak to Newcastle fans today they still say that moment is engrained in their minds, that it proved without doubt my commitment to the club. The truth is I would do anything to score goals, but my commitment against Portsmouth left me in plaster and out of action for months. Still, I lay on the sofa at home playing with Natasha and Melissa, and it was great to spend some quality time with my girls. I spent much of the time watching films by Steven Spielberg or starring Jack Nicholson, and I managed to hobble down to the bookie's every now and then too.

By the middle of October the club was bottom of the Second Division, its worst ever League placing, and £4.6 million in debt. Furthermore, Newcastle's only player worth big money – yours truly – was injured. Despite being up the Tyne without a paddle, Ossie was still being bravely upbeat – either that or he was losing his marbles. 'These kids are good. We'll get promotion,' he told the *Today* newspaper.

I admired Ossie as a footballer and as a man, and it was frustrating having to watch from the sidelines as we careered from defeat to defeat. The New Year came and went and we were still struggling at the foot of the table, and in early February 1992 we were stuffed 5–2 away at Oxford. It was a dire and embarrassing performance and our travelling fans rightly booed us off the pitch. Ossie was finally whacked.

Then a rumour began to sweep the city, and all Tyneside held its breath. There was a fantastic suggestion that the man known to the Toon Army as the Messiah was returning as manager. Then I heard it was true. My boyhood hero Kevin Keegan was on his way back to St James's Park.

15. THE MESSIAH AND JUDAS

'You fuck with me, you fuck with the best!'
                    Al Pacino as Tony Montana in *Scarface*

For a decade there had been a piece of graffiti on a wall in the quayside in Newcastle that said, in big white letters, KEEGAN IS GOD. He'd probably walked across the Tyne and written it himself. It referred to the glory days of the early eighties when the England star had galvanised a failing Newcastle team and dragged them back into the top division. Alongside Keegan were youngsters Peter Beardsley and Chris Waddle as well as seasoned campaigners like Terry McDermott and David McCreery, but everyone agreed that Kev's passion and leadership had been the decisive factors.

Driving into training on 5 February 1992, I didn't need to be told the news that Keegan was back. All of Tyneside was going bonkers. Fans were out in the streets in their black and white strips, the excitement on their faces clear to see. A huge group of supporters had gathered at the Benwell training ground, and when I went inside everyone at the club was buzzing. Just as before, Keegan's mere presence at once captivated the region. United's disgruntled supporters became excited, expectant ones overnight.

We were told to report to the gym, and we fanned out in a semi-circle as Kev and his assistant Terry McDermott breezed in to a round of applause. He then gave a rousing speech of the sort that would become familiar over the coming months. 'This is a new beginning for the club,' he said. 'Players who have been out of favour will have every chance. I will take a look at everybody.' Afterwards he came over to me as one of the senior players, shook my hand and said hello. I was made up.

It was the Second Coming, and I was definitely a disciple. Kevin was my boyhood hero. I had watched him in awe from the Kop when he starred for Liverpool and loved his brashness and style. Fans love a player who runs his nuts off for the shirt, and Keegan played like a terrier, combining a never-say-die approach with pure skill. He was the same whatever he was doing, whether it was a five-a-side in training or TV's *Superstars*, during which he famously fell off his bicycle going like shit round a bend. I had posters of him on my bedroom wall, and when I played with my mates I always pretended to be Kevin. I loved his flash dress sense, the wing-collared shirts and the flared suits; I loved his bubble perm and the way all the girls on our estate thought he was the cutest thing around. He was my idol, and now he was going to watch *me* play. It was a dream come true.

Terry McDermott predicted immediately that Kev would do for Newcastle what Bill Shankly had done for Liverpool. He said Newcastle would be challenging for a European place in three or four years' time and Kevin would be recognised as one of the all-time great managers. Many people laughed at him at the time because it was Kev's first managerial position and Newcastle were in the deepest shit and apparently heading for the Third Division. It was a desperate position, even for a man of Keegan's powers, but Tyneside businessman Sir John Hall was also taking control of the club and promising to bring in much-needed new investment, and to stop all the boardroom squabbling.

I had met Kevin before, at the races. Like me, he was mad keen on horses and owned several with Mick Channon. I found him good company. He was a man of obvious charisma, and he was also knowledgeable about racing. But I was worried how his appointment would affect my career at Newcastle. Ossie had made me central to his plans at the club and had been quick to acknowledge my importance both on and off the field. Kevin had a private chat with me soon after his arrival and calmed my fears. He took me to one side after training one morning and insisted, 'Micky, you are very much part of my rebuilding plans here. But make sure you are ready when you come back. You can't rush injuries like yours.'

I was now back in training and was desperate to face Port Vale at the end of February. 'I'm itching to play and I hope I do because I've got dozens of family and friends coming to watch,' I told newsmen. Kev made no secret of the fact that he wanted me to get out there and score some goals. 'I want him in as soon as possible,' he told the *Today* newspaper. 'But we have to temper his eagerness with common sense. He has come back remarkably quickly and I don't want a setback now.'

I played, but I failed to find the net. I had indeed come back too early, and my lack of fitness showed. Keegan dropped me to the subs bench for the home relegation clash with Brighton the next week, but the following Saturday I was back in to face Swindon. In the days before the game there had been rumours that Keegan was already pissed off with the club, that the board had not produced the cash they had promised him before he took the job. Kev was openly critical of Sir John Hall, saying, 'It's not like it says on the brochure.' Despite the rumblings of discontent we played well, and I popped up to score the winner in a 3–1 victory. I had a shower afterwards and went for a beer in the players' lounge.

As I emerged into the car park, reporters surrounded me.

'Keegan's walked out!' one of them yelled.

'You what?' I replied. 'Kev told us before the game that there would be some changes in the boardroom, but he didn't say anything about quitting.'

Sure enough, Kevin had spat out his dummy and pissed off down the motorway just 38 days after taking charge. I was completely shell-shocked, especially as we had actually won the game that day, which for that season was an achievement in itself. The Sunday papers were full of how the club was now £6 million in debt after losing £3 million in the last year. There were demonstrations outside the ground with WE WANT KEEGAN

BACK banners, the works. I thought Keegan was holding the club to ransom, but Kev can walk on water up there and soon the chairman had promised him cash and he was back at St James's.

I was in and out of the team for the remaining months of the season, and to put it bluntly I was pissed right off. Keeping that club from being relegated to Division Three meant everything to me and I wanted to be out there on the park battling away. With my goalscoring record at the club, I believed I should have been in the starting eleven. So when a reporter from my Portsmouth days asked for an interview about Keegan's management style, I was happy to oblige. I told him how Kev was in his first management job and that he was finding his feet. Then, speaking off the record, I said that I thought some of his decisions and training methods were incredibly naive. Kev and Terry had come in saying they were going to make training more fun, but instead, when things weren't going well, they would come in with faces like slapped arses and all the players would feel like topping themselves. Unfortunately the paper spun the story up a bit. I think the headline was NEWCASTLE IS A SHAMBLES UNDER KEEGAN, SAYS MICKY QUINN.

A muckspreader full of shit had hit the fan. Double quick, I got on the phone to Terry, who was known as the Buffer for his go-between role. I had always got on well with Terry as he was another big racing fan. Every morning he would ask, 'What do you fancy today, Quinny?' Anyway, I told him how I'd had a chat with a reporter I knew and that things had been blown up. I told him I was thinking about suing. Terry insisted he would smooth things over with Kev, but on the Monday Keegan called me into his office. The former England captain was sitting behind his desk with a look of contempt on his face. To my horror, I noticed that the newspaper article was pinned to his noticeboard. There were none of the usual pleasantries and banter.

'You have let me down personally and you have let down everyone at Newcastle United Football Club,' he said as soon as

I entered the room. 'I hope you made a few quid selling this story because you will never play for this club again.'

He hadn't even given me a chance to explain myself, so I completely lost my rag. 'Not a fucking problem,' I shouted back. 'If you want me to go, I'll fucking go.' With that, I stormed out and banged the door behind me. I hadn't received a penny for my comments to the paper and I felt I had been done up like a kipper. I was fined two weeks' wages, some £2,400, and was axed for the crucial trip to Leicester City that would decide our relegation fate. Keegan told the *Sun*, 'What Quinn said was ill-timed and totally out of order. I can't allow things like this to happen and I have nipped it in the bud.'

In characteristic fashion, I wasn't going to go quietly. I told the *Today* newspaper, 'The manager told me I have no future at the club. He said he's prepared to sell me and wants a few quid. I don't want to leave like this, but he's made it clear I'm not wanted. The story was blown up out of all proportion and I'm seeking legal advice.' In the meantime, I was consigned to the footballing equivalent of Outer Siberia and trained with the stiffs – that is, the kids and the reserves.

Keegan used all his motivating skills to gee up his team for the final contest against promotion-chasing Leicester. He said, 'We need a result, and we'll get it, survive and take off.' Full marks to Kev. He produced a minor miracle and stopped the Magpies from tumbling into the Third Division for the very first time in their history.

In the close season, I heard that a few clubs were interested in signing me and I expected to take the best offer available, but amazingly Keegan surprised me by wanting to kiss and make up. 'Let's let bygones be bygones,' he told me. 'I want to start from scratch with you because I think you're a great goalscorer.' I was more than happy to make my apologies, as I loved the club and my life in the north-east. To this day I don't know what changed his mind.

I spent the summer chilling out with Sheila and the twins. I took them to Disney in Florida. I don't think the girls were over impressed, but I loved it and I went on every ride. In the end it was me going on the rides and them watching me and waving as I went round. It was like a fantasy world, and just like *Star Trek* and *The Wizard of Oz*, I couldn't get enough of it. When we got home we went back to Liverpool to see Little Michael and the rest of the family at Cantril Farm. In July I did a bit of PR work, even opening the North of England Motor Show at Whitley Bay. I arrived in the back of the actual car from the hit film *Chitty Chitty Bang Bang* and felt a bit of a prick. Still, I got a few quid plus all I could drink – which is a fair bit – in the hospitality area.

Then it was back to the grind of training. As I was known as a bit of a drinker, I always knew I had to work very hard to prove to managers that I was fit enough to play. Again, I worked out my own training regime in the close season. I worked really hard on my fitness, determined to break back into the first team. First day back at pre-season training, I arrived in the changing room and raised a few eyebrows when I pulled out a bin bag of the sort boxers wear in order to shed the pounds. Then I pulled out a huge stopwatch.

John 'Bez' Beresford, who I had known at Portsmouth and who had just joined the club, said, 'What the fuck's that for, Quinny?'

'To time myself on the run,' I replied. As one of the slower lads at the club, I used to set off first for the run to the bridge on the way to Durham.

'How many minutes are you expecting to do it in, Quinny?' Bez added.

'Minutes?' I replied. 'My stopwatch only works in hours.'

I had first bumped into Bez in the Intermediate League when I was playing for Stockport Reserves and he was with Manchester City Juniors. We'd clashed in a couple of hefty challenges.

He'd squared up to me once and growled, 'Stop fucking treading all over me in your fucking size ten Pumas, pal.' I didn't take any shit in those days and turned to him and bellowed, 'Stop fucking squealing like a pussy just because you play for a big flash club. Fucking get on with the game.' And he got on with it. Bez reminded me of this years later. It was the sort of thing I said to most players when I was at Stockport. Bez later paid me a great compliment when he said, 'I can't remember who coined the phrase, but Mick was known as the fastest player in the club – over a yard. It was true, though. In front of goal he was as sharp as anyone I have ever played with. He was brilliant at toe-ending it. Obviously that is not something coaches like to see, but he could turn and spin and with no backlift toe-end the ball into the net. It was a real skill.'

I was in the side that played Edinburgh team Hearts in a pre-season friendly, but I failed to find the net. Afterwards, I said, 'I feel as sharp as ever. Now I aim to make up for lost time after missing so much of last season through injury. I'm so determined to do well that I trained during the summer and returned to training lighter than when the season started.' Still, when the 1992/93 season proper started, I was on the bench. Kev told me, 'You will have to be patient and wait for your chance. When you get it you will need to score goals to make it yours.'

We won our first three League games – the club's best start in 84 years. Before the fourth game against Luton, Keegan paid me an extraordinary tribute that was kind of double-edged. 'We'll have the best finisher in the First Division, if not the country, on the bench,' he said. 'It's very comforting for me, but it may not be so comforting for him. I don't know how long it can continue.' If he rated me so highly, why the fuck wasn't I playing? I said publicly, 'If the chance comes along, I'll be ready to take it. There's a big squad here and competition for every position, so every player is in the same boat. You just have to wait and grab the opportunity if it comes along, and I'm prepared to wait.' But I was actually becoming more and more pissed off. I needed to be out on the pitch in the limelight, scoring the goals, making the headlines and being the centre of attention. To make things worse, the press were speculating that Keegan was in the market for another striker – Dean Saunders from Liverpool, or Swede Kennet Andersson – which would put me even further down the pecking order.

On 12 September my old team Portsmouth were the visitors, and first-choice striker Gavin Peacock was injured. Keegan told me midweek I was back in the team. I was buzzing with anticipation. I always loved putting one over on my old clubs. Kev told the papers, 'Mick has paid his fine, apologised and worked hard. He's too good not to be in the side, and I want to keep him.' On the big day 29,885 fans crammed into St James's with another 3,000 locked out. I was pumped up in the dressing room after having spent so long on the sidelines, and I had something to prove to Kevin Keegan.

Ten minutes before kick-off, just as Kev was giving his team talk, the club physiotherapist burst into the dressing room and said, 'Phone call for Mick Quinn.'

Keegan made a face as if someone had just farted in front of him, and said indignantly, 'A phone call for Quinny? Do you know there's a very important football match about to start?'

The physio replied, 'Er, sorry, gaffer, but it's the chairman.'

A scowling Kev said, 'Well, you'd better go and take it then, Quinny.'

I went into a nearby office and Sir John Hall said to me, 'Hello, Mick. Just wanted to wish you luck for today's game. Not that you will need much incentive against your old team, but, anyway, I will give you a crate of the best Krug champagne for every goal you score today.' You have to hand it to the chairman. He certainly knew how to get me frothing at the bit.

When I got back to the dressing room, Kev was twitchy. He clearly couldn't stand the fact that one of his players had been summoned by the club chairman, who was a knight of the realm no less.

'What did he want just before a game?' Kev asked. So I told him about the champers.

In the game I scored a double, had another disallowed for offside, and made the third for David Kelly in a 3–1 victory. I was also named man of the match. Sure enough, when we trooped back into the dressing room there were three crates of Krug below my peg. Get in there, my son. I could see Kev eyeing up my stash. He was about to give his talk about the game when the physio came through the door again.

'It's the chairman on the phone for Quinny again,' he said.

This time, Kev just nodded and I went to take the call.

An excited Sir John raved, 'You were magnificent today, Mick. I threw in the third crate because I didn't believe you were offside. Well done, and have a great night.'

I went back to the dressing room. Keegan turned towards me and, nodding towards the champers, said, 'I hope you're going to share that with the rest of the lads.'

'Of course I fucking am,' I replied. I have always paid my way and bought a round, and with a windfall like that I was always going to share it with the lads. I think what was really irking Kev was that he didn't like the way the chairman had chosen to speak to me without going through him first.

It was great to put one over on my old team, and nice to see some old friends from Pompey again. The press were all over me after the game, but mindful of how my mouth had got me in trouble with Keegan before, I would only say, 'Ask the gaffer about my performance – he's my spokesman.' Kev told reporters, 'Quinn did a fantastic job. He has answered all his critics.' What else could he say?

I scored again in the Coca-Cola Cup against Grimsby in midweek. It felt good to be back centrestage scoring the goals again. Kev and I had patched things up and I was back playing for the club I loved. But come the following Saturday and the home game against Bristol City, I was on the bench again. Gavin Peacock was back from injury, and despite waiting for my chance then taking it with both hands, I was out on my arse again. I was deeply hurt. I felt I had worked as hard as possible on the training ground then taken my goals when given my chance.

I went to see the gaffer in his office. I knocked on the door and he called me in.

'Boss,' I said, pointing to my arse, 'I've got a problem with this.'

'What is it, Mick?' he said. 'Have you got a knock?'

'No,' I replied. 'I've got splinters in it from sitting on the bench every game.' He laughed, so I went on. 'What's the problem, gaffer? You told me in the summer that I had to wait for my opportunity, and when I got it I had to make sure I took it. Well, I waited, trained hard, then took my goals when I was called back in.'

'You've been unlucky, Mick,' Kev said. 'You have done well, but I'm trying out a different system on Saturday. Don't worry, you'll be back.'

The Magpies thrashed Bristol City 5–0, and after the game a source close to Mick Quinn – so close, in fact, that it was Mick Quinn – told the *Daily Mirror*, 'Mick is confused. He doesn't know what he has to do to win a regular first-team place.' With Peacock again injured I was back in for a midweek second-round tie in the Coca-Cola Cup at home to Middlesbrough, then I scored a double against Leicester City in the Anglo-Italian Cup. It was my fifth goal in five games. As Keegan prepared to drop me yet again for a visit to London to take on Brentford, he came out with an amazing tribute: 'Quinn is the best finisher I've ever seen. His awareness is uncanny. The game against Leicester was probably his best since I came to the club. He can't do any more than he is doing.' No wonder I was confused.

I went knocking on Keegan's door once more, and yet again I swallowed his explanations. At the time, the then England number two Lawrie McMenemy commented, 'Kevin can be hard – ask Mick Quinn. He suspended him last season, yet he's still there. He's not a regular, but whenever he plays he scores goals. Keegan doesn't do anything by half measures.'

I was back in the team to play Grimsby, then dropped yet again. This time I nearly took his door off its fucking hinges. I stormed in and made no pretence of small talk or pleasantries.

'Are you taking the fucking piss out of me or what?' I growled.

Keegan ducked out of a confrontation and tried to calm the situation. 'Mick, football is now all about systems and squads,' he said.

'Look, Kevin, just put me on the fucking transfer list if you don't want to play me. I'm too old to fuck about in the reserves.'

'Mick, you're still very much part of my plans,' he insisted, and that was that yet again. The game of cat and mouse went on.

Come November, we were due to play Charlton Athletic away in a midweek fixture. The idea was to travel down on Tuesday by train, have a meal and an early night, and then the next day have a lie-in followed by a walk and a good lunch. Then it would be tea and toast, the game, then a long and tiring journey back to the north-east. The squad went up on the dressing-room wall on the Monday at the training ground at Durham University. I was on my own in the dressing room when Keegan walked in, his normal bouncy self.

I hadn't made the team, so I asked, 'Gaffer, am I on the bench on Wednesday?'

He replied, 'No, you're in the squad.'

Now, I had a young family, and I didn't want to make an 800-mile round trip to London if I wasn't even going to be a sub. I had better things to do with my time, like spend time with the kids or go to a betting shop.

'I might as well stay here and play with the reserves, then,' I said casually, to see if he thought it was a sensible option.

But Keegan's reaction was astonishing. He looked as if someone had stuck a red-hot poker up his arse. 'You what?' he barked. 'Are you refusing to travel with the Newcastle United squad?' He paused, wild-eyed, his chin jutting aggressively forward. Then he repeated his question: 'Are you refusing to travel with the Newcastle United squad?'

I had begun the conversation calmly, simply questioning the point of travelling all that way if I had no chance of playing, but his reaction was, I felt, well over the top and it really rattled my cage. I felt the anger of the last few weeks well up in me, and Keegan suddenly took on the form of every authority figure who had ever fucked me around: teachers, cops, screws and managers.

'Well, if you put it like that,' I screamed, 'then yes, I am refusing to travel with your fucking squad!'

Keegan stormed out of the dressing room after that, and I had waved my Newcastle career goodbye. I was sent into football purgatory and made to train with the kids on a pitch that was like a cabbage patch compared to the bowling-green surface the first team played on. John Beresford said later, 'Mick could have scored a hatful of goals at any level. I'm sure if he had been our centre-forward in our promotion season he would have scored 50.' But it was all over for me on Tyneside. I don't think Keegan had ever really forgiven me for the original bust-up. We were never destined to be bosom buddies anyway. He was the model pro ex-England skipper with a squeaky-clean image; I was Mick Quinn. I think he thought I had got too big for my boots at Newcastle. I reckon seeing me driving around in a flash BMW put his nose out of joint.

Since then I have seen Kev at Mick Channon's yard and bumped into him at the races. We nod and say hello, but we are never going to be on each other's Christmas card list. Still,

I look on it as a professional spat only, and I am full of praise for what he achieved with Newcastle. He turned the club from skint non-entities about to drop into Division Three into one of the world's biggest clubs with a 52,000-seat arena packed with fans watching Champions League football.

Leaving Newcastle was one of the biggest wrenches of my life. I loved the city and the football club, and what's more, the Geordies themselves. I still get a great reception every time I'm in Newcastle doing media work or at the races. I get stopped in the street by Toon fans, and I'm more than happy to have a chin-wag about the old days. It is a mark of how highly the Toon Army rated me that you can still buy prints on the Internet of the greatest Magpie players. Called 'Newcastle's Heroes Past and Present', the line-up is Malcolm Macdonald, Jackie Milburn, Alan Shearer, Temuri Ketsbaia, Wyn Davies, Peter Beardsley, Paul Gascoigne, Tino Asprilla, Andy Cole, Kevin Keegan – and Mick Quinn.

Ron Atkinson at Aston Villa was interested in signing me at the end of 1992, but Newcastle didn't want me to go to such a big club. Then I got a call from my agent Mel Stein, who also looked after Gazza. He told me that Coventry City, then in the Premiership, wanted me on loan. 'Do you fancy chatting to them?' he asked. 'Newcastle say you can go for £250,000 if the loan works out.'

'Tell them I'm on my way down the fucking M1 now,' I said.

16. SUMO IS BORN

'Made it, Ma, top of the world!'

James Cagney in *White Heat*

'You're not drunk if you can lie on the floor without holding on.'

Dean Martin

On 21 November 1992 I jogged out on to the pitch at Coventry's Highfield Road stadium knowing that, yet again, I had to win over another set of fans, another group of players and another manager. But just as important for me was to prove that I was still a top goalscorer and therefore ram Kevin Keegan's words down his throat. Highfield Road is a tight little ground with the sort of friendly atmosphere you'd expect from a family club. I was introduced to the Coventry fans, but I didn't receive quite the wild adulation the Toon Army had given me. Still, I was back on the big stage in England's top division.

I was well up for the game against Manchester City and threw myself into some heavy challenges early on. On twelve minutes winger John Williams broke down the right and with a great turn of pace got to the byline and whipped in a beautiful cross. I shook off the City defence and met the ball plumb in the centre of my forehead. It thumped on to the post and rebounded into the net as City keeper Tony Coton flapped around helplessly. The emotions of the last few months exploded like a cork from a champagne bottle. For a few moments I stood completely still as everything around me seemed to run in slow motion, then I let out a huge animal-like scream and went apeshit. I ran to the front row of Coventry fans and threw myself at them. Some geezer in a sky blue shirt – he must have been twenty stone and had long, lank, greasy hair – pulled me tight to him and gave me a lovely big sloppy kiss on my tache. That one's for you, Mr Keegan.

I was buzzing. In the second half, Terry Phelan was a bit hesitant with the ball, so I went in, nicked it from him, then set off for goal. I seemed to have so much time as I ran towards Coton. Shall I chip him, shall I go round him, or shall I just smash it as hard as I can? Tony made my mind up for me. He made the goalkeeper's cardinal sin of going to ground too early. All I had to do was chip it over him. Wallop. Goal number two. This time the Coventry fans went absolutely nuts, and as play restarted a chant began high in the stand that in a few moments was echoing around the four sides of the stadium. It got louder and louder, and there was no mistaking who it was intended for: 'Sumo, Sumo, Sumo, Sumo!' One game into my Coventry career and I had become a cult hero. Man City actually clawed their way back and won the game 3–2, but that night I went out and celebrated like we had won the cup. Sumo was born.

Later, fans would turn up in comedy mullet wigs and stick-on moustaches with cushions stuffed up their shirts. Comedian Harry Enfield's Scousers characters were big at the time, and the Coventry fans would jump up and do the 'calm down, calm down' catchphrase every time I got in a ruck with another player on the pitch. It was hilarious, and I really enjoyed being the centre of all the attention. I had always loved terrace banter, especially when it was humorous. I even played up to it – football is, after all, supposed to be an entertainment industry. I even used my new celebrity status as a marketing ploy. When I bought a horse for a racing club I started, I called it Sumoquinn – and it proved a winner as well.

Even fans from other clubs seemed to warm to me, and if I was ever stopped in the street or a bar by a supporter I'd stay for a chat. The supporters are the people who pay the wages after all. I had been a terrace favourite at Portsmouth, Newcastle and Oldham. A big reason for that was all the goals I scored, but I also like to think the ordinary bloke in the stands understood where I was coming from. They knew I was a working-class lad who liked a pint and had an eye for the birds. I was living the sort of life that many of them, perhaps working away in mundane manual jobs, dreamt of. And perhaps because of my physique and lack of athleticism compared to some Premiership players, mine was more of a Roy of the Rovers story.

At the age of 30, I was back on the big stage where I knew I belonged. I had arrived in the Premiership just as football's financial revolution was going into overdrive. Sky TV had just got involved and big money was pouring into England's elite division, turning it into the world's most exciting league. And the players that starred in the Premiership became superstars. Football was the new rock 'n' roll.

Coventry were favourites to be relegated from the Premiership every season, but somehow they always managed to avoid the drop. The joke in those days was that if they had painted the *Titanic* in Coventry's sky blue colours it would never have gone down. I'd had £500 on Coventry to be relegated in the summer of 1993; in the end, my goals sank my own bet.

It was Bobby Gould, the Coventry manager, who'd been on to Keegan asking if he could have me on a month's loan. I knew next to nothing about Bobby or the club, but I jumped in the BMW and headed down to City's training ground. I was greeted by one of the lads, Brian Borrows, who wished me well and asked, 'Have you brought an agent, Quinny?' I looked at him quizzically. Brian went on: 'Because Bobby hates agents. He had some blonde dolly in here the other day who was acting for Ricky Otto. He said she kept uncrossing and crossing her legs like Sharon Stone in the film *Basic Instinct*. Bobby even reckoned she flashed her knickers at him. She was acting like she owned half the players in the League. But Bobby wasn't impressed and threw her out and the transfer fell through.' I winced. I knew exactly who he was referring to. The bird in question only worked for my agent Mel Stein. Luckily, he wasn't involved in the talks for the loan period.

Bobby ushered me into his cramped office. I immediately warmed to him. He was witty, dry and morose all at the same time. Like me, Gouldy had moved around a bit in his career – he'd had ten clubs – and like me he was known as someone who liked to socialise and express his opinion while he was playing. Coventry-born, Gouldy was a tough little striker who had played for his hometown club, Arsenal, Wolves and West Ham among others; he'd also been a successful manager. He was the mastermind behind Wimbledon's David versus Goliath victory over Liverpool in the FA Cup in 1988. In his flat Midlands tones, Gouldy wooed me by saying, 'Quinny, I've basically got a great little team here but we're not scoring any goals. I believe you are the man to do that for us and I'm sure you have the ability to play in the Premiership. I think you can come in here and do a job for us and liven the place up at the same time. Do well on loan and I'll make the move permanent.' After all the uncertainty with Keegan, this was just what I wanted to hear.

Bobby's number two was Phil Neal, ex-England star and Liverpool skipper. Anyone who has seen the famous documentary *The Impossible Job* about England manager Graham 'Turnip' Taylor's failure to qualify for the 1994 World Cup will know that Phil had a habit of agreeing with everything Taylor said. Taylor: 'Gazza looks fucked'; Phil: 'Gazza's fucked, boss.' Well, he was exactly the same with Bobby at Coventry. You would think a manager would want another view on things from a number two, but Phil the Parrot seemed to agree with Bobby's every word.

After that two-goal debut, I again found the net against Ipswich and Southampton, and at the end of my month's loan I had six big fat Premiership goals in four games and I was getting praise all round. Writing in the *Daily Telegraph*, Clive White said, 'In an age when the English game is increasingly giving itself over to the athlete as opposed to the artist, it is reassuring to see a thirteen-and-a-half-stone roly poly like Quinn, through sheer wit and sharpness of mind, regularly putting one over defenders with more brawn than brains. Certainly, as goalscorers go, £ for lb there are few better than Coventry's bargain.' Bobby pulled me in for a chat and said he wanted to make my move permanent. I decided it would be best not to bring Mel Stein in person to my negotiations, but I liaised with him over the phone. Bobby never did find out that Mel was my agent.

I knew that this would be one of my last big contracts so I wanted to get the personal terms right. They were offering a two-and-a-half-season contract at £1,500 a week with a £150,000 signing-on fee. I nearly bit their fucking hands off. The first instalment of my signing-on fee was due the day I signed, but it was a tight time financially for the club and they asked me if they could delay the payment for three months. I agreed, as I was desperate to move. Keegan proved to be a man of his word and kept to the £250,000 price tag he had agreed before the month's loan. After banging in the six Premier League goals, that was a snip, so fair play to him. I knew I would miss the unique spirit and friendliness of the city of Newcastle and the club's wonderful fans, who had treated me like a hero from the first game. Sir John Hall sent me a lovely note thanking me for my services and offering me his best wishes for the future. I really appreciated that gesture from such a powerful man.

But now I was a Coventry man with the chance to play in some of the greatest stadiums in Europe against some of the best players. Life felt good again. When I did my first training session with Bobby and the lads I found them to be a great bunch. The team then included England left-back Kenny Sansom, Irish international Phil Babb, veteran goalie Steve Ogrizovic, Scottish striker Kevin Gallacher, Brian Borrows, Robert Rosario and Dave Busst, later to break his leg and quit the game.

Then fate came along and kicked me in the bollocks. I showered after the session and asked Phil Babb where the nearest betting shop was for my usual afternoon punt. Walking out into the club car park I was surprised, to say the least, to see Ray, Newcastle's stadium manager, standing beside my gleaming, bright red, 528 injection £20,000 BMW given to me by Ossie Ardiles when I signed my new contract for Newcastle.

Ray said sheepishly, 'I'm really sorry, Mick, but I've been asked to come and get the car. The club want it back.'

'You've got to be fucking joking,' I said. 'Ossie said I could have the motor. I can't believe they're being such a petty bunch of bastards.'

But back the car went. I at first refused, but the club responded by threatening to withhold wages and other monies I was owed under the terms of the transfer. Keegan got the last laugh after all. Ossie had definitely promised me the motor if I reached the end of my contract or went to another club without asking for a transfer, but Ossie had been sacked, and with him had gone our verbal agreement. It was my stupid fault for not getting it down on paper. As I said, I think the fact that I had such a flash car always got up Keegan's nose.

My relationship with Sheila finally went south the same time as I moved to join Coventry. At first I continued living in Hexham and commuting down to Coventry, then I rented a flash pad in Kenilworth in the Midlands with Sheila. But after nearly ten years together we had finally reached the point of no return. We were no longer in love; the rows had put paid to that. We were living separate lives, and for the sake of the girls we had to split. Sheila took the kids back to Liverpool. I had bought a lovely house in Formby on Merseyside with the idea of returning to my hometown when I retired; now I handed the keys over to Sheila. It was the least I could do, even though it meant I wouldn't see as much of Melissa and Natasha as I would like, which I found very hard.

I'm sure Sheila would say I had always led the bachelor life when I was with her, but now that I was no longer under her watchful eye I really threw myself into birds, betting and boozing. Gambling was like eating and sleeping for me, part of my daily routine. I would usually arrive at the bookie's before the first horse race to read the day's cards. I would warm up with two or three dog races, then get stuck into the horses and bet on every race. My rule of thumb was don't do multiple bets, and if the price is 5–1 or higher go each way. I could have five winners in a day and not break even, and I often lost £500 a day.

Still, the more goals I banged in the more popular I became with the birds. City players would go out en masse in the city centre and women would mob us. No chatting up was required. They would come up to you and say, 'Take me home, I want to shag you.' It would have been rude not to. TGI Friday was my favourite haunt; it had a bit of class and the birds loved it. My favourite tipple then was a Bellini: champagne, vodka, peach schnapps and orange juice. Lovely. In TGI I got pally with a couple of real characters called Noel Innes, a boxing MC, and his sidekick Stretch, so-called because he shot up from three feet to six feet in a few months when he was a teenager. They were both of Irish descent, as are many folk in the Coventry area, and were what you might call loveable rogues, a couple of Del Boy-style wheeler dealers.

One day, chairman Bryan Richardson called me and Lee Hurst into his office and said, 'I'm not happy with the type of person you're mixing with.' He was referring to Noel and Stretch.

'I get them a ticket for the games and then have a beer with them afterwards,' I replied. 'I'm bit too big a boy for you to be telling me who I should and should not be mixing with.'

Bryan snapped back, 'They are a bad influence on a young lad like Lee.'

'As far as I know they are good lads, and I will mix with who I want,' I insisted. I hate being talked down to, and after that I stormed out of the room, slamming the door behind me. But I then poked my head back round the door and said, 'Are you coming, Lee, or what?'

Lee stood up and, without a word to the chairman, followed me out of the door.

TGI was also a stop-off point for jockeys based in the south coming back from meetings in the Midlands at places like Leicester and Nottingham. It was here that I first met jump jockey Luke Harvey, elder brother of my co-writer on this book Oliver. Luke, dual Grand National winner Carl Llewellyn and Jenny Pitman's stable jockey Warren Marston had stopped off for a few beers and were giving it loads at the bar. They looked like three Munchkins from *The Wizard of Oz*. When they talked about riding they didn't necessarily mean the horses they had sat on that day. I have so much admiration for jump jockeys who put their neck on the line every day for a fraction of the reward of their flat-racing counterparts. I had a couple of Bellinis with them and had a right laugh. Just like footballers, their preoccupations seemed to be ale and shagging.

I was having the time of my life, especially as the goals continued to flow for me at Highfield Road. Bobby understood my playing style, which was basically being a fox in the box. He didn't want to see me chasing back to defend, which suited me fine. 'If I see you in our half I'll fine you, Quinny,' he once joked. At least, I think he was joking.

I was at the top of my game. I had the instinct of being able to grab goals combined with the experience that comes with age. I now knew exactly when to time a run to get into the right place at the right time. Scoring goals is a gift, an art form. Bob Latchford, Ian Rush and John Aldridge all had the precious gift. There aren't too many strikers around who can guarantee you twenty goals a season, which is why they go for extortionate prices. Unfortunately, I missed out on the extortion. Goalscoring is a natural gift. It's a split-second thing that you don't have time to think about. Suddenly the ball is in the net and you're not sure how it happened. If you take the time to think about it, you will usually miss.

Among the first clubs to visit Highfield Road after I signed was Liverpool. I was made up to be playing them and managed to round up twenty freebie tickets for friends and family. Graeme Souness was their boss at the time and they were going through a rocky patch, which for them meant they weren't top of the League or champions of Europe. They were still a footballing Rolls-Royce to Coventry's Skoda, and they were still my boyhood team – the team I had on my bedroom wall. And we murdered them. Totally tore them apart. In front of my dad, Mark and my closest pals, I scored two goals in a 5–1 rout. After I scored the fifth I ran to the halfway line with one hand over my eye and the other grasping my leg, as if I could score blindfold on one leg. It was a cheeky piss-take. We might have given them a footballing masterclass but they deserved more respect than that. Liverpool rammed the lesson down my throat later in the season when they thumped us 4–0, but just to be walking on the hallowed turf at Anfield that day was a dream for me.

17. PIES

'I don't mind that I'm fat. You still get the same money.'

Marlon Brando

'Who ate all the pies? Who ate all the pies? You fat bastard, you fat bastard, you ate all the pies!'

Ten thousand Aston Villa fans are trying to wind me up, as usual. Coventry City are playing their great Midlands rivals in a crunch Boxing Day Premiership game. In one of those quirks of English football, Coventry fans detest their Villa counterparts, even though Villa supporters regard Birmingham City as greater rivals. No one hates us, we don't care.

The light is fading fast, and the frost in the air gives you smoky breath under the floodlights. I have barely touched the ball all game and can see our substitutes stretching and warming up. Gouldy may be looking to replace me at half-time. Kevin Gallacher sprays a ball forward to me from midfield but it's a few feet short and I fail to get on to it. That is met with a huge cheer from the Villa fans and a chorus of 'Fat Scouse bastard, fat Scouse bastard!' Our fans, some with their curly wigs, stick-on taches and cushions, respond with affectionate chants of 'Sumo, Sumo!'

Suddenly, Phil Babb gets the ball wide and puts a looping cross into the box. My big strike partner Robert Rosario nods the ball on as I scream for it on the edge of the eighteen-yard box. The ball seems to hang in the frosty air, but with a quick shimmy I have beaten my marker and I wait for the ball to connect with my left foot. Wallop. Goal! Love it. I spin around to face the Villa fans, one hand cocked to my ear, the other pointing at my gut which I push out so that it's pulling taut on my shirt. Not bad for a fat bastard. It feels like an orgasmic release. The City fans sing my praises: 'He's fat, he's round, he scores on every ground, Micky Quinn, Micky Quinn!' It's enough to give you a weight complex. In the second half big Robert breaks down the flank and puts in a beautiful cross that I thump home for my second. 'Sumo, Sumo, Sumo, Sumo!' I repay the compliment by putting Robert through for the third. I have always needed a big strike partner to play off and to bring out the best in me. Robert certainly did that.

The pies thing might have got to lots of people but it didn't bother me. I actually took it as a compliment at times because fans don't often get on the back of bad players. I've always been built like a brick shithouse, but when I was in my prime I didn't have an extra pound on me. No manager ever complained to me about my weight and I always made sure I burnt off the pints on the training pitch. Fat bastards don't score 231 goals in 512 League appearances. Mind you, that Coventry kit didn't do me any favours. It was a horrible sky blue acrylic, and the style of the time was to make everything, shorts and shirt, small and tight. I looked like the Incredible Hulk just before he bursts out of his clothing. But I'd rather be the Pieman, Sumo, the Flying Pig, the Mighty Quinn or plain Fat Bastard than some boring model pro no one has ever heard of or cares about. If any player ever asked me why I was such a fat bastard, I would always retort, 'Well, every time I fuck your missus she gives me a chocolate biscuit.' I always did love the banter, and I've never been afraid to laugh at myself.

Once, when I was playing at West Ham and we won a corner at their end, over 20,000 Cockneys were giving a beautiful rendition of the 'Pies' chant when some prat lobbed a chicken and mushroom pie at my head. I reached out, caught it in mid-air and started scoffing it down. The crowd loved it. Another time I was doing a bit of TV work for Sky at Newcastle. The thousand fans in the Gallowgate spotted me in the TV gantry and thought it was more of a laugh to sing 'Pies' at me than watch the match. At half-time I went to the bar and on the way back I bought 50 pies. Then, to the shock of thousands of Geordies, I started to play the pieman and gave them out to punters in the Gallowgate.

Throughout my career fans and fellow players loved to give me nicknames, some of them endearing, others not so. After my stretch in Winchester nick, I was Fletch after the lead character from the BBC comedy *Porridge*; I was Bob, too, because with my moustache and black hair I looked like comedian Bob Carolgees who starred on *Tiswas* with his puppet Spit the Dog. I was playing at West Ham again when some joker in the crowd – like Scousers, all Cockneys fancy themselves as comedians – shouted, 'Oi, Bob, where's Spit?' I grabbed my bollocks and shouted, 'Ask your missus!'

Whatever happens in life, and I've had more than my fair share of ups and downs, you have to keep laughing. And I was certainly still laughing as 1992 turned into 1993 because by then I'd scored thirteen times for Coventry in twelve games and was being touted for an England cap. There was an injury crisis with Alan Shearer and David Hirst both out for February's World Cup qualifier with San Marino at Wembley. I was on the top of my form and my confidence was sky high. I'd recently told the papers, 'If Graham Taylor wants someone to put San Marino to the sword, then I'm the man. I'm grabbing goals – now give me an England cap.' If there was an England team for cocky bastards, I would have been made skipper. In typically understated manner, I went on: 'It has been my lifelong ambition to represent England, and if Mr Taylor feels there is a crisis, I am convinced I can provide him with the short-term solution. I've heard all the jokes about me being fat and round, unable to get over the ground. But I'm banging in the goals at Premiership level – and surely that should count for a bit extra in Graham Taylor's mind.'

It certainly helped my goalscoring form that we were a close bunch of players at Coventry. And one night a few of us got very close. We were on an away trip to Norwich, and the night before the game we had a few drinks. Robert Rosario, who had played in Norwich, knew a local woman who was a nymphomaniac and who boasted that her record was sixteen blowjobs in one session. I was rooming with him and he invited six players back to our suite to meet her. I didn't get involved – honestly, it wasn't really my scene – but it all took place in my room and I watched it all unfold. She gave at least five of the lads a blowjob and was wanking them off two at a time. She was like a well-oiled and finely tuned machine. It was unreal. It only stopped when one of the lads farted, everyone burst out laughing and no one could get a hard-on. Probably not the perfect preparation for a Premiership game, but we held Norwich to a 1–1 draw.

That January, I thought it was time to settle a few scores with Keegan. After being dubbed the 'transfer sensation of the season' in the papers I wanted everyone, especially Newcastle fans, to know what had really happened. The previous week my old strike partner Mark McGhee had been interviewed on Sky Sports and had revealed that in the summer Keegan's number two Terry McDermott had told him I wasn't in Newcastle's plans for the season. Yet I had thought at the time that we had patched things up and Keegan had told me I was playing for my place. I chose Sunday red-top the *People* to launch my verbal Exocet against Kev. Over a double-page spread, I accused Newcastle's Messiah and favourite son of being a hypocrite and a liar.

'What really brassed me off about Keegan was that he wasn't man enough to look me in the eyes and admit he didn't fancy me as a player,' I told the paper. 'Instead he kept telling me the shirt was there to be played for and that I should make it mine. Every time I wore it, I got goals. But immediately afterwards he dropped me. I wanted to believe that he meant what he said. I couldn't have tried harder because I loved Newcastle and those fanatical fans. But every time he dropped me it was another kick between the legs, and in the end I came to believe I was being frozen out.' Keegan, as you might expect, went nuts. The Messiah branded me a Judas in the pages of the *Sun*. 'There used to be only one Judas, but now there are a number of them, all after their 30 pieces of silver,' he said. He went on: 'Quinn's just another Judas to me and that's the finish of it. There is no way Quinn can slag us off after what we did for him. I even sent him a telegram before his first game for Coventry, wishing him all the best.' He added, 'Now I hope he feels really good.' He meant the exact opposite. It still seems bizarre that I should have had such a massive falling-out with my boyhood hero, the man who inspired me to become a professional football player, but at the time I felt that, if nothing else, I had set the record straight with the Toon Army.

In the spring, Coventry began to struggle. The board decided to sell Robert, without Bobby's full backing, to Nottingham Forest for a paltry £200,000. Robert provided 90 per cent of my goals, so as a result my strike rate slowed. That April, Coventry's bankers rubbed their hands with glee when top-of-the-table Manchester United paid us a visit. Highfield Road was a sell-out, but the disappointing thing was that the majority of fans were in red shirts, making it more like a home game for United. Their team included Eric Cantona, Mark Hughes, Paul Ince, Bryan Robson and goalie Peter Schmeichel. Ryan Giggs had also broken into the team. His pace on the pitch was frightening – I did not want to get into a chase for a loose ball with him. It would be like sending out a five-furlong sprinter against a four-mile chaser.

With Highfield echoing to the sound of 'Glory, Glory Man United', the Reds dominated the game. Five minutes before half-time Denis Irwin collected a Lee Sharpe pass and blasted home a right-foot drive from 25 yards. I was feeling wound up by the fact that United seemed to be swanning around our ground like it was Old Trafford, their fans having turned the ground into a sea of red. Then, with three minutes to go Lee Hurst made a late lunging challenge on United skipper Steve Bruce on the edge of their penalty area. There was a bit of a mêlée between the rival players but it was all very much handbags at dawn stuff. Then Schmeichel came goose-stepping out of his goal, mouthing off and trying to get involved. I put my arm across his chest and warned him, 'Fuck off back to your goal, sunshine, this has got fuck-all to do with you.' Next thing I know Schmeichel is on the turf and is clutching his face like he's been shot by a sniper in the crowd. Ref Roger Gifford held up the red card and waved it in my face. I had to make an 80-yard walk of shame off the pitch with 16,000 United fans screaming 'You fat Scouse bastard!'

Sitting alone in the changing rooms, I felt disgusted at what had happened. Then Schmeichel rubbed salt into the wound by slating me to the press boys. The next day I was all over the papers. The *Sun* headline was FIGHTY QUINN, while the *Mirror* ran their piece under the banner SCHMACK! The Dane told the *Sun*, 'Quinn lost his temper – yet again. It was just stupid. He couldn't complain it was not a foul in the first place, but he was having a go at us right through the game. Quinn was trying to antagonise a few United players. He had a go at me in the first half, studs first. He hit Brucie and he also caught Denis Irwin. It was a push, not a punch. It was crazy for him to behave like that. He doesn't need to do it, because he is a good player and should rely on his ability. I'm afraid he just spoils himself.'

Bobby told me to keep my mouth shut. He even thought I might be able to sue Schmeichel for libel. Coventry striker Roy Wegerle stuck up for me, saying, 'Schmeichel took a dive. He dived, and I'd be prepared to go to a hearing as a witness for Mick.' He explained that the ref had had his back to the incident and had relied on one of his linesmen to make the decision. Just days later the FA cleared my name after studying the match video, but they took no action against Schmeichel, believing that he'd fallen because he'd been 'surprised'. In my opinion, the FA bottled it by not having a go at him. Now, every time I see Schmeichel's face on the telly I want to kick the set in. Next time, I vowed, my phasers definitely wouldn't be on stun.

By the end of the season I had scored 17 Premier League goals in 25 games and had proudly worn the captain's armband. City stayed in the top six well into March, and despite a tailing-off which saw us finish fifteenth, the season was by Coventry standards a huge success.

That summer Bobby Gould thought his men needed toughening up, so he took us for pre-season training to the army barracks at Aldershot, where 30 pampered and spoilt Premiership footballers, a bit puffy around the middle after a month off, were given the full boot-camp treatment by some suitably gruff sergeant-major types. We were taken on night manoeuvres and were taught the art of survival and how to make a shelter with a groundsheet and branches. It was like a Boy Scouts outing with all the lads in high spirits. We trekked for six miles from the base, and after cooking our rations around the camp fires the order for bed was given at 10 p.m. But the lads weren't ready to sleep.

I decided it was time to have a laugh, and victim number one was Phil Neal. Phil had obeyed the 10 p.m. call for lights out (I'm sure he said 'Yes boss' to the sergeant major) and was tucked up in his tent with the other coach Harry Roberts. Me and some of the other lads, including Phil Babb, let their tent down a couple of times and Phil laughed along, but when we did it again he came out screaming: 'If you fucking do that again I'll make you run the six miles back to camp.' We apologised like guilty schoolboys and went back to our tents. As soon as it had quietened down we regrouped and launched a broadside at Phil's tent with branches and lumps of turf. Judging from the squawks from within we ruffled a few feathers. All very childish, but that's professional footballers for you.

Babby and I were still not done. We wanted to pull one on the gaffer. We found Bobby's tent and could see the outline of his body against the side of the canvas. Babby is a great impressionist, so he pretended to be one of the squaddies on sentry duty. He poked a large stick into Bobby's back and barked, 'Name and rank!'

'Bobby Gould, manager of Coventry City, sir,' came the reply.

Phil and I looked at each other in amazement, desperately trying to stifle our laughter.

Babby responded in military manner: 'At ease, Gould, and keep an eye out for them daft footballers.'

Next day, when we were back at camp, in the officers' mess we overheard Gouldy complimenting the sergeant on the night manoeuvres. Bobby told him, 'I was very impressed with one of your boys last night. He crept up on me SAS-style and put his gun in my back. I didn't hear him coming. If I had been the enemy he could have slit my throat.'

Babby and I were shitting ourselves laughing. The gaffer never did find out who the SAS men really were.

The boot camp, however, had one terrible consequence. Lee Hurst, a lovely guy and a talented player, slipped while tackling one of the walls on the assault course and snapped his ligaments. His career was over. It's a pity the club couldn't be arsed to organise a testimonial for him to earn some much-needed cash to give him a new start. The way in which Lee's career had been snuffed out at its height hit a lot of the lads hard. It certainly made me determined to make the most of my football career while I had the chance.

Coventry then went to Scotland for a few friendlies. One night Mick Harford asked out a couple of very pretty girls from behind the counter in Ladbrokes, and I joined him to make up the foursome. We went to a local pub, and when that kicked out the only place for a late drink was a local hotel where a wedding reception was taking place. The wedding party welcomed us like long-lost family members and we ended up posing for pictures with the bride and groom and having a beer with them. Then we lured the two Ladbrokes girls back to the team hotel. It turned out that one of them was a great singer, and she belted out a note-perfect rendition of 'Gloria On My Mind'.

Suddenly, the door burst open and there stood a fuming Bobby Gould. 'That was beautiful, love,' he said. 'In fact it is one of my favourite songs, but I'm afraid I'm going to have to ask you to leave the hotel. These boys have got a football match to play tomorrow.'

I did behave myself in pre-season, lost a few pounds and got fit, and come the opening day of the 1993/94 season I really fancied my chances in the Premiership – so much so that I had £50 on myself to finish top scorer at 50–1, and in typical Quinn style I gave it the big one to the papers that I was a good thing. We travelled to Arsenal for our first game. Highbury is one of football's great theatres, and, having never played there before, I was buzzing. I was up against one of British football's greatest ever defences: Tony Adams, Lee Dixon, Nigel Winterburn and Andy Linighan, with David Seaman between the sticks. Arsenal had just completed their £16.5 million new luxury stand, and after winning both the FA and League Cups they expected to brush small fry like Coventry to one side. But I was like a pitbull straining at its leash to get at Adams and co.

After twenty minutes Roy Wegerle was tripped in the box and I demanded the ball. Facing me in goal was England legend David Seaman, but I felt supremely confident and knew exactly where I was going to place the ball. I turned, struck it to Seaman's right and clenched my fist as the ball rose and hit the top right-hand corner of the net. John Williams and I had had a bet before the game that if we scored we would do the funky chicken dance, which basically involves bending your arms at the elbow and flapping them while strutting about like a cockerel. We looked a right pair of prats flapping about in front of the North Bank, and the footage was later used on *Match of the Day* and on Sky Sports.

Ten minutes after the break Roy laid on a lovely ball for me on the right-hand side of the box. I hit a lovely left-foot shot into the right-hand corner past a flailing Seaman, one of my best ever goals, for 2–0. The star-studded Arsenal team were left standing with hands on their hips looking on again at my wild funky chicken goal celebrations. Two minutes after that I was away down the right wing, cut inside near the box and unleashed a Quinn Exocet off my right peg. It hit exactly the same spot on the net as the last one. It was lovely watching Seaman picking it out of the back of his goal. I ran to Gouldy on the halfway line and performed the funky chicken for him. He looked at me like I was mad. Micky Quinn, Sumo to the fans and roly-poly hitman to lazy newspaper sub-editors, had scored the first hat-trick by a visiting striker to Highbury in 40 years. In fact, we were all over them and should have scored seven or eight. They even pushed Tony Adams up front for the last twenty minutes.

Afterwards, Ian Wright made a point of coming over and shaking my hand. 'Quinny, that was some of the best finishing I have ever seen,' he told me. I was absolutely made up. Wrighty, now a huge TV star, was one of the greatest finishers of his generation and a player I had buckets of respect for. At the time he'd just released a naff record called 'Do the Wright Thing', and to remind the Highbury faithful to go out and buy it he had made sure advertising leaflets had been left all around the ground – including the away dressing room. Before getting back to the dressing room one of the Coventry lads who wasn't playing had written on one of Wrighty's record leaflets: 'Forget Wrighty, Quinny did the right thing'. He'd then slid it under the Arsenal dressing-room door. I heard later that Wrighty and manager George Graham went apeshit.

I was typically understated after the game. 'I should have had four. I missed a golden chance late on,' I told the press boys. When asked about an England call-up, I insisted, 'I can score the goals to take England to the [1994] World Cup finals.' What a cocky bastard. Wrighty paid me another massive compliment when he said, 'I've got a lot of respect and admiration for the way Coventry played. They came to Highbury with a great team spirit, played some lovely football, and Quinny did us with three excellent finishes.' Gouldy was on top form too, saying, 'Quinny was exquisite today. Maybe he should quit now while he's ahead.' Cheers, Bob. Then, of course, it was back to TGI Friday in Coventry for a monumental piss-up.

Next up, Kevin Keegan. My beloved Newcastle had won promotion under the Messiah and they came to Highfield Road just four days after that Highbury triumph. Kev ratcheted up the tension by insisting he had been right to sell me. He added, bizarrely, 'My thoughts on Mick Quinn have never changed. I think he is the best finisher I have ever seen.' So, again, why the fuck did you sell me, Kev? He went on: 'I believe I was justified in what I did. I wanted to play a different way and he was too good a player to be stuck on the bench. He got a very good move out of me. Whatever happens on Wednesday it's not about him and me.' Maybe he felt like that, but I was desperate to score against him to underline the huge clanger he had dropped by booting me out of the club I loved.

It was a scrappy game, locked at 0–0, but then our pacy winger Peter Ndlovu broke through for a one-on-one with Toon goalie Pavel Srnicek. Nuddy pushed the ball past him but Pavel brought him down inside the box. Penalty and red card. I raced over and picked the ball up. This was one penalty I was definitely going to take. Then Newcastle decided to bring on their substitute goalie, my old team-mate Tommy Wright. In those few seconds my mind was working overtime. I usually stuck the ball hard and low into the bottom right-hand corner, but Tommy would know all about that. I placed the ball on the spot. This is for all the hurt, Kev. I took two paces back, composed myself, and went to strike the ball. In the moments before my foot connected with the ball I decided to hit it into the top corner instead to wrong-foot Tommy. Whack. I gave the ball a right good thump. Up it went towards the top right-hand corner, but it carried on going; it actually sailed over the temporary hoarding where City were building a new stand. I think the ball boys are still looking for it. Shit. I fell on my knees on the wet turf and imagined Kev's face.

Sitting in the stands, scoring a penalty seems the easiest thing in the world for a professional footballer who is paid thousands a week. But it isn't. It doesn't matter if you're David Beckham or Michael Owen or whoever, your ringpiece still twitches like a sparrow dying in the snow. My misery was eased a bit when we fought our way back into the game and beat them 2–1. New signing Mick Harford, a tough centre-forward and a great lad, came off the bench to score with his first touch, a looping header, with ten minutes to go.

That night I had a few bevvies in the players' lounge before going out on the piss in Coventry with Mick and a few of the other lads. We went on to a club where Mick, in very high spirits, announced he was to perform his party piece: a handspring over a bar stool. He placed the stool in a quiet area of the bar, took a run-up, launched himself into the air and came crashing down on the small of his back. We were crying with laughter. The next morning at training Mick told Coventry physio George Dalton that he had a mystery back ailment. When George asked him how he'd got it, Mick replied, 'Sitting on a cold, stiff bench for 80 minutes during yesterday's game.' Mick suffered for that night of high jinks. It took three operations and fifteen months to put things right.

There were more high jinks courtesy of midfielder Micky Gynn, who'd been part of Coventry's FA Cup-winning side in

1987. Micky was a good bloke to know. His missus worked for Guinness and could get VIP tickets for sporting events like the Open and the Grand National. An even bigger bonus was that these events were attended by Guinness Girls, there to promote the black stuff, who dressed in sexy black uniforms. Micky knew I was a racing nut so he got me and fellow striker Roy Wegerle tickets to Cheltenham. We soon started to knock back the Black Velvets – Guinness and champagne – and got to know the Guinness Girls. South Africa-born Roy, a class act on and off the field, was known as the John Travolta of football. He was a good-looking lad and a slick mover, and we soon had the girls eating out of our hands. After the racing finished we wanted the party to continue, so Roy and I invited a couple of the girls back to my house in Kenilworth. More drinks flowed, and I moved in for the kill. She was gorgeous, with short, dark, bobbed hair, a curvy figure and long, long legs. I manoeuvred her into the lounge and on to the sofa. She didn't waste much time before undoing my kecks and going down on me. I was in ecstasy when I heard the door creak and saw Roy poking his head round. As the girl carried on, Roy gave me the thumbs up as if to say, 'Go on, my son.' Then he left me to it. Weighed in. Looking back, I must have had a thing about uniforms – Guinness Girls, Ladbrokes girls and barmaids.

About this time I was getting well into R & B music, especially a US singer called Joe, and also R Kelly. I loved R Kelly's Mr Lover Man attitude; his songs 'Sex Me' and 'Bump and Grind' speak for themselves. A mate sorted me out some free tickets for an R Kelly show in Wolverhampton, and me and Mick Harford took a couple of birds along. We made a day of it and were absolutely arseholed when we got there. We had fantastic seats in a box high above the stage, and when R Kelly came on Mick, for some reason, decided to hang from the outside of the box. R Kelly was singing and looking up nervously at this mad footballer doing his best Tarzan of the

Apes impression. Eventually two bouncers rushed over and told Mick to calm down. But you don't tell Mick Harford to calm down. He swung back into the box and there was a terse stand-off before the security men backed off and we continued to enjoy the show.

The 1993/94 season saw Coventry City having their best start since 1937, but behind the scenes financial pressures were increasing. Bobby Gould had already been forced to sell Robert Rosario and Kevin Gallacher, and rumours continued to abound of money problems at the club. Things began to go tits up. The board wanted to cash in on £3 million-rated Peter Ndlovu, but Bobby was trying to build a team, not to sell players. Coventry had sold too many good players in my short time there to make the transition from a team always facing the drop to a team challenging for honours. Even their bonus scheme was structured around staying up. You got more for finishing fourth from bottom, rising with every place.

Then, in October, we were stuffed 5–1 at QPR. Bobby was really upset, and he resigned there and then. We were all upset for him and very shocked. Bobby had got some great results for Coventry on a shoestring. On the journey back to the Midlands on the coach, I sat next to Bobby and tried to talk him round. 'Bobby, the lads love working with you. We can turn this around for you,' I pleaded. I was so upset that I told him I was going to put myself on the transfer list if he went. Bobby told me not to be so bloody stupid and to fight on under a new manager. I took his advice, but in hindsight it would have been a good time to leave. I thanked him for all he had done for me and left him to his thoughts. Bobby said later that managing Coventry 'had been like racing Formula One in a Mini Metro'. It was a good line.

We wondered who would replace him. Would it be a big name? I was dumbstruck to hear that Phil Neal would be taking over. With Phil's 'yes boss' philosophy, I couldn't see him standing up to the board; I thought he'd prove to be to football management what Douglas Bader was to tap dancing. He came in on a trial basis, and if results went his way he would be made full-time boss. The first game we drew 0–0. Next up, Everton at Highfield Road, and I put two past big Neville Southall as we beat them 2–1. Then Arsenal at home, and I bagged the winner. In Phil's month on trial we won seven points out of a possible nine, and I had scored the winning goal in two of the games. My goals had helped Phil land the job.

Phil brought in Ron Atkinson's former number two at Manchester United, Mick Brown. Phil insisted Mick take first-team training, but his methods were a throwback to the sixties. Phil was actually a great coach who knew all the modern techniques, but Mick had us doing circuit training, with squat thrusts and bunny hops. It was just like *Superstars*. The game had moved on, and we used to moan at him, dubbing him Jurassic Mick. We took the piss out of Mick, but he's a real character and he laughed it off.

In November, Manchester United visited Highfield Road. I was my usual shy and retiring self in the build-up to the game, telling the *Daily Mirror* that I 'hated' Manchester United. However, I added that it had nothing to do with my bust-up with goalie Peter Schmeichel the season before. 'What happened with Schmeichel is water under the bridge,' I said. 'The real reason I want to sink Peter and the rest of his side goes far deeper than that. Coming from where I do, brought up as a self-confessed Anfield nut, the simple fact of the matter is that I hate Manchester United. It's in the blood. It's something that's bred into you. It's an emotion so strong that I hate United even more than Everton.' The lessons I had learnt on the Kop as a kid certainly did run deep, and in that respect I was really a football fan who was going out to play Premiership football every Saturday. United won 1–0 with an Eric Cantona header, and Schmeichel made two world-class saves to keep me off the scoresheet. Afterwards, I refused even to mention his name, simply referring to him as 'the goalie'.

My relationship with Phil Neal deteriorated as the season wore on. We just didn't see eye to eye, and he dropped me more times than in the rest of my career put together. I'd picked up a niggling Achilles tendon injury that forced me to miss a few games, but Phil just didn't fancy me and I was getting pissed off playing with the stiffs. Neal said publicly, 'People might wonder what's happening when I drop my leading scorer, but it had the desired effect. He was not doing himself or the club justice.'

I did enough to help Coventry have another successful season, though. Towards the end of the campaign we beat title-chasing Blackburn and drew 0–0 at Manchester United. A young kid called David Beckham played that day; he made some good touches and obviously had class. Coventry finished a creditable sixth in the League, which for them was like winning the European Cup.

18. KAREN

'My history of relationships with women is very poor – very macho, very stupid, but pretty typical of a certain type of man, which I was I suppose: a very insecure, sensitive person acting very aggressive and macho. Trying to cover up the feminine side, which I still have a tendency to do, but I'm learning.'

John Lennon

I was in the bar at Worcester racecourse one balmy August afternoon in 1994 with fellow Scouser and Coventry player Paul Cook when a stunning blonde caught my eye. She had amazing high angular cheekbones and beautiful big blue eyes, and was showing off her shapely figure in tight blue jeans, white shirt and smart blazer. I was at the top of my pulling form and thought I looked the dog's bollocks. Dressed in dark Gucci slacks, loafers and waist-length black leather jacket, my hair bouncing on my shoulders in the then fashionable mullet style, I felt sharp. I pointed her out to Cookie. He said he knew her through racehorse trainer Frank Jordan and offered to make the introductions.

'Hi love, I'm Micky Quinn, the Coventry footballer,' I said, hoping to impress her.

'Never heard of you,' she replied, and carried on reading the form for the next race in the *Racing Post*.

'Well, that's my trump card out the window,' I thought. 'This one's going to be a little more tricky.'

I bought her a gin and tonic. She told me her name was Karen Davies. She was 21 and had been doing modelling and promotional work. The afternoon progressed, the vodka flowed and the Quinn magic began to work. She was gorgeous-looking, intelligent and had a great sense of humour. I was completely smitten.

The last race finished, but I didn't want to let her out of my sight. We all went back to the Cross Keys pub near Risbury in Herefordshire where a huge piss-up ensued. That night I ended up in Karen's bed – with Cookie. Me and Cookie passed out on Karen's bed fully clothed in her mum Sue's house, and she couldn't budge us, so Karen went back to her place a few miles away and left us snoring together. Next morning, over a fry-up, I got Karen's number, then I pestered her until she went out on a date with me. The electricity between us was amazing, and the sex was mind-blowing. We began to see each other more often, and soon we were spending most nights together.

My personal life in my first season at Coventry had been a mess. I'd spent most of the time living in a hotel in the town and going out boozing and shagging with the lads. Meeting Karen changed my life for ever. I thought I had been in love before, but this was different.

Karen might not have known much about footie, but her knowledge of racing was impeccable. That was hardly surprising as she was the daughter of ex-National Hunt champion jockey Bob Davies, who won the 1978 Grand National on Lucius, and her mum's brother Terry Biddlecome was also an ex-champion jump jockey who had shared the title one year with Karen's dad. Karen herself was an accomplished horsewoman and a very talented show jumper. We could talk about my love of horses, and she helped increase my knowledge of horses and racing.

Our first date, however, probably wasn't the romantic occasion it should have been: I took her dog racing at Hall Green. To make matters worse, a curvy brunette I'd been on a couple of dates with approached us, gave me a peck on the cheek and started nattering away. I looked over at Karen and, quite understandably, she had a face like thunder. Luckily, Cookie was with us, and after the girl left he made a joke about it and thawed things a bit. I got a second date, anyway.

Barry, Sue's partner who owns a successful double-glazing firm and is known as Barmy Barry for his raucous behaviour, wasn't sure about me at all. He kept warning Karen, 'This Quinn bloke has been to jail, you know. He's a criminal, and he's bad news. Watch out for him.' So one night when we were out for a beer, Karen said, 'I hear you've been to jail and are a bit of a bad boy.' I pointed out that I had been inside for driving offences, which, while serious enough, were hardly in the same league as rape or murder. Later, Barmy Barry and I became great friends, but I was none too pleased with him at the time. Coventry had signed Paul Cook in the summer, and Phil Neal also had a warning about me. 'Don't hang around with Mick Quinn,' he told Cookie. 'He likes a beer and a bet and will be a bad influence.' But Neal's words went in one ear and out the other. From day one Cookie and I palled up. We were inseparable.

Karen brought some much-needed stability and structure to my life. I was the wrong side of 30 and it was time to slow down a bit. The conveyor belt of drunken one-night stands had begun to become boring. With her by my side, I was more enthusiastic than ever about my racing. I owned a half share in a horse called Va Utu in training with Mick Channon. I was spending more and more time down at Mick's stables watching the horses work on the gallops and chatting to the stable lads in the yard. I loved the atmosphere, and it helped me switch off from the pressures of football. At the time I also ran a tipping service – punters phoned a premium phone line to get my tips – and I set up another club, the Mick Quinn Racing and Sporting Club. For £250 ordinary working people could experience the thrill of owning a racehorse. They could go in the parade ring at the races and visit Mick's stables in Lambourn in Berkshire where the horses were trained.

Surprise, surprise, again things didn't run smoothly. We didn't get enough members, and I was left having to pick up the shortfall on the training fees. Then disaster struck: one of the horses, Hat-trick Hero, had a freak accident on the gallops and had to be put down. To replace him we leased a horse we named Sumoquinn from Mick Channon. Why not cash in on my cult status? Sumoquinn proved rather quicker than his footballing namesake. He cost just 2,000 guineas as a yearling and went on to win six races in two months, including the prestigious Rockingham Stakes at York, worth nearly £10,000 to the winner.

Because the club had only leased the horse, Mick Channon eventually sold it to Hong Kong for £80,000. One of the club members got uppity about this and decided to call the *News of the World*. The story ran under the headline WHERE'S OUR CASH, MICKY? PUNTERS' FURY AT SOCCER ACE QUINN. It was all bollocks, as Sumoquinn had only been leased. The members got a lot of fun out of that horse and I had actually propped the club up with my own cash. I couldn't believe they would moan to the papers like that.

Karen also helped me focus on my career. I was determined to win back my place in the Coventry team. That summer the papers were full of stories that Coventry were going to let me go on a free and that Sunderland were interested. After my time at Newcastle that would have been a tough move, and winning over the Mackems – as Sunderland fans are known – would have been next to impossible. Nothing came of it in the end. Publicly, I said, 'All I can say is that I have a year of my contract left to run and I want to play for Coventry City.'

I was 32, and I knew that if I was to have a good season in the Premiership I would have to shed a few pounds and be as fit as possible. Three weeks before we were due back at training I cut out all the bacon butties and chips and got back on the pasta and veg. I stopped boozing, too, and the weight fell off. I devised my own training programme, which included swimming and a spot of tennis with team-mate Brian Borrows. I had been playing Brian ever since the previous season ended and thought I had the measure of him. Then he went on holiday and was bullish about a rematch, giving it the big one that he was going to thrash me. I had a little wager with him: the loser buys dinner. Brian came out like Bjorn Bjorg, aceing me all over the place and smashing me off the park. It was a complete thrashing.

Later, over the meal, I said, 'Fucking hell, Bri, you were Wimbledon class out there.'

'I've got a little confession to make,' he replied. 'I went on holiday to Florida and enrolled in the Nick Bolletieri tennis school. One of the other blokes he taught in the past was someone called Andre Agassi.'

'You cheeky git!' I shouted, laughing.

The tennis and everything else did the trick, and I returned to Coventry as slimline as I was ever going to get and raring to go.

The 1994/95 season began with a draw at Wimbledon and an away drubbing at Newcastle. Next up were Blackburn. We started well, and were holding them at 0–0 with just eighteen minutes left on the clock. I was chasing back over the halfway line when the ball ricocheted off my hand. The ref, Graham Poll, insisted it was intentional and pulled out the yellow card.

'What the fucking hell was that for?' I screamed.

'I heard that clearly. You're off,' he replied.

Red card for the ball accidentally hitting my arm. I couldn't believe it.

As I trudged towards the dressing room, Phil Neal came running down the touchline screaming blue murder and jabbing his finger at me. 'You should have kept your fucking mouth shut!' he yelled. 'You've let the whole team down!'

Revved up, I shouted back, 'Shut the fuck up! If you've got something to say, say it in the dressing room.'

As I walked down the tunnel I heard a huge cheer. Chris Sutton had scored from the free-kick I gave away. Then Blackburn banged in another three to make the score 4–0.

Back in the dressing room, Phil was seething. 'Quinny, you were out of order out there. I want you to apologise to the rest of the team right now. Look at their faces and see how knackered they are. They were running their tits off because you got sent off.'

I apologised – I had been wrong to swear at the ref – but then tried to argue that the first goal wasn't my fault. The free-kick was on the halfway line after all.

Phil snapped back, 'I'm fining you the maximum two weeks' wages.'

I accepted the £3,000 fine and let it drop. That was that as far as I was concerned, but next morning I picked up the Sunday papers and Phil Neal was all over the place slagging me to the hilt. I was pissed off to say the least. Any decent manager would have dealt with it face to face and kept it in-house without going public. Phil had been at Liverpool long enough to know how to do things the Liverpool way. Despite my anger, I decided not to respond when I went in for training on Monday morning. We had a derby match with Aston Villa coming up and I didn't want to rock the boat.

After a good training session, Phil asked to see me in his office.

'I'm afraid you're dropped for the Villa game, mate,' he said straight away.

I had taken the verbals from him after the Blackburn game, the £3,000 fine, and the slagging in the papers. I'd also apologised to the other lads, so this was the final insult.

'Why the fuck are you dropping me?' I demanded. 'Is it for the red card?'

'It's not because of the sending-off,' he replied.

'Why am I being dropped, then?'

'Because I said so, that's why. End of story.'

I stared at him, thinking, 'What an arrogant bastard.' Then I exploded. 'You can stick Coventry City up your fucking arse. I want a transfer.'

That night Sky TV invited me to be a guest panellist for the Villa game. I told viewers exactly what I thought of Phil Neal and how I had demanded a transfer. Nothing wrong with putting yourself in the shop window. Two weeks later Phil granted me my request. I told the *Daily Mirror*, 'It's time for a change and I will go to any club. I have always been the sort of person who has bag, will travel. I will go anywhere. Last season wasn't very good for me because the team didn't create that many chances. But I still have confidence in my ability and will score goals at any level.' I even joked, 'I might even consider going back to Newcastle to become Andy Cole's strike partner.'

Phil wanted to strengthen the Coventry squad, and he brought in Liverpudlian Mike Marsh from West Ham. As soon as he arrived, Neal pulled him into his office and said, 'Stay away from Quinny and Cookie. They're either at the races or in the pub. It's not the sort of image you want if you want to get on at this club.' Mike 'mine's a lager' Marsh ignored him and became the third leg of a Scouse trio.

We were partners in crime. Straight after training we would go to a little row of shops in Stychel. We would grab a sarnie and be in the bookie's for the first race. We would stay there most of the afternoon and then go to TGI Friday or the Hilton. Mike also got the nickname Hilton Burger because that's all he seemed to eat. If there wasn't a match coming up, it was off to a club. That would be the routine at least three or four nights a week. I would describe my consumption at the time as that of a heavy social drinker: four or five pints followed by a few vodkas with alcopop mixers and perhaps a few brandies as a nightcap. I always knew when to stop. I've never been the sort who needs a hair of the dog just to get through the next day.

One day, me and Cookie, my TGI mates Noel and Stretch and a couple of their mates had a kind of works outing to nearby Stratford races. We got absolutely bladdered and ended up in the champagne bar. One of Noel's party got into an argument with some bloke and ended up twatting him. I knew it was time to go and I made a swift exit to another bar on the course. We carried on drinking after the races had long finished, then Cookie challenged me to a race down the home straight. Bevvied up and in our best suits, we ran hell for leather down in front of the stands, taking an open ditch in full flight. Cookie jumped it like a stag, but I didn't quite see a stride and went arse over tit. By now the course was locked up and we had to climb out over the fence to get home.

Next day, I was told to report to Phil Neal's office.

'We have been told you have been in trouble again,' he said, his face crumpled up as if I had just had a crap on the floor of his office. 'This time you were involved in a fracas in the champagne bar at Stratford races.'

'Not guilty,' I complained. 'I was in the bar, yes, but I wasn't involved in any way with the scrap. I saw it, but it had nothing to do with me.'

Phil left it at that.

I was down TGI one day when Duran Duran singer Simon Le Bon came in with a large entourage. One of his mates recognised me and asked me where they could get a late drink. I said we were going to our usual bar, a country club in Leamington. Simon came over and we got on really well. He invited me along for the late drink, saying they had a people carrier waiting outside. I'd actually moved in with Noel by this time, and I thought it was a great opportunity to pull a little stunt.

'I'd love to join you, Simon,' I said, 'but can we stop off at my gaff first? I've got a little trick I want to play on someone.'

We pulled up outside the house and I sent Simon to knock on the door. He played his part to perfection. Noel answered the door, and from my seat in the people carrier I could see his face contort in amazement.

Simon said, 'You must be Noel. Hello, I'm Simon from Duran Duran. I hear you're a bit of a mover and shaker in Coventry and was wondering if you fancied coming to a party. It will be girls, champagne, the works.'

Noel couldn't get his best togs on quick enough. The singer led an eager Noel to the people carrier and pulled back the door to reveal me shitting myself laughing inside.

'Gotcha!' I said through my giggles.

We went on to the club and had a great night. The birds were buzzing around us, and Simon was a great laugh, a really nice bloke. At the end of the evening he gave me his number and said I was welcome to come and visit him and his beautiful wife Yasmin in London whenever I liked. I never got round to following up his kind offer.

My social life was curtailed in November 1994 when I was persuaded to join Plymouth Argyle, then in Division Three, on a month's loan. Their manager was ex-England keeper Peter Shilton who, as a hardcore punter, was doing his best to gamble his career earnings away. I think Shilts only brought me to the club for my racing knowledge and the fact that I was mates with Mick Channon. On my first day down at Plymouth I knocked on Shilts's door to introduce myself and ask him what role he wanted me to play on the field. The conversation went like this:

'Hiya, Peter –'

'What do you fancy in the 3.40 at Uttoxeter?' Shilts butted in. 'What does Mick Channon fancy? Does that thing in the last like the ground?'

Calm down, Peter. There was no 'Hello, how are you?' No explanation of why he had brought me to the club and what he expected of me. It was racing, racing, racing. It seemed Peter had signed me on loan just to pick my brains on the horses.

I did score down there and won a man of the match award, but the loan deal wasn't renewed. I reckon that had more to do with the tips I gave Shilts rather than what I achieved on the park. I think I put him even deeper in the shit – I don't think

I gave him a winner in the whole month I was there – and had I stayed any longer I would have sent him under.

I returned to Coventry, but I couldn't get in the squad let alone the team. It was frustrating. I was still on good cash, but I hated languishing in the reserves. I wanted to be playing in the Premiership, but when Phil signed striker Dion Dublin I was further away from the team than ever. As Christmas rolled into the New Year the results remained dreadful. Then, on St Valentine's Day 1995, Phil called a surprise meeting at the café area of the training ground. Everyone – the apprentices, the pros, the coaching staff, even the kitchen workers – shuffled in to see a disconsolate Phil standing there. In a trembling voice he told us he had been sacked. As he explained the reasons for his dismissal, his eyes began to well with tears, and to the amazement of everyone he began to sob. I was also tearful that day, because my equine hero Red Rum had died. Like all managers I'd had spats with, it was nothing personal with Phil, and if I see him today I'll nod and say hello.

In came 'Big Ron' Atkinson, Mr Bojangles himself. He brought with him his big-time talk, flash manner and big-time spending. Ron told me, 'Whatever grievances you had with Phil is water under the bridge. It's time for a fresh start. I'm a Scouser like you and know you like a laugh. You'll have fun working under me, and the door to the first team is very much open.' He added, 'You know I tried to sign you when I was at Aston Villa. I think you are a natural goalscorer. Go out there, work hard, and get back in the team.'

Nice one, Ron. I hardly trained with the first team while Ron was there, let alone got back in the squad. I really worked my bollocks off in training, lost weight and thought I had done enough to be picked, but it was reserve-team football for me, despite the fact that the club was hardly setting the Premiership on fire. Ron joked, 'I'm still the best five-a-side player at the club. Mind you, that's probably why we are in the position we are in.'

I got a call from my old gaffer from Newcastle, Jim Smith, who was now manager at Portsmouth. The Bald Eagle said, 'Quinny, do you fancy another spell at Pompey? You are still loved down here and you know you and I work well together. I'm looking to bring you in on loan. Give it some thought, and we'll speak in a couple of days.' I was flattered by the offer and would have loved to recreate my glory days on the south coast, but then Jim called again and said, 'Quinny, everything is in place for the loan deal. There is just one problem: I've been given the sack and Terry Fenwick is taking over.' Just my fucking luck.

I carried on in Coventry reserves, but I desperately wanted first-team football and there were other loan offers: both Watford boss Glenn Roeder and Bristol City's Joe Jordan wanted me. With Bristol City struggling badly in the relegation zone and Glenn's team still in with a chance of the play-offs, in March I went south to Watford.

19. A 'PLAY A MATCH WITH THE HORNETS' RAFFLE

'My only regret is that I didn't drink every pub dry and sleep with every woman on the planet.'

Oliver Reed

I jogged out at Watford's Vicarage Road stadium to an atmosphere that would shame a morgue. Early in the game I turned an opposition defender, hit the ball on the half volley from 30 yards and watched it thump against the woodwork. At Newcastle the shot would have been greeted by wild applause and a chorus of 'The Mighty Quinn'; at Watford they put down their egg and cress sandwiches and gave me a polite ripple of applause. Vicarage Road is hardly one of football's hotbeds. Anfield, it ain't. After playing in front of passionate supporters at Fratton Park and St James's Park, it felt very tame.

Manager Glenn Roeder wanted to add a bit of experience to his strike force. He told me he had a hotshot kid who he believed could go all the way to the top. Glenn introduced me to this youngster, who reminded me of a raggedy urchin, in training. He held out his hand and said, 'Hello, my name's Kevin Phillips.' I could tell Kevin had class in training and it was no surprise that he went on to play for Sunderland and England. He was only a kid then, but he had what it took. I used to give him a few tips about making runs and getting into good positions.

But personally, after so long on the sidelines at Coventry, I was woefully short of match practice, I lacked fitness and I didn't do myself justice at Watford. If I thought the Watford fans were on the tame side, their opinion of me certainly wasn't, as the following article from a Watford fans Internet site shows.

The fan who wrote this was a little unkind, but I love humour and I'm not too far up my own arse to laugh at myself.

The Hall of Arse: Mick Quinn by Ian Grant

It is unavoidable, and there is no polite way of saying it, so let's get it over with: MICK QUINN WAS A FAT BASTARD. When he arrived on loan from Coventry towards the end of the 1994/95 season, the latest in an endless procession of players who weren't Paul Furlong, his fat bastardness was not headline news. It had always been so – indeed, Quinn had turned his ample girth into something of a sales gimmick during a successful career as a top-flight goal poacher.

And there's something vaguely admirable about that. Quinn's very obvious refusal to commit himself to anything even slightly resembling an athlete's lifestyle was ultimately just dull, laddish indulgence. But today's sleek 'n' soulless world lends such grease-caked memories a certain nostalgic quality. It's hard to imagine, for example, Mick Quinn ever being asked to appear in one of those hell-awful *Match of the Day* title sequences. It's rather fun to picture it, though: Alan Shearer looks hard and menacing, Michael Owen looks like a pop star, John Hartson kisses his badge tenderly, Mick Quinn gets stuck into his eighth pint of best down his local . . .

But this is The Hall of Arse, and Quinn was an absolute arse at Watford. It may be feasible to be an utter slob and a footballer in your twenties; it's just not possible on the 'experienced' side of 30. He was laughable, waddling around at a pace barely discernible from a stroll in a manner that suggested some fat geezer who'd won a 'Play a Match with the Hornets' raffle. He couldn't win the ball in the air because getting such excess weight off the ground was impossible without the aid of a crane. He couldn't run with the ball because he couldn't run as fast as the ball. Even the trademark 'right place, right time' striker's instinct was worthless because by the time he'd huffed and puffed his way to the 'right place' the referee had blown for full time, the fans had gone home and the last one to leave the ground had turned the floodlights off.

Mick Quinn started four matches for the Hornets and didn't finish any of them, perhaps because Glenn Roeder feared a fatal collapse at any moment. On each occasion, it was difficult to avoid the impression that he'd been propping up the bar in the Red Lion half an hour before kick-off. Which could bring forth warm images of yesteryear – goalies smoking fags during quiet spells, players warming up with a nip of the hard stuff, rain-soaked balls heavy enough to demolish buildings, that kind of nonsense – were it not for a wage bill that definitely didn't belong to yesteryear.

The feeling's mutual, pal.

Before I went to Newcastle I'd had the chance of signing for Watford, then under manager Steve Harrison, for a much higher wage. I'd decided to go to St James's Park for a lot less cash because I wanted to play for a club full of passion and desire, not one with no ambition, few supporters and no future. The atmosphere at Vicarage Road is about as tame as one of Elton John's slushy albums. If I had gone to Watford I would probably have disappeared into mediocrity, never to be heard of again.

When I got back to Coventry after this loan period, Big Ron gave me a free transfer and my City career ended in the late spring of 1995 without me being able to say a proper goodbye to a set of fans I loved. Ron said, 'Quinny, you've worked your bollocks off to try to get yourself back in the team, but it's not going to happen. I'm playing kids with half your talent, but you're the wrong side of 30. Good luck, mate.' Big Ron also sold off Cookie and Marshy – the former to Tranmere Rovers for £250,000 and the latter to Galatasaray in Turkey for £500,000. Fans joked I was going on a free plus 10,000 mince pies.

My big regret about my time at Coventry was that Bobby Gould didn't have the sort of cash to build a team that was given to Phil Neal and Big Ron. I think Bobby could have established Coventry as a top-half-of-the-table Premiership side.

The Players Football Association sent out a circular alerting clubs that I was a free agent. I was looking for £2,000 a week, but Premiership clubs were loath to pay that sort of cash for a 33-year-old striker. I got an offer from Japan but I didn't take it seriously as I would be too far away from the kids. The best offer that came in was from a club called PAOK Salonika in Greece. They were a big club in the country's top division and were offering £800-a-month wages, but with some extraordinary, sliding-scale bonuses based on home results. If you beat one of the top sides like Panathinaikos you could get anywhere between two and five grand. On the other hand, if you lost any of the games you were supposed to win, you paid *them* two grand. PAOK were unbeaten at home the previous season. I didn't want to drop down the divisions in England like an old boxer taking on opponents he would have wiped the floor with in his prime, so I discussed a move to Greece with Karen and we decided to go for it. We thought it would be a new and challenging experience for both of us.

One day that summer I woke up, looked in the mirror and decided it was time to lose the muzzy. The moustache had become something of a Scouse trademark, especially with footballers. John Aldridge, Ian Rush, Terry McDermott, Tommy Smith – the list goes on. The tache had become part of my image, but it had to go. It's easy to hide behind a moustache. At first I felt naked without it, but it had become a cliché. Fans still stop me in the street and say, 'Where's the moustache, Mick?' I also got rid of the mullet. In a way the change of image was a sign I was growing up. It was also a sign of the added maturity that Karen had brought to my life. In her, I was sure I had found my soulmate.

I was a bit surprised when I received the PAOK contract in the post. At English clubs, you get reams and reams of the stuff; this was just one badly typed page. It did set the alarm bells ringing, but I signed it anyway and sent it back. I linked up with the squad on a pre-season tour of Germany and was introduced to manager Ari Haan, who had been part of Holland's World Cup final team, and the rest of the players. Mick Quinn from Cantril Farm was going to be a continental football star.

20. BLOWIN' IN THE WIND

'How many roads must a man walk down, before you can call him a man?'

Bob Dylan, 'Blowin' in the Wind'

'It was like living in a foreign country.'

Ian Rush on his time in Italy playing with Juventus

I'd just put the bags down on the bed in my Bavarian hotel room when my mobile phone rang. I pulled it out of my pocket and saw Dad's number flashing on the screen.

'All right, Pops,' I said, but I immediately knew something was wrong. There was no cheery hello, no funny gag.

'Mick, you're not going to believe this,' Dad said, his voice cracking up. 'Sean's dead.'

My whole world came crashing in. My kid brother was dead. He was only 26. I felt like I'd been twatted with a gigantic boxing glove, and I just sat there with a sick feeling in my gut. The tears flooded out of me. I couldn't accept I would never see my kid brother again. He was just setting out in life. Sean had always looked up to me as I was the eldest son, and I had always looked out for him. We had had a special bond.

Sean, or Sinbad as we called him, was a big character, a joker and the archetypal loveable rogue who danced through life. He would have £1,500 on Monday then nothing on Friday. Sean lived more in his 26 years than many do in a lifetime, and I'm sure he would have found a successful path through life. Sean was a fit lad who'd been an apprentice at Liverpool and Portsmouth, but he died in his sleep on our living-room sofa. The autopsy uncovered traces of cannabis and alcohol in his blood, but not enough to kill him. Doctors blamed it on a sort of adult cot death.

He was the youngest of the three brothers, and as the baby had been allowed to get away with murder, but he wasn't a bad lad. When he nicked Ian Rush's boots while an apprentice at Liverpool, he didn't try to sell them to make a few quid but gave them to one of his mates who idolised Rushy. As the eldest, I had always tried to help Sean in life. When things went tits up for him at Liverpool I had got him an apprenticeship at Pompey. Everyone was impressed and thought he was a great player, but after he had landed the contract he thought he was already a seasoned pro who didn't need to work hard at the game. Instead of getting in at 8.30 a.m. he was rolling in at 10.30. He lived the life of a pro footballer even though he wasn't one. In the end, it didn't work out for him. He went to Oldham but had to retire from the game after busting his knee while playing five-a-side. If I had been born with his pace and athleticism I would have played for England; if he'd had my attitude and commitment he would have played for Liverpool.

I flew back to Liverpool in a daze. Mum was especially devastated. No parent wants to bury a child. We all rallied round and decided to give Sean the send-off he deserved. Mark bought a huge American-style oak coffin with gold handles, similar to the one Elvis was buried in. As a Catholic family, we asked the undertakers to bring the coffin back to 16 Round Hey the night before the funeral. We are a well-known family on the estate, and dozens of people lined the streets to see the coffin pass. The undertakers unloaded the coffin and slowly moved towards the door of our semi, but the Elvis-style casket was so big it wouldn't fit through the front door. We had to take it round the back and pass it over the fences of seven of our neighbours' gardens. It was like something out of *It's a Knockout*. Scousers are never scared to laugh at themselves, and the whole family had a right giggle. Sean would have loved the ridiculousness of it all.

'Sean's up there laughing his head off,' Dad said. 'I think he planned this.'

We eventually got the coffin into the house by taking the back door off its hinges and passing it through on its side. I sat with Sean and mourned him.

The next day, dozens of folk from Cantril lined the streets as we walked the coffin from number 16 to St Albert's Church. It was like a lap of honour of the estate for him. The people of Cantril gave him a great send-off. Afterwards, as the coffin left the church where we had spent so much time as kids, Sean's favourite song, Bob Dylan's 'Blowin' in the Wind', boomed out from the PA system. I looked around and saw Mum and the rest of the family crying their eyes out. It really broke me up to see that. Sean had been the apple of Mum's eye.

Sean's death made me realise how short life is and how important family and loved ones are. I was determined, more than ever, to live life to the full. I still think about him every day.

When we arrived at the airport in Greece, Karen and I were greeted by a throng of PAOK fans with bouquets of flowers. They had heard about Sean's death and wanted me to know they were thinking of me. It was an amazing gesture and a mark of the hospitality of Greek people. It really moved me at a time when I needed all the support I could get.

We moved into a plush three-bedroomed flat overlooking the marina in Thessaloniki, the northern capital of Greece, where PAOK are based. The apartment, which looked out over the deep blue Aegean Sea, had marble floors and Sky TV showing live Premiership games on a Saturday. From our balcony you could look right around the marina and down on to a parade of lively restaurants and flash clothes shops. The city, with a population of some 750,000, was a very cosmopolitan place. It was a bustling industrial centre but had a history dating back to the days of Alexander the Great.

I was pleasantly surprised by the apartment, but it was when I took possession of the club car that I got an inkling of what I had let myself in for. It was a 25-year-old white Mercedes, a one-time taxi that looked as if it had gone round the clock five times. There was no tread on the tyres, no speedo, and only two of the doors opened. It looked as if a strong gust of wind would have blown the thing apart.

I knew next to nothing about Greece; the only Greek-sounding place I had ever been to was Toxteth. Ian Rush was once asked what it was like moving to Italy to play for Juventus, and he replied, 'It was like living in a foreign country.' No shit, Ian. But now I knew exactly what he meant. The language was literally all Greek to me. The one word I knew was *mallacha*, which means 'wanker'.

There were no bookies in Greece, but after two months Karen and I found somewhere that sold the *Racing Post*. It was a half-hour drive from our apartment but I religiously made the trip every day. It actually did me a lot of good to get away from the betting-shop culture, to break the habit of going there every lunchtime. It also allowed me to put a bit of cash into a pension, for the first time in my career. It was also good to get away from English alehouses for a bit. I developed a taste for a nice drop of wine and ate lots of kebabs, paella and pasta – they don't do too many roasts over there. The kebabs were gorgeous, nothing like the gristle-on-a-spit stuff you can get here.

The lifestyle was great, too. Because of the heat we would start training at 7 a.m. and finish at ten. We would then go back in at 9 p.m. and train again. It meant Karen and I could spend every day together and enjoy some quality time. It was just what I needed after Sean's death, and Karen was a great strength and support to me. We hit the shops together. There was a McDonald's and a Marks and Spencer, and the cinemas there had all the Hollywood films in English with Greek subtitles. Even better, you could buy a beer at the cinema and take it in with you. We also did the culture bit and went round all the museums. I remember the vases with paintings on them of blokes with cocks the size of baby's arms.

Karen was there for me in my darkest moments as I attempted to come to terms with Sean's death. We often talked late into the night and she held me when I needed comforting. We'd been close in England, but we now found a love deeper and stronger than I had ever known.

I was a bit disappointed, however, with the style of football in Greece. I was used to the action-packed Premiership, but over there it was slow and laborious. They would string fifteen or twenty passes together before they crossed the halfway line. Sometimes I felt like tackling one of our own players and hoofing the ball 50 yards upfield. But the fans in Greece are unbelievably passionate. The PAOK supporters made Millwall's New Den seem like a Sunday school outing. They modelled themselves on English hooligans, wearing scarves around their faces and holding up banners in English saying stuff like BLACK AND WHITE DEATH. I was very popular, for simply being English and also for my never-say-die playing style. My name was translated as 'Miki Koyin' in Greek.

My first game for the club, a cup tie in Crete against a Third Division side, was a real eye-opener. It was a tiny ground, but they had somehow managed to squeeze in 3,500. The place was heaving, and our hardcore hooly element were letting off flares and generally going mental. In the first minute, I challenged the keeper and he went down like a sack of shit, writhing around on the ground and clutching his face. It was a tough challenge but it wouldn't even have raised an eyebrow in the Premiership. It was a performance Laurence Olivier would have been proud of. I was still on the ground after the challenge when the next thing I knew someone was kicking me in the back. I got up, and another player spat in my face. Then, as I turned round, someone else pulled my hair. You don't do that to someone from Cantril Farm. I turned around to face the players and made a little motioning gesture with my hands. 'Come on then, you c***s, I'll take you all on.' Their fans went crazy.

From then on, it was murder. Every time I went anywhere near the touchline the fans started throwing plastic water bottles at me full of piss. It was as if it was raining water bottles. One of them hit a linesman. He turned round and grabbed his bollocks in a gesture of defiance, so the fans launched another 50 at him. Three policemen then rushed on to the pitch, waving their arms around like orchestra conductors to try to calm things down. The crowd let them have it, too. Then the police started to pick up the bottles and began lobbing them back at the crowd. It was like something out of a Carry On film. The game was stopped for twenty minutes, but we somehow managed to get through to half-time. By then, the fans were all clustered round the halfway line and the ref decided it might be better if we stayed on the pitch. I felt like Michael Caine in *Zulu*.

Then, five minutes into the second half, I only went and scored. Well, that was it. They started lobbing coins, stones, more bottles – the lot. But the biggest miracle, apart from the fact that I managed to avoid having my head smashed in, was that we managed to finish the game. And it didn't end there. We had to be chaperoned off the pitch by the home players and were then besieged in the dressing room for an hour as the fans tried to break down the door. By the time the coach came to take us to the airport, all the windows had been smashed and we had to lie down in the centre aisle.

Welcome to Greece.

A couple of months after my debut, PAOK were hosts to AEK Athens. We had 43,000 in, and when we went 3–1 down with 25 minutes to go the fans decided they'd had enough. They started ripping up the concrete terracing and launching it at the AEK fans, but half of it hit their own supporters. It turned into a huge riot, and it was very scary. The ref was laid out, there were bodies everywhere, casualties numbered 38 and the game was abandoned. And they'd already been banned from Europe because of crowd trouble the season before.

The Greek FA had no option but to come down on PAOK like a ton of bricks – highly appropriate, considering the circumstances. We were sentenced to having to play our next six home games away, and outside a 100-mile radius too. We were out in the sticks playing in front of 900 fans. Consequently, there was no money coming in – though this was hardly anything new for the players. A few weeks after playing in front of 43,000 in the AEK game, we were watched by just 747 diehard supporters. And that was more frightening because they could take a run-up when they were lobbing things at us.

Our wages, paid in cash, were always three weeks late, and the club had still coughed up only half of the previous season's European bonus. Once I was paid in Deutschmarks, but I was just happy to get some dosh. One of the young players burst out crying, telling me that he didn't have enough money to feed his family. Things got so bad that the chairman started to receive death threats. He used to drive around with a gun in the glove compartment.

Finally, the players decided to go on strike. The general manager rang the chairman and within half an hour he had banned us from both the training ground and the club. At this point, the chairman said he could no longer afford any foreign players, so I was on my bike.

It had been a crazy seven months. I had played all over England at places like Millwall and Leeds, but they were tame compared with what I experienced over in Greece. I was spat on and pelted with coins and bottles full of piss – and that was just when I nipped out for a paper in the morning. But it was wonderful to experience a different culture and way of life. It was also great to spend some much-needed quality time with Karen without the distraction of horses and pubs.

My parting shot was a major blast at the chairman in the press because the other players were too scared to do it themselves. On the day it appeared, I went to say goodbye to the lads and they gave me a standing ovation. After seven goals in fifteen games, Miki Koyin was on the next plane to Heathrow.

21. TRAINER

'When I was young, I didn't want to get beaten and go back with excuses. It was every man for himself. You went out to win. Yes, I did cut up one or two, and them me. But you can't do two things, do your best to win all the time and be careful all the time.'

Lester Piggott

The plane touched down at Heathrow on a freezing February afternoon in 1996. I was 33 years old and after seventeen years as a top pro footballer I had fuck-all to show for it. No house, no car, no job and three kids to support. Sue and Barry picked us up from the airport and drove us up to Risbury, near Leominster in Herefordshire. They said we could stay in their beautiful three-bedroomed cottage while we got ourselves straight.

I could easily have found another English club in one of the lower divisions to take me on, but the last thing I wanted was to drift down the League. It had taken a long time to work my way up to the Premiership, and I didn't want to end things playing in front of a few men and a dog at some provincial khazi of a ground. It was time to knock it on the head while I was still in one piece. I had scored 231 goals in 512 League appearances, but the limited pace I did have was starting to fade. I wasn't even quick over a yard any more. I hated watching once great boxers turning into flabby, embarrassing parodies of themselves by carrying on fighting too long. I didn't want to become the Joe Bugner of football. The sight of my hero Muhammad Ali barely being able to walk or talk was enough to tell me you've got to quit at the top.

Despite nearly two decades of rough-and-tumble football, I had steered clear of serious injury. My worst knock was doing my cruciate ligaments chasing that no-hope goal for Newcastle against my old club Portsmouth. When I see my good mate

Mick Channon shuffling around with crippling arthritis from injuries picked up in football, I know I got out at the right time. I believe my brick-shithouse physique helped me avoid injury. I didn't get knocked about all over the park like some of the slighter lads. The slog of jogging about in the mud on a cold winter's morning was over. No more booing fans, gobby managers or ungrateful chairmen. It also meant no more adulation from the terraces, no more dressing-room banter and no more thrills from scoring goals, so I knew I was going to have to replace the buzz with something.

Looking back, my golden period in football was undoubtedly the season I banged in 36 goals at Newcastle. My only regret was that when the club finally got its act together and got promoted to the Premiership under Keegan, I wasn't there to be a part of it. Still, I had my Division Two runners-up medal with Pompey and two Golden Boot awards for my scoring feats, and I'd played for some of English football's biggest names – Keegan, Gould, Royle, Neal, Shilton, Roeder – and three World Cup finalists in Argentina's Ossie Ardiles, England's Alan Ball and Holland's Ari Haan. There'd been tantrums, industrial language and thrown tea cups, but that was just me.

Throughout my career I'd had my fair share of run-ins with centre-halves, too. I didn't mind hard but fair tackling, but if it started going beyond that I just used to say, 'Look, if you want a war then you'll fucking get one.' That old Luigi Silvano fighting spirit – it usually did the trick. As for the best defenders I played against, I would have to say Alan Hansen, Mark Lawrenson and Gary Gillespie at Liverpool. They were so bloody good it was like chasing shadows. In the end you'd feel like kicking them, but you just couldn't get anywhere near enough to do it. They would be so relaxed. It was like they were standing around having after-dinner cigars, stroking the ball effortlessly between them. I'd be running around like a headless chicken trying to get a touch. Different class, they were.

I believe I made it in the game when thousands of young hopefuls didn't because of my attitude. Despite all the pies stuff, I was always one of the hardest workers at every club I played for. I also had the supreme confidence in my ability that I believe every top sportsman needs. Ask Muhammad Ali. Sometimes my confidence bordered on cockiness. Once, when I was at Coventry, we were playing Chelsea and Glenn Hoddle, then in his twilight years as a player, came up to tackle me. I slipped the ball through his legs to nutmeg him, and as I moved upfield with the ball I shouted back to him, 'Nuts!' The worst thing you can do to a pro footballer is to nutmeg him, and we had this little thing of shouting 'Nuts!' at a player when we did it on the training pitch. It infuriated players so much it often led to scything tackles and even fisticuffs. Doing it during a five-a-side on the training park is one thing, but to do it to Hoddle, one of England's most skilful ball players, during a Premiership match was the ultimate piss-take. Unlucky, Glenda. I fucking loved it.

Summing up my career in the *Independent*, I said, 'A lot of clubs probably steered clear of me because I did enjoy myself while I was playing. Any manager I played under will tell you I trained as hard as anyone, but I liked to enjoy it at the same time. That doesn't mean I was stupid and went swinging from the chandeliers with just my underpants on, but I did have a good time. But I did get a name, especially as I was outspoken as well, and that went against me while I was playing.'

I toyed with idea of going into management. Football was what I knew best, and I considered myself tactically aware with the leadership qualities needed for success. Plus, I wasn't sure if I wanted to cut the umbilical cord with football just yet. Soon after arriving back from Greece I did apply for the vacant Burnley manager's job. I did it on a whim, really, but I managed to get down to the last three. Adrian Heath, who had played for them, got the nod in the end, but I was chuffed to have got that far. Then I was offered the chance to be player–manager for a Vauxhall Conference club, but I didn't give the job a moment's thought. I didn't fancy scratching about at that level after playing at Anfield and Old Trafford.

Just a few weeks after returning I got the awful news that Mum had been diagnosed with lung cancer. I was left numb. I just couldn't face losing her so soon after Sean. Karen and I visited her and she said she was having chemotherapy and believed she could beat the disease. She told me, 'Michael, I'm fine. I'm sure I'll get better. I'm only 52 after all.' Mark, Trisha and Dad, even though he and Mum were separated, were there for her.

Life at Sue and Barry's was quiet, and it gave me time to reflect on what I really wanted to do with the rest of my life. After a few weeks R & R in Risbury, I picked up the phone and dialled Mick Channon's number.

'Mick, it's Quinny. I need your advice. I've been turning it over in my mind for ages and I've decided I want to train racehorses for a living.'

After owning thoroughbreds for nearly a decade, I'd realised it was racehorses rather than racing that I loved and I wanted to work with them on a daily basis.

'Are you nuts?' Mick demanded. 'Do you realise the shit you will have to go through, especially being an ex-footballer? The odds on you making it are tiny.' Mick explained that the Jockey Club was strict over who it awarded licences to, and as an ex-footballer I would have to work doubly hard to prove myself to the racing community. Mick also warned me: 'Because of who you are, a Scouse ex-footballer, if you ever did anything wrong the racing hierarchy would come down on you like a ton of bricks.'

But I had made up my mind.

'You know I'm nuts,' I told him. 'I've thought it over, Mick, and I'm determined to do it.'

'Well, get your arse down here then, boy,' he said in his strangulated carrot-cruncher accent.

It was a brave step for me – the boy from Cantril Farm mixing it in the sport of kings – but I was never going to be one of those ex-footballers who ended up running a pub or selling insurance. The snobby side of racing has never bothered me. I think I've got just as much right to be at Royal Ascot as anybody else.

After a bloody hard slog, Mick is now one of the country's top trainers with a string of 130 horses. I have always seen him as an inspiration and a mentor. The only other footballer to become a trainer was ex-Manchester City star Francis Lee. He also enjoyed considerable success, but ended up packing the game in. Franny and Mick played many times for England. My only cap is a baseball cap, but they'd both showed that footballers could make the switch to racehorse training.

Many footballers are totally hooked on racing. Racehorse owners include Sir Alex Ferguson, Michael Owen, David Platt, Alan Shearer, Robbie Fowler, Steve McManaman and Kevin Keegan. Footballers usually come from a working-class background where betting is an important part of the culture. When they get a bit of dosh it's only natural that they want to shell out on their own racehorse. Sir Alex, who owned wonder horse Rock of Gibraltar, and the rest of football's racing fans have given the sport a big boost, not only in financial terms but by putting racing in the spotlight. The football crowd offer something different to the usual aristos, business tycoons and Arab sheikhs who own horses.

Mick explained that to become a trainer you have to show the Jockey Club you have two and a half years' experience as an assistant trainer, so I went down to Mick's Upper Lambourn Stables in the so-called Valley of the Racehorse in Berkshire and started to learn about racing from the bottom up. I began literally by shovelling shit and caring for the horses with the rest of the stable lads. I learnt how to arrange the straw and wood shavings in a stable so the horses were comfortable, and how to muck them out properly. I was taught how to groom them and wash them down after exercise, and what rugs they needed to keep them warm. Mick's head lads, Jim Davies and Ted Waite, taught me the art of feeding, which is so important for producing winners. Just like the other lads, I took horses racing, travelling for hours in the horsebox to far-flung meetings, and learnt how to saddle them properly. I remember going on one long haul in the horsebox from Berkshire to Hamilton in Scotland. It took hours, and when we got to the course we had to make sure the horses were fed and watered and the bed was made before we could attend to our own creature comforts. I stayed in the racecourse digs with the other stable lads. It was a culture shock after the five-star hotels and flash club cars of the Premiership, but I loved every minute of it.

It was a real crash course, but I was in my element in the yard. I had loved horses ever since as a kid I'd sneaked over the fence at Aintree, and to learn all about their husbandry was a real thrill. I even had a bash at riding the horses – not the thoroughbreds, but the stockier types (unless they start racing shire horses I don't think I'm ever going to make a jockey). The *Sun* soon heard about my career change and sent a reporter and photographer down to watch me at work. The article appeared under the headline MUCK QUINN, and I was pictured in shorts and trainers with a pitchfork in my hand, mucking out a stable. It was great to be learning so much, to be given responsibility after so long in football being told exactly what to do and when to do it. I hope my time at Mick's put paid to the theory that I wasn't a hard worker. Due to my size many had thought I was never one for hard graft on the football field, but that was absolute bollocks. My ex-football managers will tell you how hard I worked.

I watched closely how Mick worked his horses on the gallops. He trained them very much like footballers. They had pre-season training to give them basic fitness, then once they'd started running in races he gave them one big blow-out a week. The day after a race, just like a footballer, the horse is given a day off to have a stretch in the field. Horses, of course, don't sup twelve pints of lager after exerting themselves, which helps them to recover quicker.

As I became more experienced, Mick let me stand in for him when he had runners at more than one meeting. He would go to the big southern tracks and I would go to the smaller places up north. I acted as the trainer on Mick's behalf, taking care of the welfare of the horses and saddling them before they ran. I also had to entertain the owners and deal with the press. Thus I became his full-time assistant, and to start with it was nerve-racking. If you're the owner of a horse you're shelling out a grand a month to keep your horse in training. Had anything gone wrong, I would have been for the chop. Thankfully, it didn't. Mick was careful to teach me the finer points of racecourse etiquette. 'You've got to tone down your language a bit for the owners, Mick,' he told me. 'I'm going to limit you to one fuck per sentence.'

Mick and his lovely wife Jill really looked after me. I listened to everything he told me and learnt the importance of the form book and how to place horses in races. Mick knew what he was talking about, and has gone on to become one of Britain's biggest trainers. One of his pearls of wisdom that has stuck with me is this: 'Don't believe your geese are swans.' By that he meant don't believe your horses are better than they are, and run them in races of the right quality. His other piece of advice to me was 'Always make sure the owners pay their bills.'

Mick also brought a sense of humour into the game. I remember standing in the parade ring with him before a race as he gave a young jockey his orders. The kid was barely out of short trousers and had even brought his dad with him. Mick's instructions were to hold the horse up to the final furlong, take close order going round the final bend, then kick and win by three lengths. The kid nodded nervously, then Mick added, 'If you don't I'll give you the biggest kick you've ever had in your life. In fact, I'll kick you that hard you'll have three Adam's apples.' The kid went absolutely white. Then I chipped in. 'You'd better do what he says, because I used to play with him at Portsmouth and he doesn't often miss.' We were both being sarcastic, but the lad obviously took it on board. He rode exactly as Mick had instructed and won the race by exactly three lengths. Mick has a friendly and down-to-earth manner, but behind that is a real pro who won't stand for anything less than the highest standards for his horses. One of his mottos is 'Piss-poor preparation leads to piss-poor performances.'

My other big hero from the training ranks was Bill Marshall, one of racing's all-time great characters. An RAF war hero, Bill left Britain for Barbados, and it was there that I met him. I was on holiday with Neale Doughty, my jockey friend from my Newcastle days, and a load of other jocks including Steve Smith Eccles and Graham McCourt. Neale had been a conditional or trainee jockey for Bill, and we were invited to a barbecue at his wonderful home. He told us some amazing stories about his monster gambles and his daredevil wartime exploits. Bill once flew his Spitfire under the bridge at Marlow in Buckinghamshire to impress a girl. He was court-martialled and was put in charge of a squadron full of misfits and rebels as a punishment. They ended up getting more hits than any other squadron. Bill was shot down twice by the Luftwaffe. On one occasion he escaped by stealing a German plane and flying it back to England. He'd always lived on the edge, and would pawn his missus's jewellery to have a punt. He told me that when they took horses to tracks a long way from home, he and the wife would sleep in the car and use the money they would have spent on a hotel to gamble. Bill is in his late eighties now but is still training in Barbados, specialising in winning the island's big race, the Cockspur Cup.

I didn't get paid for the work with Mick, so Karen and I were skint. We lived on the philosophy that something always turns up. I was chasing my dream, and my relationship with Karen was getting stronger and stronger, but I was worried about Mum, who was still battling lung cancer and undergoing chemotherapy. In early September 1996 I picked her up from Cantril Farm and took her, Melissa and Natasha out for lunch. As she walked towards the restaurant from the car I noticed for the first time how frail she had become. She was terribly short of breath and walked in small, faltering steps. She was obviously in pain, and it broke my heart to see her like that. She loved seeing the girls and fussed over them and me. We laughed together, talked about the old times on the Farm, the degree in Sociology she'd finally managed to get from Liverpool University, and my training aspirations. Then I asked her how she was. She smiled, and said, 'Michael, I'm fine. I'm feeling a lot better actually, much better. I'm more worried about you getting on in this training lark. I'm really proud of everything you've achieved, Michael. You know that, don't you?' It was a funny thing to come out with unprompted. I dropped her home, kissed her on the cheek and said goodbye.

Ten days later, Dad rang me late in the evening. His voice was husky and distant. 'You'd better get up here, your mum's taken a turn for the worse.'

I set off for Liverpool early the next morning. I had got as far as the Midlands when the mobile rang again. It was Dad.

'She's gone,' he whispered.

I pulled over in the next lay-by and wept uncontrollably. Mum was just 52. Why had she been taken away so young? First Sean, and now Mum. What had we done to deserve this? Mum had held the family together. She was a warm, strong and intelligent woman. Had she been born twenty years later she would have gone to university at eighteen and been a successful career woman.

It was back to St Albert's Church at Cantril Farm for another Quinn family funeral. You don't expect to bury both your kid brother and your Mum in a little over a year. It was a very dark time for me and I spent long hours mulling over what life was all about. Mum had always been so supportive; I could do no wrong in her eyes. Even when I had been jailed, had messed up another relationship or left myself skint through gambling, she had unquestioningly forgiven me and given me love. She would say to me, 'You'd be living in a mansion now if you didn't bet.' But she knew I thrived on the buzz of having a punt. My big regret now is that I wasn't up in Liverpool more when Mum was ill.

The deaths of my mother and brother hardened me as a person. Once you've experienced grief like that it is difficult not to have a more cynical view of life. If I heard someone moaning about having a boring job, or about their car breaking down, I felt like grabbing them by the collar and screaming, 'Listen, mate, I'm really cut up about your car but my mum and brother have just died.'

I went back to Mick's totally focused on getting my licence. I divided my time between Channon's place and Sue and Barry's. I was living off what was left of my Greek cash while my brother Mark sorted me out a Toyota Carina to get around in. Joining Mick's yard was financial madness. Technically I was his pupil assistant, but in reality that meant unpaid stable lad. Most of our spending money was coming from a good run I was having with the punting. By now I was reading the form book like it was the Bible, and my favourite bet was the placepot. For this bet you have to find a horse to be placed in each race on the card. Just when it looked like everything was going tits up, I would bang in another placepot – £1,500 here, £1,000 there. My best placepot win was £3,500 from virtually my last £40.

Mick approached me in the feed room at his yard one day and said, 'Mick, you need to be confident in your own ability.

I think you have the talent and experience now to start training on your own.' It was a special moment, coming as it did from someone I respected as much as Mick. He had taught me so much in such a short space of time.

I enrolled on the British Horse Racing Board's respected trainer training course at Newmarket's racing school. It was a residential course with modules in staff, business and stable management. I was one of the first to enrol on the course, alongside Grand National queen Jenny Pitman's son Mark, Dorothy Thompson and Lawrence Squires. It was like being at boarding school. I had to make my own bed every morning before lectures in a classroom. I knuckled down and really enjoyed it.

One night, the pupils decided to slip out for a couple of beers in a nearby pub. Mark and Lawrence seemed to be rubbing each other up the wrong way. At closing time we bought a bottle of whisky and continued drinking back at the hostel. Eventually, Mark went back to his room, but Lawrence, fortified by the scotch, felt he had unfinished business with him. Lawrence, now a photographer, barged into Mark's room as he slept, grabbed the bin and emptied its contents on to his head. Mark came charging into our room in his boxer shorts and went for Lawrence. I managed to get between them and calmed things down, suggesting to Mark that he sit down and have a scotch. A drunken Lawrence muttered, 'He was lucky. I've trained with the SAS. One flick of my finger and I could have killed him.' Moments later he crashed out, and it was time for Mark's revenge. He shaved off one of Lawrence's eyebrows and put mascara on him. They had another pop at each other in the morning.

I passed the course and was then ready to apply for my licence. I began to sound out potential owners who would have horses with me. Liverpool's German midfielder Didi Hamann and Everton striker Duncan Ferguson both came on board, and my old mate Paul Cook, then at Stockport County, also offered to get involved. Paul 'Byo' Byatt, who played Mike Dickson in TV soap *Brookside*; restaurateur John Dooley, who owns Jalons, a great eaterie in Liverpool; and businessman Steven Astaire also had horses with me. Chelsea vice-president Gary Pinchen bought a horse and named it Zola after the club's Italian midfielder Gianfranco Zola. Dad, Mark and his mates chipped in, and Sue and Barry said they would have a horse or two as well. I even gave an interview to drum up some publicity and hopefully a few more owners, saying, 'I'm sure there are a lot of people out there hoping that I fall flat on my face because I'm imposing on their world.'

I had taken out a seven-year lease on a lovely stables in the pretty Oxfordshire village of Sparsholt. Nestled into the Lambourn Downs near Wantage, East Manton Stables was just a mile from the famous prehistoric chalk white horse and close to the ancient ridgeway track. Racehorses have been trained in the area for as long as there has been racing because the chalk downland drains quickly, which stops the gallops being turned into a quagmire. The whole area is dotted with racing yards following the sweep of the downs. My 30-box red-bricked stables is steeped in racing history. A previous tenant of the yard was Matt McCormack, who trained Royal Ascot winner Horage. With its wood-timbered, thatched cottages, genteel Sparsholt couldn't have been more different from Cantril Farm. Mum would have loved Sparsholt, and I really wish she could have seen it. She would have loved to walk on the downs and spend time around the yard. I know she would have been so proud of me.

I now had a yard, gallops, staff, horses, owners and a business plan. I felt I had earned my wings as a trainer through hard graft in Mick's yard. I had seen the heartaches and headaches, the ups and downs of racing, at first hand. I knew I would be starting off in the Dr Marten League while Mick was in the Premiership, but I was chomping at the bit to get started. The last hurdle I had to face before getting my licence was to convince a Jockey Club committee I was fit to train.

So, suited and booted, I got the train down to Portman Square in London, walked into an imposing committee room and sat down in a chair in front of a three-man board. They questioned me on my financial situation and my racing experience. It was like being in court again. I was then told to wait outside while they discussed my application. A few minutes later I was called back in. It was October 1997, and I was the new master of East Manton Stables.

It was one of the proudest moments in my life. Football had been a natural progression for me, but I was now joining a totally different world. I knew I was putting everything on the line and that if I failed it could all end in bankruptcy and me looking like a right prat – another ex-footballer who fell flat on his face after leaving the comfort of football. I realised there were people out there who thought I was about to do just that. It was like when I was fifteen and the job creation bloke wouldn't take me seriously when I said I wanted to be a footballer. It just made me more determined to succeed. I would be lying if I said I didn't have some nerves, but I knew in my heart of hearts that I could train horses to win races. Karen, as always, was there to reassure me over any doubts. My adrenalin was pumping, and I couldn't wait to have my first runner.

Simon Barnes, writing in *The Times*, summed up with real feeling the risks I was taking. 'Quinn has unbelted a fair amount of the readies, and staked his future, his credibility as a person. It is hard and brave to do, this, even if you have been bred for the task and brought up in the smell of it. To do so from the world of football, a world not only unhorsey but in many ways quite unreal, is an act of rare courage. And love and folly of course, but nobody goes into horses (or stays in horses) without lashings of those two things. It is the courage that is exceptional. Sumo Quinn sprinkles salt on to the arena of combat, adjusts his loincloth and crouches on his mark. Let battle commence.'

22. I WILL LOVE IT, ABSOLUTELY LOVE IT

'If you are first, you are first. If you are second, you are nothing.'
Bill Shankly

Watching Katie's Cracker walk around the paddock at Southwell on 8 December 1997, I felt a bigger thrill than when I walked out at Anfield. Katie's, a two-year-old filly, was my second runner as a trainer. Fairy Domino had run earlier that day and tailed off last, but Katie's was classy and I really needed her to run a big race for me. I stood with owner Jim Miller as the horses walked around us. The sun beat down on a crisp winter's afternoon. Katie's had a twinkle in her eye and her coat shone – all signs that she was fit and healthy and would run well. Her paddock rug was emblazoned with a logo: MICK QUINN above a football. It's good to have a gimmick. Standing a few feet away were the connections of Cutting Anshake. The trainer was my old gaffer, Mick Channon. Anshake's jockey was wearing the colours of Mrs Jean Keegan, wife of a certain bubble-permed football manager. I turned to Jim and said, in the words Kev had immortalised in his TV rant against Alex Ferguson, 'I will love it if Katie's beats his horse, absolutely love it.'

I legged up jockey Peter Murphy and made my way to the owners and trainers section of the grandstand. Katie's came out of the stalls well and Peter had her handily placed at the halfway stage, but it was Cutting Anshake who was leading the field as they passed the furlong pole in the home straight. Then Katie's began to motor, just like I had seen her do on the gallops at home. She flew down the last furlong and pulled alongside Cutting Anshake. I was screaming myself silly in the stands, but as they flashed past the post Keegan's horse found something extra and got up by half a length. The Messiah had put Judas in his place again. Anshake's jockey, Richard Perham, who I knew well from my time at Mick Channon's yard, shouted to me, 'Sorry, Mick!' as he entered the winners' enclosure.

The battle between Keegan and me was not lost on the press. I actually got more much-needed publicity than if I had won. Under the headline MICK AS A PARROT: CHANNON AND KEEGAN FOIL QUINN'S FIRST-DAY STRIKE, the *Sun* reported me as saying, 'The guvnor has turned me over. It's what Tommy Docherty used to call the old one-two. I'm still happy with the result as it shows we are on the right lines, especially as my first runner, Fairy Domino, got completely outpaced and finished last in the previous race.' The *Sporting Life* said that I was taking 'one giant leap for Scousekind' in my second professional career, which I thought was quite funny.

I concentrated on flat racing with one or two jumpers. I love the idea of buying a yearling at the sales then educating it and moulding it into a racehorse. Then, when the horse runs, a piece of you goes out on the course with it. I found it more exciting than playing football. In that first season I had a fourteen-horse string that was a little short on class, but you have to start somewhere. I'd inherited many of the horses from other trainers and they'd already failed on the track or picked up bad habits. I charged £200 a week training fees compared to the £350 a week that the big Newmarket trainers were asking for, but the owners weren't exactly flooding in. Everton and ex-Newcastle striker Duncan Ferguson, who had become a friend of the family, sent a two-year-old called No Regrets to us, but it couldn't have a had a less fitting name. It was the only living creature which was injured more often than Big Dunc, which is some feat. At the time, though, it wasn't funny and I did everything possible to try to get the horse right.

Duncan had become a great pal of my brother Mark, a true blue. They'd met in a box at Everton and hit it off. The first time

I met Duncan was at the Adelphi Hotel – Liverpool's most famous hotel. We had a few beers – well, a lot of beers – and Dunc said, 'Where are you staying tonight?'

'Probably at the old man's,' I replied. 'I've just got up here from Oxfordshire.'

Dunc wouldn't hear of it and paid for a suite for me at the hotel. It was typical of his generosity. He is an incredibly warm and welcoming man, and a great striker. I went on Dunc's stag 'week' to Benidorm, which was a riot. On the second night Dunc and one of Mark's mates Dicky decided to have a drinking competition. The bet was who could be first to knock back a whole large bottle of vintage £500 XO brandy. They both slapped the equivalent of £500 in pesetas on the table and started swigging. Dunc's a real competitor, and after 35 minutes he had knocked back the whole lot. It took him just as long to walk to the next bar just a few yards away. He was falling about all over the place. Unsurprisingly, he didn't show for days three and four, but he was back on the piss on day five.

Karen and I complimented each other really well as a team. She is a good rider, she worked hard in the yard and was also great with the accounts, and after years of sitting in bookmakers I knew form and bloodlines backwards. I loved being in the yard at 6.30 a.m. to feed the horses and check them over. I feel I have horses in my blood, which many might think odd coming from a Scouser from Cantril Farm. I often think it must come from my great grandfather Quinn, who apparently kept horses in Waterford in Ireland.

Karen and I worked bloody hard, doing much of the shit-shovelling ourselves because we couldn't afford many staff. Despite the financial pressures, I was never happier than when I was up on the Lambourn Downs, my little string of horses emerging from the mist as they worked up the gallops. When they finished they would walk around me and I would assess their fitness from how hard they were blowing and decide when they were ready to run. I loved being around horses every day, handling them and getting to know the character, the likes and dislikes, of each animal.

The *Independent* ran a feature about my new career under the headline HE'S FAT, HE'S ROUND, A NEW CAREER HE'S FOUND. The reporter, Richard Edmondson, asked me if I had any tips. 'Don't put black polish on brown shoes and don't wipe your arse with broken glass because it hurts,' I told him. Edmondson wrote: 'This was going to be different than talking to trainers Major Dick Hern or Captain Tim Forster.' And there is a class thing in racing. It's an expensive business being an owner, so obviously the jet set and the super rich are involved. When my racing club's horse Sumoquinn won the Listed Rockingham Stakes at York, owners of other horses in the race included Sheikh Maktoum Al Maktoum, Sheikh Mohammed and tycoon Robert Sangster. When you see such people in the parade ring and beat them in a top race with a horse that cost £3,500, it is a moment to savour. It is a buzz for a boy from Cantril Farm to be mixing with aristos and Arab sheikhs, but I'm not fazed by it. There is a place for everyone in racing, and the sport of kings always has to remember that it is the ordinary punters in betting shops up and down the country who are the lifeblood of racing.

I also had to contend with not coming from a horsey or rural background. Many in racing are born to it. Trainers often have as good a racing pedigree as their horses. They are often ex-jockeys, or their parents were owners. I always tell people I was brought up on a farm – though they probably don't realise that the nearest concrete Cantril came to farm animals was the Black Angus pub. But I have always felt a natural affinity with horses. I love being around them and handling them. I don't see why you have to be born with a plum in your mouth in a country mansion to train racehorses well.

I had now settled in at Sparsholt, which despite being a tiny village has got a great social life. It's all racing, racing, racing.

Jockeys Luke Harvey and Graham Bradley lived in the village. Lambourn, horse racing's biggest centre after Newmarket, is just over the downs. Sparsholt has a nice pub called the Star, and Sunday is the big piss-up day. Racing people often work a seven-day week, but there isn't much racing on a Sunday and Karen and I would meet a few of the racing lads in there for a cider or two. Luke was a journeyman jockey who had won the Welsh Grand National and had a Cheltenham Festival winner but was coming to the end of his riding career. I gave him his last ever ride. Both loud characters who like a beer, we get on well. Luke went on to have a successful career as a TV and radio pundit after he hung up his boots. He also runs the Blowing Stone pub with sister Jessica in Kingston Lisle near Sparsholt. Champion jumps jockey Tony McCoy lives just around the corner, and some evenings there are more jocks in the Blowing Stone than in the weighing room at most racecourses. Luke does his best to drink away the profits while being rude to the customers. People come from far and wide to have the piss taken out of them by him – it's the pub's big selling point. If we are having a real drink, celebrating a big winner or something, we'll do the Magnificent Seven – that is, a bottle each of the different Bacardi Breezers. If things get out of hand we'll then try to go through all the optics. Despite cutting down on the boozing, I can still turn it on, on a big occasion.

So the social life was good, but after nearly two months as a racehorse trainer I had failed to break my duck. It was like going on a barren spell as a striker. Seven of my runners had finished in the frame but I had yet to experience that winning feeling. Racing is a cut-throat business, and I'm sure some of the tweed brigade were muttering, 'What do you expect from a footballer? He probably doesn't even know which end a horse shits out of.' But I was confident in my ability to train horses. As always, Mick Channon was quick to lend some sound advice. 'It will come, Quinny,' he said calmly. 'Be patient. The horses are getting in the frame so you must be doing something right. It'll come.' Still, I was becoming frustrated. My finances were perilous and I couldn't afford to fail. Just as important, my ego would not let me fail.

At the time, a nice little filly I owned called Miss Dangerous was looking great on the gallops at home. I spent hours scouring the form book looking for a race for her, and eventually I found a modest contest I believed was ideal. The Bilston Selling Stakes on the artificial turf – or dirt, as it is known in racing – at Wolverhampton on 21 January 1998 was hardly Royal Ascot. In fact it was more like a Leyland DAF first-round cup game at Torquay than a Premiership fixture at Old Trafford, but on the big day, as Karen and I watched Miss Dangerous stride around the parade ring, my heart was beating harder than when I was playing in front of 50,000 people. It was a cold, grey day, and most of the sparse crowd had stayed in the bars to keep warm.

I legged up jockey Tony Whelan, watched Miss Dangerous canter to the start, then paid a visit to the betting ring. I got a ton on at 3–1 and went to stand in the area reserved for owners and trainers. I could hardly bear to watch. She broke well from the stalls and Tony eased her into a handy position. Coming into the home straight, Tony kicked for home and moved up to nearest rival Tilburg. As they battled up the straight, Karen and I screamed ourselves hoarse. At last, with a heart bigger than Ron Atkinson's gob, Miss Dangerous pulled away to pass the winning post a length and three quarters in front. I punched the air and Karen and I hugged each other tightly. I proudly led Miss Dangerous into the winners' enclosure as my mobile began to buzz with congratulatory calls. It felt better than anything I had achieved on the football field.

The next day, Karen and I were splashed all over the front of the *Sporting Life*, holding Miss Dangerous in the winners' enclosure under the headline QUINN ON THE BALL AT LAST. Karen likes to joke that the only time I like leading the horses round is when they have won a race, or the best-turned-out prize. She reckons I run over and snatch the leading rein off her. I told reporters, 'It wasn't a great race, but the tap-ins appear in the paper the next morning just like the 25-yarders. It's like football when you go three or four games at the start of the season without scoring a goal. Now I can relax a bit. I hope it's the first of many.'

My horses weren't the classiest bunch, but as 1998 progressed I began to see more of the winners' enclosure. In April, Miss Dangerous became my first winner on turf when she landed the Chatham Claiming Stakes at Folkestone under Tony Whelan at 9–2. A few days later I turned the tables on Mick Channon when my two-year-old Snap Cracker ploughed through the heavy ground at Sandown to win the Bow Street Maiden Fillies Stakes to beat his Palace Green, which was favourite. Mick was the first to congratulate me. 'You're getting a bit handy at this game,' he told me. 'I'm going to have to watch my back.' It meant a lot to me to win praise from Mick, who is my mentor in racing. For me, training racehorses is all about common sense, but it's like football or any other career: you have to work very hard to get results and to earn the respect of other people in the game. I wanted to make sure people didn't think I was just some flash ex-footballer doing it as a hobby. And, slowly, the winners were coming and I was being sent more horses.

I concentrated on the less fashionable tracks like Southwell and Wolverhampton because my horses weren't yet quality enough for the top courses. I would rather win at Southwell than come sixth at Sandown. It wasn't until August 2000 that I proved I could mix it with the big boys at the grade one courses when I sent out Foley Millennium to score at Newbury. The two-year-old colt was the 7–1 outsider of four, but he battled home under jockey Jimmy Fortune. It was a wonderful feeling walking into the winners' enclosure at such a famous and prestigious course as Newbury. It also showed I was ready and capable of stepping up a class.

I threw a party in Newbury that Christmas for my stable staff. The group included Karen, Luke Harvey and our apprentice jockey Gary Oliver. Gary, then eighteen, is a tiny, baby-faced bloke, and the nightclub we were going to was for over-21s. Me and Luke coached him on what date of birth to give to the bouncers. 'Tenth of the fifth 1979, Gary. It's easy,' I told him. But he looked very, very nervous.

When we got to the door I explained to the bouncer that Gary was a jockey, hence his small size.

'What's your date of birth, son?' the bouncer growled.

Gary looked flustered. 'Er, er, tenth of the fifth 1989,' he spluttered.

'Well,' the bouncer came back with a laugh, 'we don't let eleven-year-olds in here, sorry.'

We walked back down the road disconsolately – Newbury's not exactly flush with nightspots. Then we spotted a billboard outside a club: TONIGHT, BAD MANNERS. The eighties ska band led by man mountain Buster Bloodvessel were playing. We didn't have many other options so we gave it a go. We all got completely bladdered and had a top night. We went mental on the dance floor to hits like 'Lorraine' and the Can Can. Buster, who makes me look like Kate Moss, has definitely eaten all the pies, but what a showman!

In my first season as a trainer I had twelve winners, in my second I had ten, and in my third, eleven. The size of my string steadily rose to twenty, and, more importantly, the quality of horses was improving. I know the form book and bloodlines like an encyclopaedia and was beginning to pride myself on picking up bargains. I got a call once from football agent Willie McKay who looks after a lot of French players like Manchester City striker Nicolas Anelka and West Ham front man Frederic

Kanoute. He wanted me to buy him a horse and have it in training with me. He was full of bullish talk, so I went to Doncaster Breeze-up Sales and picked out a few I liked in the catalogue. But when a yearling filly walked into the auction ring I was bowled over. She had a beautiful, intelligent face, her eyes sparkled, her coat shone and she flicked her toes proudly as she walked around the ring. I knew this was a horse that would win races.

When the bidding started, I got Willie on the mobile and stuck my mitt in the air. I bid £5,000; someone else bid £6,000. 'Go again,' Willy said. I went to £7,000; they went to £8,000. 'Another five hundred,' barked Willie. Then, 'Going, going, gone, to the large chap with the black hair.' I was chuffed to bits. I knew I had got Willie a bargain. The filly, called Dragon Flyer, came back to Sparsholt and settled in immediately, but when I rang Willie to report on her progress and arrange for him to send me a cheque, I couldn't get hold of him. I left messages all over the place but heard nothing. As the days passed I realised he was deliberately not taking my calls. The double-crossing bugger didn't want his horse any more.

Dragon Flyer didn't know about all the hassle, and as soon as we worked her on the gallops I knew we had a flying machine on our hands. I managed to offload her to some more owners – civil engineer Danny Major and builders Paul and Vince Kilkenny – but I kept a share myself. Willie had talked of running her in selling races – the lowest of the low – but she was better than that. A lot better. A five-furlong speed merchant, she won £60,000 in prize money in her first season. Tough shit, Willie old lad.

I like to think I can spot a bargain – which is lucky, because most of the horses I buy are from the bargain basement. They are usually cheap yearlings which for some reason others don't fancy, or a talented horse from a talented stable which has lost its way. Communicating with owners is a big part of the job.

Some of them are on the phone every five minutes, others you hardly ever hear from. Owners are madly protective of their horses. They would rather you shagged their missus than tell them their horse isn't any good. My policy has always been to be honest. I tell them what I think of the horse, and if it picks up an illness or a knock I immediately tell them. Handling the owners is just as much a part of the training game as handling horses. They are just as flighty and unpredictable. But I have a laugh with my owners, and I think, after years of owning horses myself, I know what they want from a trainer. Racing is very much an entertainment industry and I try to make it as much fun as possible for them. Many of them like a bet themselves, and I am happy to offer advice wherever I can. I go each way if the price is over 5–1, usually avoiding complicated multiple bets and ignoring handicaps. You have to rely on the handicapper's skills which stack up the odds against you even more. I like backing two-year-olds where their form is easy to work through and you can tell a lot from the bloodlines. I also like betting in novice hurdles, conditions races and group races.

The yard really picked up into the new millennium, and I won a nice race with Hagley Park, owned by Steven Astaire, our fifth winner of the 2001 campaign. Then, in February, foot and mouth disease swept the country and racing was suspended indefinitely to stop the virus spreading further. Karen and I had been working solidly for three and a half years, so we decided it was time for a holiday. We went up to Liverpool for a week, saw Melissa and Natasha, had a pint with Dad and Mark, then jetted off to Tenerife.

23. THE BAN

'The odds are against us and the situation is grim.'

Captain James T. Kirk

'We're in some really pretty shit now!'

Bill Paxton as Hudson in *Aliens*

Sitting by the palm-fringed pool of the four-star Hotel Bitacora in Tenerife, I raised my glass of pina colada and proposed a toast. 'Here's to training more winners,' I said to Karen, and we chinked our glasses together.

It was our first holiday in nearly four years; we had been working like crazy to get the training operation off the ground. With us were Karen's mum Sue, her partner Barmy Barry, and ex-jockey Luke Harvey and his then girlfriend Françoise. The day had begun with a full English breakfast, and then we went straight out to the pool. As the girls stretched out on the sunbeds, Barry, Luke and I decided to have a 'sports' day. This involved a round-robin competition consisting of pool, table tennis and that air hockey game, plus a crate of San Miguel. Then it was a stroll into the local town, Playa de las Americas, for a bit of paella with some nice red wine. On the way back, Luke, by now falling about all over the show, bought three sombreros for us. He was that pissed he managed to barter the stallholder from 80 pesetas a pop up to 100 pesetas. Us lads staggered up the street looking like the Three Amigos. Back at the hotel I changed into my Newcastle number nine shirt with QUINN on the back, shorts and flip flops, kept my sombrero on, and started on the cocktails. A group of Liverpool fans spotted me and came over for a chat and a beer, and we had a great laugh.

I joined Karen on a table by the pool armed with a couple of pina coladas. The sun was beginning to set, the crickets provided a background hum, and the setting couldn't have been more romantic.

'We really deserve this, Karen,' I said. 'It's been a tough last few years but I finally think we're going places in the training game. We're a great team, Karen. We've done it together.'

I was interrupted by the shrill ring of my mobile phone.

'Hello, is that Mick Quinn?' a sober voice said.

'The one and only. Who's this?'

'This is the *Daily Mail*, Mr Quinn. We've received information that three horses in your care in a paddock are in a very poor condition, and that the RSPCA have been called in.'

'What are you talking about? You print that and I'll sue the arse off you. Listen, I'm on holiday abroad, mate. The horses are being looked after by my experienced staff. They were fine when I left.'

I told him I didn't want to say anything else, then desperately phoned the stables. I was told by my staff that a woman whose home overlooked the paddock had rung the *Daily Mail* and the RSPCA to say that three horses I trained – Zola, Winsome George and Arab Gold – were in poor condition. I told my staff to bring the horses in immediately.

I jetted back to Britain trying to put a brave face on things, but I was absolutely bricking it. I was finally beginning to make an impression on the racing game, and now this. John Maxse, the Jockey Club's press spokesman, advised me to tell the *Mail* that the Jockey Club was now carrying out an investigation after being contacted by the RSPCA. A couple of weeks later the *Mail* ran the story, saying I was facing a Jockey Club disciplinary committee over allegations of neglecting horses. They said the three horses were thin and were suffering from rain scold – irritation on their skin from being out in the weather. I told the paper, 'It's just one in particular, Winsome George, who hasn't done very well. It has been a harsh winter. It has been so wet there has not been much grass, and one of them has lost a bit of condition. My staff were down there feeding them twice a day all winter. The horses are back in now and are doing fine.' I added, 'I'm trying to make a name for myself for the right reasons, and when you are trying to attract new owners you need this like a hole in the head. The game is hard enough without this happening. It is very unfortunate as the staff work very hard and love the horses.'

When racehorses are taken out of training, they lose condition very quickly because they are not being exercised every day. The muscle falls off them in a matter of days, and they need to be rugged up if they are turned out in a paddock. My three horses had been rugged up and fed twice a day. The problem was the harsh weather and the fact that two of the horses were driving Winsome George away from his food, and he kept throwing off his rug. I absolutely love horses and would never do anything to cause them harm. All this happened when I was on holiday, but I realised, as boss of the operation, that I was going to have to take the rap.

Within three weeks of the horses being brought back in, they looked better than ever. They were sold, and all went on to run again. Zola won a point to point, and Arab Gold also won a race, thus proving their health. I was never charged with cruelty by the RSPCA, but I was in breach of Rule 51 of the Rules of Racing because the horses' condition had fallen 'below that expected of a licensed trainer'. I was told by John Maxse that if I held up my hands and admitted the offences I was likely to face a big fine only, and with luck would escape a ban. But Mick Channon's words of warning when I announced I wanted to become a trainer flashed through my mind: 'Because of who you are, a Scouse ex-footballer, if you ever did anything wrong the racing hierarchy would come down on you like a ton of bricks.'

The hearing at the Jockey Club's forbidding headquarters at Portman Square in central London was set for 28 June 2001. I was represented by lawyer Susannah Farr of the National

Trainers Federation. She also advised me to admit the offence, and thought I would get off with a fine. But when she stood up to speak she seemed to me like a rabbit caught in the headlights. She tried to come up with some mitigating circumstances but I wasn't at all happy with the way she outlined my case.

I was sent out of the chamber for a few agonising minutes while the committee came to a decision, then I was called back in. I was shaking in a cold sweat. The chairman said, 'Mr Quinn, in light of the seriousness of these charges the committee is banning you from training racehorses for two and a half years.'

I gripped the desk in front of me as the colour drained from my face. I was absolutely shell-shocked. The gobby Scouser had finally been put in his place. Bewildered, I walked slowly out of the room, refusing to comment to waiting reporters, and blinked back tears as I faced the photographers outside. The Jockey Club had taken away my livelihood, my dream. I felt physically sick. The ban would destroy me. I was in the middle of a costly lease on a yard, and with no cash coming in, it would mean bankruptcy. It looked like I would end up running a pub or selling insurance after all. What else was there for an ex-footballer and disgraced racehorse trainer with one O-level?

That night, Karen and I comforted each other as best we could. As usual, she was a tower of strength. We had so enjoyed building up the business together, but now it looked like our dream was over. I barely slept that night. I slipped out of bed at 5 a.m. and went out into the yard, followed by Rizzie, our border terrier. It was a summer's morning but there was still a chill in the air. Tearfully, I went round each box to say good morning to each of the horses. I gave them a pat, then went to mix their feeds. To see this lot go, after all the work Karen and I had put in to build up the yard, would break my fucking heart. Karen came out too, and we fed the horses together. For once there was none of the laughter and joking. We were like a pair of zombies.

Racing's big names were hardly queuing up to support me. Richard Hannon, the Marlborough trainer, was one of the few exceptions. He blasted the decision, saying, 'It's a disgrace to take a man's living away like that. OK, fine him four or five thousand, but to do what they have done seems harsh.' Others who backed me were trainers Brian Meehan and Jack Berry, and Mick Channon, as always, was there for me. My family and close friends rallied around, as did many of my owners, and letters of support from the public also poured in. The *Daily Mail* gleefully reported my downfall under the headline BANNED QUINN FACES RUIN, but those in the know said I had been harshly treated. So I did in life what I've always done when life kicked me in the bollocks, the same as I did when Mum and Sean died, and when 10,000 people were calling me a fat bastard on the football pitch. Just like my hero Muhammad Ali, I took the blows, got off the ropes and fought back.

In order to lodge an appeal, the first thing I needed was a good brief. I hired top lawyer Peter McCormick, who represented Chelsea's John Terry after his nightclub bust-up. He knew his stuff, and he did what he could to pick up the pieces, though I was told before the hearing that Karen wouldn't be allowed to apply for a licence in her name. The appeal was chaired by High Court judge Sir Edward Cazalet with two Jockey Club members, Anthony Mildmay-White and Fiona Whitaker, in support. It was a very austere environment, and I was shitting myself, but Peter was the consummate pro and he handled the case brilliantly. The committee listened to the evidence for two hours and deliberated for a further hour and a half, by which time my nerves were completely frayed. They eventually told us that my ban was being reduced by twelve months. In the circumstances, it was a result.

I rushed for a waiting cab, saying only, 'I just want to get out of this building.' Peter spoke to the press on my behalf: 'Obviously in an ideal world we would have liked to have had the suspension wiped out altogether, but being realistic, we never thought that was seriously on the cards. So to persuade the appeal board to take a year off the suspension was good news, and Mick is now going to concentrate on trying to keep his business together for the eighteen months that remain.'

That night I went down the Star in the village for a few pints of cider. I spoke to Dad later.

'Mick,' he said, 'you must be mad to think about going back into racing. Let it go. They don't want upstarts like you in the game.'

'Fuck it, Dad,' I answered. 'I will go back to the sport I love. Training racehorses is all I want to do.'

24. TALK, TALK, TALK

'Remember, my sentimental friend, a heart cannot be judged by how much you love, but by how much you are loved by others.'
The Wizard to the Tin Man in *The Wizard of Oz*

I was sitting at home in Sparsholt, can of cider in hand, watching Channel Four's football show *Under the Moon*. Chris Kamara, ex-manager and player, was giving his views during a phone-in and I was getting more and more irate with what he was saying. So I dialled the programme's number.

'And our next caller is Mick Quinn from Sparsholt near Wantage,' Kamara said. 'What do you want to say, Mick?'

'Well, Chris, if you sit on the fence any longer you're going to end up impaling yourself on it,' I snapped. 'You're talking complete and absolute boll– baloney.'

'Er, that's not Mick Quinn the ex-Newcastle striker by any chance, is it?' he asked, looking embarrassed. The studio audience were in stitches.

Footballers often go to pieces when a microphone is stuck in front of their faces. They either trot out the old 'over the moon' or 'sick as a parrot' clichés or become so tongue-tied that they mix their metaphors and come out with a load of rubbish. My favourite is 'I can see the carrot at the end of the tunnel' by Stuart Pearce. One David Beckham classic from an interview was 'My parents have been there for me ever since I was about seven.' You can't blame them; their gift is with a football. Everyone who picks up a microphone makes a prat of himself at some time. Even, very occasionally, me.

One thing I have always been able to do is talk. I've got an opinion on everything – ask my managers. After my licence was taken away I needed cash quickly, and the media seemed to be my only way forward, so I threw myself into the business.

Most of my owners had stuck by me. They knew I loved horses and that I would do nothing to purposefully harm them. I decided the best way to keep the owners onboard would be to suggest that they send their horses to Graham McCourt, who trains close to Sparsholt in a village called Letcombe Regis. That way I could keep a close eye on the horses. The owners who stuck by me included Steven Astaire, Danny Major, Barry Edwards, John Dooley, Paul and Vince Kilkenny and Paul Byatt. I wasn't banned from looking after horses, just training them, so Karen and I wrote to 60 trainers saying we were up and running for pre-training and breaking horses. We didn't receive one reply, so if I was going to save myself from going bankrupt I was going to have to get off my arse and do some work.

I had already been doing bits and bobs for the Racing Channel, SIS (the TV service piped into betting shops) and Sky. I was still in a betting shop most days, but these days I was talking from a TV screen. Racing Channel bosses Mick Embleton and George Irvine have always been very supportive of me. I also found work with Talk Sport radio, filling in on the important morning slot, and began working for The Quay, a new radio channel for the Portsmouth area covering Pompey games every Saturday. It was nice to get back to football grounds, see a few old faces and soak up the atmosphere from the stands. I always got a great reception from the fans, especially at Newcastle, Portsmouth and Coventry.

The media stuff came easy to me, I didn't have a problem being on camera and, as I said, I've got an opinion on everything. I don't follow any one political party, but I'll give my view. Refereeing is something that really makes me irate, as it did in my playing days. Refs can and often do turn a whole game with their decisions. Why the fuck aren't referees professional? Until you get paid referees, you are going to have amateurs making amateur decisions. Ex-players, people who should know something about the game, should be hired on a decent wage. I only know of one ex-player, Steve Bains, who is currently refereeing. Instead you get school teachers, bank workers and anyone else who fancies themselves as a little Hitler. Ex-footballers need to get more involved in every level of running football.

Drugs in football troubles me, too. I remember the urine sample Mick Kennedy had to give, or rather couldn't give, in my Portsmouth days. He'd topped it up with lager and the test had come back fine. I suppose they must think it's normal for a footballer's piss to be almost pure lager. I never saw any drug use in football, but the authorities need to keep a lid on it.

Another issue that winds me up is kids of fourteen, fifteen and sixteen getting bungs to join top clubs. Kids should be doing it for the love of the game, and joining a club they feel is best suited to them. Clubs shouldn't be throwing money at youngsters, at a time in their lives when it's likely to spoil them. Are they going to work as hard if they get a heap of cash so easily? In contrast, racing's big problem is a lack of prize money. Owners can win two or three races with a horse, albeit moderate contests, and still make a loss on the year when training fees have been taken into account. It doesn't exactly encourage people to get involved, and it leaves small owners needing to have a bet on their horses to make ends meet. My TV and radio work allowed me a platform to spout off about these, and other, subjects.

After working my bollocks off in the media for a few months, I decided that Karen and I deserved a break. We chose to go skiing in Val d'Isere in France with Luke Harvey and a few others – all very posh, but a right laugh. After putting on my fleeces, windcheaters and skiing gear, Luke said I looked like Michelin Man's fatter brother. I had never been skiing before but, still bevvied up from the night before, I thought I was a natural. After a few lessons on the nursery slopes, I decided to join the others on a downhill run. I soon built up speed, but I hadn't quite mastered the art of stopping. I careered down the slope and ploughed through a family at full speed, sending them flying. This plummy bloke got up covered in snow and screamed at me, 'You are a fucking disgrace and a liability! You shouldn't be on the slopes!' I told him to calm down, adding, 'We don't have many mountains in Liverpool.' It was a corker of a holiday.

Back in Britain, I came up with the idea of writing this book. I thought it would be nice if it made a few bob, but my main driving force was that I knew I had a story to tell which others would find interesting and, above all, funny. Virgin Books agreed with me.

As 2002 broke, I began to plan my return to training. I could apply for my licence on 1 January 2003, which meant I would need to get the horses in and fit and ready to run several months before then. I was continually surprised by the support I received from owners without really trying. Blackburn and England star David Thompson came on board immediately and bought two yearlings.

I was back in the spotlight in the week leading up to Christmas due to David Beckham's new mullet hairstyle. After years in the fashion wilderness, the two hairstyles in one – short at the sides and top, long at the back – was in vogue again thanks to football's biggest icon. The *Sun* did a round-up of the great mullets in history, from the pharaohs to Chris Waddle. I made the cut, and my caption read: 'With this mullet it's difficult to see how Quinn scored on or off the pitch.' Cheeky bastards. I was sandwiched between US president George Washington and singer Curtis Stigers. I was chuffed to bits to be in such great company.

During the Christmas week I did the morning show at Talk Sport, and on Christmas Eve, with little sport to talk about, we ended up discussing last-minute shopping. I told listeners I had yet to buy Karen a Christmas present and asked them to call in with ideas. Tony from Chepstow said: 'How about a white cane and some dark glasses?' Steve from Nuneaton added: 'A bone for the guide dog.' And Mike from Stafford chipped in with: 'Do the girl a favour, buy her membership to a dating agency.' It was a right laugh, and afterwards the producer said he thought it was one of our best ever shows.

I was juggling the media work with my preparations for starting training again. On 29 December the Jockey Club sent out a team to inspect the yard to make sure it met the requirements. East Manton has been a licensed yard for two decades, so it was something of a formality, but nonetheless, Karen and I were still very nervy. We went over and over the health and safety regulations to make sure everything was right. I showed the inspector around the yard, and in the end it passed without incident. Everything was now in place for New Year's Day. I had a string of thirteen horses, some supportive owners, a great yard and gallops, and a financial plan to kickstart my career. All I had to do was convince the Jockey Club that I was fit to hold a licence again.

25. TWENTY-FIVE DAYS IN JANUARY

Looking out of my living-room window I can see the beech trees on top of the Lambourn Downs where my string of thorough-breds exercises each morning. Karen and I like to be in the yard by 6.30 a.m. to feed the horses and decide what they will do that day. When I was a footballer, I would just about be leaving the nightclub at that hour and looking for a kebab van. Rizzie, our border terrier, follows me around as I visit each box to check that the horses are OK and to give them their breakfast. Despite the pies gags, I kept to a pretty strict diet of pasta in my playing days – albeit with fifteen portions of garlic bread – so the importance of nutrition for the horses isn't lost on me. Up on the gallops the other trainers favour green wellies, corduroy trousers and tweed jackets, but I prefer a shellsuit, baseball cap and trainers. I'm sure many of them think I'm a Scouse oik, but I really couldn't give a shit.

Just like football training, there is pre-season conditioning for horses, initially in the form of light exercise with the accent on building stamina. Once the season proper starts, there's more serious work, a good blow-out once a week and the inevitable resting periods – hopefully just between races and not as a result of injuries. We are nicely self-contained at East Manton Stables with two four-furlong gallops, one grass, one dirt. We also take the horses two miles up the road to Moss Hill, the same gallop on which Peter Walwyn used to train his Derby winner Grundy. I get a real buzz every time we go up there. We walk and trot them on the way up there as part of their warm-up.

By 8.20 a.m. we're inside for a coffee. After a quick glance at the *Racing Post* I'm on the blower to my owners. I open the office at nine, making entries for upcoming races and declaring, that is confirming, the horses that will run in the next few days. Then it's either off to the races if we have a runner, or out for the second and third lots – the next strings of horses to be exercised. At 4 p.m. I do a round of all the horses. I feel their legs to check for injuries, assess their overall health and organise their evening feed. I love the daily routine of a racing stables. I'm as happy as a pig in shit.

I think it is a real achievement to succeed in two sports. The only other footballer currently training racehorses is my old mate Mick Channon. When they took away my licence to train horses it was like shooting me in the head, but I knew I would bounce back, just like I've always done.

The Jockey Club contacted me and said I had to appear before their licensing committee in the second week of January. It looked like a good thing but experience taught me not to count my chickens. Journalists began to call and the *Sun* jumped the gun a bit by running a piece headlined QUINN BACK IN BUSINESS. I told the paper's Claude Duval: 'If I get the green light, I'm ready to rock n roll.'

As the days rolled by slowly, I spent every minute I could in the yard with the horses I would hopefully have in training. I had to start mapping out races for them and getting them fit to run even though I wasn't sure of getting my licence back. It was a tense time but Karen and I pulled together and got on with it.

On the big day it was back up to the Jockey Club's Portman Square offices. It was becoming a second home. Suited and booted, I was like a nervous schoolboy as I sat before the committee. The sweat was running down the back of my freshly ironed white shirt. I was cacking myself. I told them I now had paddocks close to the house where I could see the horses I turned out at all times. I told them I had made a mistake, taken my punishment and was ready to resume my career.

After hearing my spiel they sent me outside. For ten nerve-wracking minutes I paced the austere corridors as my fate was discussed. What would I do if the game was up? More TV and radio work? I wanted to be up on the gallops with the wind flapping against the old shellsuit as my string cantered past.

I was called back in. The chairman said: 'Mr Quinn, I'm pleased to say we have granted your application to renew your licence.' I stifled a scream, thanked him, and strode out onto the street. 'Fucking, get in there,' I bellowed. Journalists and a TV crew from Sky monstered me for an interview. The Mighty Quinn was back. Weighed in, weighed in.

On the train back home I gave the mobile a serious bashing. I called dad and Mark on the Farm and they were obviously made up. I made sure all the owners who stuck by me got a personal thank you.

I strode into the yard like King Shit and Rizzie the terrier skipped around at my heels, sensing my happiness. I was Mick Quinn, Master of East Manton Stables again.

After evening stables it was down the Blowing Stone with Karen, Sue, Barmy Barry and a heap of others for the Mother of All Piss Ups. I soon switched from the ciders to champagne and then the large voddies and alcopop mixers. What a night.

Early next morning it was back to business. I scoured the entries book. It felt like I was starting all over again.

My first runner was Hagley Park for Steven Astaire, one of my most loyal owners. On 25 January 2003, Hagley went to post in the 9 p.m. at Wolverhampton. As I watched the horse canter down to the stalls I got a lump in my throat. I tried not to catch Karen's eye because I was worried I would break into tears.

Then the Tannoy blared: 'And they're off . . .'

'Come on my son,' I screamed. Hagley Park eventually trailed in seventh. It would have been nice to bounce straight back with a winner but I was just pleased to be a trainer again.

POSTSCRIPT: ALL SHINE ON

*'I know where I'm going and I know the truth and I don't have to
be what you want me to be. I'm free to be what I want.'*
Muhammad Ali

'Well we all shine on, like the moon, the stars and the sun.'
John Lennon, 'Instant Karma'

Mad Monday at the Black Angus is one of the best nights of the
week. Dad bought the pub, not far from my childhood home at
16 Round Hey, in 1997. It has two bars, one for Everton fans
and the other for Liverpool's. In Chaos Corner in the Everton
bar Dad sets up the karaoke machine, and on Mondays, when
the ale is cheap, everyone has a good old Scouse singsong. To
give it a bit of a *Stars in their Eyes* touch there is also a selection
of wigs on the table. If you do Elvis, you can slip on a black
quiff; if you do Madonna, you can don a blonde wig. In the
afternoon the big screen comes down and the racing is shown.
There are some serious drinkers in there and everyone likes to
have a punt. Locals call the pub the Bermuda Triangle – people
go in, but they never seem to come out.

I still go back as often as possible to see the family and catch
up with old friends. Me and Dad have got a great relationship
these days. We can natter about horses and football for ever. I
hope he's proud of what I've achieved; I know I'm proud of the
way he has been there for me, backing me all the way in my
football and racing careers. Those few, awful months when every
time he seemed to call someone else had died were a nightmare.
Dad was like the Grim Reaper. He was strong then, he had to be.

When I see Dad for an ale I often bump into my old mates
like Kevin McGowan, who helped me run the Bus Stop Disco,
and Steven Ward and John 'Taskforce' Tasker from the football

team I played with as a kid. Steve and John, whose love of pie and chips was legendary, are pals with the old fella; they drink in the Black Angus and go on boozy golfing holidays with him. It's great to have an ale and a laugh. John Clarke, the other member of the Bus Stop Disco, is a physical training instructor for the prison service, and I haven't seen him for a while, which is a shame. The other lads from my little gang have mostly married and moved away from the Farm, many of them to the more leafy surroundings of The Wirral.

After the then Tory minister Michael Heseltine had visited Cantril Farm and it was declared a deprived area, the council struck on a great wheeze to rid the estate of its 'Cannibal Farm' drugs and crime image. They decided to rebrand it and give the place a completely different name altogether. The area now goes by the very posh-sounding moniker Stockbridge Village, but it's still Cantril Farm to us. Wherever I have lived the spirit of the Farm has gone with me. Every couple of months I have to go back home to get a fix. It's in my blood.

My son, Little Michael, is now 23 and lives in Dovecote near Cantril Farm with his son, Little Little Michael. Little Michael works in demolition and is a decent Sunday league centre-forward. When he was younger I got him trials at Tranmere, Blackpool and Wigan, but he didn't get the breaks. If I had got the job managing Burnley, I'm sure I would have taken him there. My twin girls Natasha and Melissa, now fourteen, have grown into beautiful, intelligent girls and are doing well at Formby High School. I haven't spoken to their mum Sheila for five years. After the screaming matches we had over the years, that's probably for the best. I have been an absent father for much of my children's lives, but I love all three of them to bits and am very proud of them. I hope to see a lot more of them in the future. Both Michael's mum Debbie and Sheila have done a fantastic job bringing them up without me around. I am eternally grateful for that.

Our Mark and his dog, Kai 2, still scare the shit out of people. He's a wheeler dealer in the best Scouse tradition. Mark is the Geoff Boycott of marriage: he's played it with a straight bat all the way through. The complete opposite to me. He and Denise have four lovely kids and live on a posh new estate not far from the Farm. Trisha gets more and more like Mum every year. She lives off Green Lane in Liverpool and has a little six-year-old called Luke.

Not a day goes by when I don't think of Mum and Sean. I wish Mum could see me walking around East Manton Stables and watching my string on the gallops. She would have been so proud. It would have been great for Sean to come down to Sparsholt for a beer and a day at the races. No one who knew either of them will ever forget them.

They say form is temporary, but class is for ever. Now into my forties, I still like a kickabout every now and again, and though the pace has gone, that touch and vision will never desert you. I play five-a-side at Wantage Leisure Centre, and every year there is a Mick Channon Stables v. Mick Quinn Stables challenge match. The games themselves are highly competitive; they are the Newcastle–Sunderland or Pompey–Saints clashes of racing. Mick, who has terrible arthritis as a result of having painkilling injections to allow him to play on while injured, takes on a purely managerial role, but I'm player–manager of my side and I slot myself in up front. I still get as big a thrill out of scoring as I did when I was a seven-year-old kid. I'm still in touch with many in the footie world, but those I would call mates include Alex Cribley, my old Wigan pal; Paul Cook from Coventry; Marky Ward from Oldham; Big Duncan Ferguson and David Thompson.

I never did marry, but Karen and I got engaged last year and one day I might just walk down the aisle – especially with the new tax breaks for married couples. Only joking, Karen. We share a wonderful life together in Sparsholt and are rock solid despite not having a marriage certificate. We love a night in with the phones off for a romantic meal and a film, and I still get the guitar out for a bit of Lennon. I adore Oasis and Eminem, too, and I'll always love Earth, Wind and Fire. A quarter of a century after first hearing 'That's the Way of the World' in Kevin McGowan's brother's bedroom as a spotty teenager, it's still my favourite record. As the song says, 'Stay young at heart cause you're never, never, never, old at heart.'

Unlike many boozing and betting men, my story doesn't end with Gamblers Anonymous and the twelve-point plan. I still like to unwind at the Blowing Stone over a pint of cider or, if it's a big night, a few large vodkas with alcopop mixers, but it's nothing like the old days. And I still like a punt. If I see value in a horse or a football match, I'll have £50 on. Nothing silly, though. Karen makes sure of that.

Racing is my life now. I want to build up a string of around 50 horses, with the emphasis on quality rather than quantity. A Derby or Grand National win would be nice, but what I'd really like is a Royal Ascot winner. Not sure if they'd let me in the royal enclosure in a shellsuit, though. I see this book as just volume one of my life. There's a lot more to come. As I've said, life has a nasty habit of kicking you in the bollocks when you least expect it, but as Dorothy said in *The Wizard of Oz*, you've just got to follow that yellow brick road. That's all you can do. Keep on going, have a laugh on the way, and with a bit of luck you'll end up in life's winners' enclosure.

The latest buzz around Cantril Farm is about a little centre-forward who the ones in the know say is one of the best kids they've ever seen. He's a big lad for his age – he's got that Wayne Rooney-type physique – but he's very skilful. Little Sean, my little brother's kid, is the next Great White Hope of the Quinn family. He kicks a ball around the same streets on the Farm that I haunted and is coached by Paul Fitzpatrick, the former Leicester and Bristol City defender. Paul keeps raving to

Dad, 'He's a gem. He's got pace like Sean and a touch and an eye for goal like Mick.' I always said that if you put me and Sean together you would have an England footballer. We've all got high hopes for him, and I'm sure Sean is up there looking down and willing him on. Shine on, Little Sean, shine on. All we have to do is make sure we keep him off the fucking pies.

CAREER

Clubs, with transfer fee, goals, appearances and weekly wage:

1978–79 Derby (apprentice) 0 in 0; £16
1979–82 Wigan (free) 19 in 69; £35 rising to £250
1982–84 Stockport (free) 39 in 63; £190
1984–86 Oldham (£52,000) 34 in 80; £300
1986–89 Portsmouth (£150,000) 54 in 121; £950
1989–92 Newcastle (£680,000) 59 in 112; £1,000, plus £85,000 signing-on fee
1992–95 Coventry (£250,000) 26 in 67; £1,500, plus £150,000 signing-on fee
1994 Plymouth (loan)
1995 Watford (loan)
1995–96 PAOK Salonika (free) 7 in 15; £1,000 a month plus bonuses

Total goals: 231 in 512 English League appearances
Approximate earnings in football career: £750,000
Cash left on retiring: £0
Cash invested in property and cars on retiring: £0

INDEX